THE MOUSE MACHINE

J. P. TELOTTE

The Mouse Machine

DISNEY AND TECHNOLOGY

UNIVERSITY OF ILLINOIS PRESS

URBANA AND CHICAGO

Portions of this work previously appeared in the
following forms:
"Crossing Borders and Opening Boxes: Disney and Hybrid
Animation." *Quarterly Review of Film and Video* 24.2
(2007): 107–16.
"Disney in Science Fiction Land." *Journal of Popular Film
and Television* 33.1 (2005): 12–21.
"Minor Hazards: Disney and the Color Adventure."
Quarterly Review of Film and Video 21.4 (2004): 273–82.
"Negotiating Disney and Technology." *Studies in the
Humanities* 29.2 (2002): 109–24.

Library of Congress Cataloging-in-Publication Data
Telotte, J. P., 1949–
The mouse machine : Disney and technology /
J. P. Telotte.
p.   cm.
Includes bibliographical references and index.
ISBN-13 978-0-252-03327-8 (cloth : alk. paper)
ISBN-10 0-252-03327-2 (cloth : alk. paper)
ISBN-13 978-0-252-07540-7 (pbk. : alk. paper)
ISBN-10 0-252-07540-4 (pbk. : alk. paper)
1. Walt Disney Company.
2. Motion picture industry—Technological innovations.
3. Television—Technological innovations.
4. Amusement parks—Technological innovations.
I. Title.
PN1999.W27T45   2008
384'.80979494—dc22   2007045204

Contents

Acknowledgments

A number of people have contributed to the creation of this book and deserve special mention. Foremost among them are Leigh and Gabrielle, who have endured far more Disney culture than might have been good for them, but who always came back for more. Their willingness to share their reactions to and thoughts on that culture invariably helped to shape my own. At Georgia Tech, a number of colleagues, particularly Shannon Dobranski and Carol Senf, consistently provided encouragement and acted as sounding boards for my thoughts on various Disney texts, while my chair, Ken Knoespel, was, as his nature, constantly supportive. And my students at Tech, especially those who have worked through my Film and/as Technology course, have always been an invaluable resource, sharing their knowledge about film, technology, and Disney while abiding my own enthusiasm. In this group there are simply too many to acknowledge, but special thanks are due to Jason Ellis, Rory Gordan, Torey Hass, Whitney Hagan, James Pittman, and Brad Tucker.

I also want to acknowledge the efforts of the editorial staff at the University of Illinois Press, all of whom have been very professional and have provided assistance and support throughout the final preparation of this manuscript.

Introduction:
Main Street, Machines,
and the Mouse

I

Disney's gift, from the beginning, was not as is commonly
supposed a "genius" for artistic expression . . . it was for the
exploitation of technological innovation.

—Richard Schickel, *The Disney Version*

In the Disney theme parks, appearance is everything. The
company's insistence on accurate research and detailed reproduction is
well known, and the Disney Main Street, while what Stephen Fjellman
has described as "a romanticized, idealized, architecturally controlled"
creation (170), supposedly modeled on the downtown of Marceline, Missouri, where Walt Disney spent his formative years, quickly affirms the
corporate emphasis on detail. The parks are also notoriously *clean*. Attendants—or "cast members," as employees are all termed—constantly
walk the streets and pathways, picking up trash, wiping and polishing,
watering the decorative flowers and shrubs, and generally making sure
that there is little to mar the planned illusions. In addition, perspective
is carefully controlled, so that guests see things—and are encouraged to
take photographs—from calculated vantages, ones that afford the most
picturesque views and that avoid glimpses of all that is "backstage." As
a consequence, much of what allows for those attractive appearances,

what makes the parks work, is never seen. For example, just underneath Main Street (and the other streets in the Magic Kingdom, as well as part of Epcot) snakes an elaborate complex of passageways, or "utilidors," as Disney terms them, providing quick access to all areas of the parks and holding the water, gas, and compressed air pipes, electrical wiring, computer cables, heating and air-conditioning ducts, and so on, that make these immense structures function so efficiently and entertainingly.[1] The appearances here are, in fact, designed not only to provide guests with a pleasurable experience, but also to obscure the fact that these parks are not fantasy worlds but great technological wonders, with their creation and propagation reminding us of how accurately Richard Schickel estimated Walt Disney's true genius.

By remaining largely invisible, those technological underpinnings are supposed to make the parks seem to work by magic, thereby adding to the "magical" atmosphere that Disney sells—as a vacation destination, a purveyor of television and radio programs, a retail sales source, and a film studio, among other things. Of course, at times the appearances do fail. Rides inevitably break down; cast members, playing one of the Disney characters in a full body costume, have been known to faint; in 2006, a forty-nine-year-old tourist died of heart failure after riding Epcot's "Mission: SPACE" attraction. And when doing so can contribute to the company's profitability, Disney itself does lift the curtain and let us glimpse the mechanisms at work. Visitors to the Magic Kingdom, for example, after paying the usual park admission, can also take the rather pricey "Keys to the Kingdom" tour, a four-to-five-hour guided exploration of the utilidors, the waste treatment plant, parade staging area, and various other logistical and operational components unseen by the usual park visitor. Other Disney parks have also added versions of this behind-the-scenes experience, such as Epcot's "Behind the Seeds" tour of the high-tech food and plant cultivation that supports the park and its restaurants, or Animal Kingdom's "Wild by Design" excursion that shows how the park operates and cares for its animal inhabitants. As Disney has learned, revealing how the "magic" works can prove a rewarding experience for visitors, as well as a lucrative extension of the company's larger synergistic strategy; in fact, such revelation provides further evidence of Disney's status as what Janet Wasko terms "the most synergistic of the Hollywood majors" (*Hollywood* 53).

The aim of this book is to follow the company's lead in this regard, to offer a selective look at some of those often-unseen—or unconsidered—technological supports or developments that, in film, television, and the theme parks, have been crucial to the success of the Walt Disney Company and, at times, also a clue to its limitations. The result, I hope, is a very different, if admittedly limited kind of studio history, one in which we focus on both the manner and the implications of the company's investment in technology and technological culture. Certainly, wherever we look at the company that bears the name of one of its founders—and throughout this study we shall use the Disney name mainly to designate the company, but at times also its original driving force, Walt Disney—we see the traces of both this technological development and a technological attitude that have become almost as fundamental to the company's identity as its trademark cartoon characters: Mickey and Minnie Mouse, Donald Duck, Goofy, and the rest. Yet those seemingly real figures and the fantasy realm they inhabit often, and even purposely, distract us from the technology that, as in the theme parks, operates just below the surface, making possible the various fantasies the company sells. By exploring the technological context for the various Disney creations, the literal foundation of the many Disney worlds, we can better understand not only Disney's phenomenal development from a small Poverty Row film studio to one of the largest and most influential media and entertainment companies in the world, but also its powerful appeal to a contemporary worldwide audience, an audience that seems increasingly aware that it inhabits a thoroughly technological, mediated environment—one to which Disney lends a most inviting and even seductive countenance.

This technological perspective should also shed some light on Disney's role within that contemporary media environment. For even as it has branched out from its early primary function as a small cartoon studio to become a key presence in television, radio, the Internet, book and music publishing, theme parks, theater, and the more amorphous leisure industry, the studio has retained something of its original character, a kind of technological fingerprint that attests to Schickel's assessment. Today Disney functions as an important part of what the cultural philosopher Paul Virilio has termed "the vision machine" (*Vision* 59), as a segment of that contemporary technological culture that conditions how we see—and inhabit—our world. Esther Leslie has observed how early discussions of the cinema frequently anticipated this impact, describing the ways in which film "obliges the viewer to see the world" in particular ways—in terms of tracking shots, master shots, close-ups, a montage of juxtaposed images, and so on (105). A wide array of subsequent analyses has tied that conventionalizing of vision to film's powerful ideological impact. But more than simply pointing towards such ideological manipulations, Virilio's development of this notion emphasizes two points that are typically overlooked. One is a kind of totalitarian force that pervades the contemporary cultural environment,[2] a force that he a bit exaggeratedly terms "a eugenics of sight," but one that might more accurately be described as a tendency towards a "standardization of ways of seeing" (*Vision* 12, 13), an inclination to control how we see. As initially noted, some of this standardization is crucial to the Disney theme park experience, which carefully organizes and controls its guests' point of view. As Alexander Wilson notes about the Epcot experience, "There is never a moment or space that is not visually, aurally, and olfactorily programmed" (122) there. But that very tendency for programming and control, this fundamental character of modern technological culture in general, also charges the entertainment experience with a kind of challenge. And here is Virilio's second key point: that the workings of such a cultural force implicate *us*, across cultures and classes, in an ongoing struggle, in our own sort of negotiation, "not in an effort to destroy it, but in order to transfigure" that environment by rendering its effects quite transparent and thus less controlling or pernicious (Armitage 157), as we negotiate between our desire for entertainment and our mindfulness of the ideological baggage often hidden in that experience.

In fact, Janet Wasko, Mark Phillips, and Eileen Meehan have already situated the contemporary work of Disney in one version of this struggle. Approaching the company as a conglomeration of globally focused entertainment technologies, they describe how various audiences have developed different strategies for addressing and coping with Disney's efforts at "standardization," and the often "dazzling" effect of those efforts on worldwide audiences. As they observe, some audiences readily recognize the manipulative and even exploitative effects found in Disney films, television programs, comic books, and other products, and resist those effects—although ironically, as Phillips notes, that resistance usually "does not stop them from liking the products produced by the company" (48). Others acknowledge some of those effects but are able "to compartmentalize Disney the business from Disney as entertainment," and to distinguish "between 'classic' Disney and current Disney" (Phillips 48), that is, between a historical set of texts, linked to Walt Disney, to which they are more kindly disposed and those elements, produced by the more recent company regimes, that immediately affect their lives and seem to emphasize a consumerist ethic. Yet another audience segment, as they offer, adopts a strategy of appropriation, incorporating the Disney experience into family or cultural rituals, thereby translating Disney from something "uniquely American" to something perceived as "mine" (Phillips 55). Thus in her study of Disney audiences in Denmark, Kirsten Drotner observes how they "form and sustain their own cultural identities" by defining "what they see as being Danish through a process of contrastive validation to what they perceive as being American" in the Disney texts (113). Through these various strategies we can begin to see the complexity of response that the technological world, and Disney as a powerful component of that world, not only elicits but almost requires of audiences throughout the world.

While the technological perspective outlined in Virilio's work has at times been charged with overlooking just such cultural strategies in favor of more formal phenomenological concerns, I would suggest that Virilio's emphasis on a sense of struggle or "wrestling with" the technological (Armitage 10, 157) links his vantage in an important way to analyses like those described above. For it points to the broader nature of this technological contention, implicating both the audience and the companies that employ it in a nexus of negotiations, and suggesting that both must similarly bargain with all that constitutes our technological climate. Since commentary on the studio has, over the last two decades, been dominated by rather strict ideological assessments that emphasize reception, treat Disney like a monolithic agent, and largely exempt technology from the equation, Virilio's perspective seems a valuable vantage to bring to such a powerful component of the media environment. Thus, a primary aim of this study is to open a broader perspective on Disney by examining the company's technological workings—i.e., both its attitudes towards technology and its efforts at relating technology to a mass audience—and hopefully rendering them far more transparent.

It is also in the context of this imperative to deal with the power of technology and the nature of modern technological culture that I see Disney playing a crucial and in some ways instructive role, one that can help to explain some of its great attraction, even for those who, as Phillips points out, generally resist the studio's work, or as Drotner suggests, approach it with a sense of "ironic enjoyment" (113). For as we shall see, throughout its history, Disney has constantly been engaged in what we shall metaphorically describe as "negotiations" with various components of the vision machine. Like most companies in the entertainment industry, Disney has, in order to survive in an increasingly competitive environment, repeatedly had to innovate or adopt new technologies or move into new media forms, and in some cases to innovate and then abandon new technologies that proved unprofitable or problematic. The development of sound cartoons and the corporate partnership with television are two obvious examples of the former path, with sound allowing the studio to differentiate its product from most other early cartoon makers, and television creating a new source of revenue and advertising, as well as an outlet for its product in a powerful emerging medium in the 1950s. As instances of the latter situation, we might recall Disney's development of stereophonic surround sound for *Fantasia* (1940) and its rather quick abandonment of that technology after its costly road-show failure, as well as the studio's move away from hybrid animation in the late 1940s after both audiences and critics responded coolly to this development. Moreover, the studio's various productions—texts that cut across all aspects of our media environment—have provided audiences with numerous sites wherein they can both observe and vi- cariously participate in these most important negotiations. In them we repeatedly encounter dramatized examples of how we might deal with the difficulties of this world, situations Disney has carefully measured and worked out for us, as in the case of *Monsters, Inc.*'s solution to the energy crisis—the substitution of laughter for screams as an infinitely renewable energy source, and analogously, the need for optimism rather than fear in addressing the obvious problems posed by limited natural resources.

Before further considering these various technological encounters, though, we should pause a moment to clarify how we might use that term *technology*, since today it often means different things to different people. For many the term simply denotes a category of mechanical or electrical tools or devices, specific *things*, while others, particularly in the area of cultural studies, liberally deploy it to describe a set of practices commonly centering on how we manipulate our world. I want to stake out a kind of middle ground between these extremes, using technology to suggest something more than what Neil Postman limits it to, that is, "merely a machine" (*Amusing* 84), but also something less than what Andrew Ross, in an example of the excesses of cultural studies, far too ambiguously defines as a "cultural process . . . that only makes sense in the context of familiar kinds of behavior" (3). In between is an area that includes both hardware and software, or perhaps more precisely, spe- cific mechanical constructs like the multiplane camera, media such as television, and even a scientific mindset that construes and constructs the world according to technological principles, such as regularity, effi- ciency, and speed. To consider only hardware or technical extensions of the body would obviously exclude most cultural considerations, while to go completely in the direction that Ross suggests, to see practically all human behavior as a form of technology, ultimately renders the term al- most meaningless. That approach creates an identity between technology and culture because it wants to emphasize human or social agency, but that perspective risks forgetting a point that has often been made: that many apparatuses, even mechanical and electronic devices, are far from neutral.[3] Ultimately, I want to suggest a more complex and, I hope, more *useful* relationship than either of those extremes usually permits.

Certainly, as we shall use it here, technology does implicate a variety of specific tools or devices that have proved crucial to the development of the Disney empire. Yet those devices are invariably tied to a certain technical mindset or context, what some might broadly describe as a cultural discourse, that has helped propel Disney's development. While the specific tools of sound technology, such as Vitaphone's sound-on-disk, Movietone's sound-on-film, or the RCA Photophone system were essential to transforming the film industry in the late 1920s, a larger discourse—i.e., both popular and scientific—about sound and about how it could affect both film production and the film experience was also crucial. So as the following chapters, in order, chronicle Disney's innovation of sound cartoons, its application of three-strip color, its efforts at giving depth to the animated image, its partnership with television, its experimentation with widescreen technology, its development of the theme park and Audio-Animatronics, and its movement into digital animation and effects filmmaking, they will also invoke a broader technological discourse or attitude, such as that involved in the space race of the 1950s and 1960s, that surrounding issues of digital representation much later, or, in several chapters, that central to the increasing popularity of the genre of science fiction. The result, I hope, is a situating of technology in what might broadly be termed a technological context, and an avoidance of the extremes that often characterize many discussions of the subject.

Within this context, we might see my initial description of Main Street and its functions as pointing towards two technological issues that will periodically resurface here, ones not only central to the Disney universe, but also crucial to contemporary culture, to that cinematized landscape we all inhabit but that Disney has made its special province. One of those concerns is a persistent challenge facing contemporary culture: how do we find an accommodation with the technological? This effort at accommodation is something that Disney as a company has, practically from its inception, practiced, almost invariably profited from, and regularly, in its films, television programs, and theme park attractions, models for audiences. In this project we find a telling explanation of why, despite its frequent nostalgic evocations, Disney has also, like no other American cultural institution, always been invested in the technological, and how it has effectively made the technological seem like a natural or complementary element of our world. As an example, we might recall how this dual effort surfaces in Disney's *Swiss Family Robinson* (1962), wherein the shipwrecked title family determines not simply to build a tree-house shelter, but, as a matter of course, to equip it with elevators, running water, fans, and a host of other modern appliances that effectively link their primitive island home with the advanced European culture from which they have come, as well as with the modern world of the audience for whom such features are simply commonplace. Appropriately, Disney has featured versions of this tree house in several of its parks, where it serves to suggest this sort of easy connection and to demonstrate the possibilities of such accommodation—an accommodation *with* technology that is also enabled *by* the technology. This attraction, located off of Main Street and just within Adventureland in the Magic Kingdom, affords an especially comforting presence for audiences who are living through accelerating technological change and its attendant challenges. In fact, it suggests that we should see a visit to a Disney theme park not so much as a retreat from the real world into fantasy, as many commentators would offer, but as a rather comforting affirmation of our ability to live *with change,* to recognize, as the Audio-Animatronic theater of the Carousel of Progress offers, that "there's a brave new beautiful tomorrow, just a dream away," and to encourage us in that dreaming by modeling it for us.

The other key concern to which I have already alluded might be described as *connection* itself, often embodied in various forms of communication. Of course, maps are distributed as guests enter any Disney Main Street or park; and maps to treasures and lost civilizations propel the action in a wide array of Disney films, from *Treasure Island* (1950) to *National Treasure* (2004). Messages conveyed in various ways, including bottles and magic mirrors, are central to *20,000 Leagues Under the Sea* (1954), *Snow White and the Seven Dwarfs,* and *The Rescuers* (1977). Television's shaping force on a child's imagination drives the two *Toy Story* movies; and both *Monsters, Inc.* (2003) and *The Incredibles* (2004) suggest that there are disconcerting and even "incredible" dimensions to our world just beyond a closet door or within the cookie-cutter suburban house next door—connections just waiting to be discovered. While at times suggesting a kind of simple wish fulfillment and firmly embedding most of the Disney product within the realm of the fantastic, this emphasis on connection also underscores an important dimension of the Disney product, the way in which it consistently points to the possibility of unseen, often denied, but also hoped-for links, ways of bridging the past and the future, connecting to others, and even of reaching other, most secret parts of ourselves, often with the assistance of some sort of technology.

In short, those concerns with technology and connectivity underlie and enable that nostalgic veneer on which most Disney commentators have dwelt, while they also help to explain why people of various cultures have been drawn to Disney and have welcomed not only its films but also its theme parks—and with them its peculiar ideologies—into their own countries. This is a point Virginia Nightingale makes explicit in her study of Disney audiences in Australia, where she observes that most of her survey respondents see Disney texts as "*not* uniquely American," but rather as "universal or multicultural" (67).

I would suggest that these concepts are linked and form one of the key Disney contributions to contemporary culture. For within the Disney universe the technological *does* seem natural or at least congruent with nature and usually fun, as the tree house attraction demonstrates. And the technological repeatedly plays an important role in enabling just the sorts of communications and connections that we implicitly sense are lacking in our world and that we most desire, so that the Disney version of the technological typically, even necessarily, speaks a message of promise or need satisfaction. While the movies allowed Disney to speak to millions and develop a media machine that could reach all corners of the earth, that could link everyone as part of a global village—or World Showcase, as the Epcot park styles it—technology as envisioned by Disney has become crucial to connections of every sort. It is precisely for this reason, I would suggest, that another of the key Disney emblems, the geodesic dome that stands as Epcot's symbol, houses a ride, "Spaceship Earth," that is devoted precisely to depicting the changing nature of our communication technologies. Much like the various Main Streets, this structure functions as an official entryway, as well as a point of divergence, dramatically conveying for all who pass through it the Disney ethos of communication and connection.[4] From here visitors may turn to visit the various technological pavilions that occupy the front portion of the park or end that experience and take the central walkway leading to the different national exhibits that comprise the World Showcase—all of them identified by traditional, easily identifiable structures that recall past glories or stereotyped characteristics of their respective cultures. Past and present, a brave new world and an equally valued old one are, as the park's technological products affirm, here able to strike a bargain, to fit in relatively easy harmony, and even to allow visitors to move almost effortlessly between them.

Of course, there is a danger precisely in the seemingly effortless nature of that ersatz harmony, in the hidden difficulties of negotiation, in the entertainment itself. Too often the Disney world—and especially every Disney themed "world"—does seem to be preaching the pure gospel of what Virilio has termed "technological fundamentalism" (Armitage 5), suggesting that we can invest a kind of absolute and unquestionable value in every new technological development. Like the complex support system of the utilidors, we seldom glimpse the great effort and difficulty involved in making that world run properly and with the sort of marvelous efficiency promised by the Machine Age into which Walt and Roy Disney had been born and in the promise of which Walt was so invested. The entertaining nature of the Disney products all too easily projects the sort of "utopian" sense that Richard Dyer argues is a fundamental effect of most popular entertainment, that Howard Segal describes as part of the aura that commonly attaches to all technological development, and that is certainly one of the bases on which technologies are commonly sold to the public, both by Disney and by much of contemporary culture.[5] One of the seductive lures of the Disney technological world, consequently, is the sense that those negotiations might occur quite naturally, without any effort on our part, and certainly without the sort of trade-offs and even crippling false steps about which a number of recent critiques have warned. As Edward Tenner has observed, any history of technological development should include a chronicle of technology's many "revenge effects," of the various ways in which our technical ingenuity has also backfired (6). But telling the story of such revenge effects would distract from the primary message here, and certainly from the entertainment factor.[6] For through its constructed worlds Disney dramatically plays out for its audiences the possibility of such negotiations, suggests that they can in various ways be accomplished, much as the Walt Disney Company would seem to have done throughout its history. As a partial corrective, this study tries not only to chronicle a number of Disney's key technological achievements, but also to begin to *denaturalize* the negotiations implicit in those accomplishments, to sketch some of the very real difficulties that have been involved in and through a range of Disney texts.

II

The Disney Main Street, as I have suggested, is an appropriate place to begin thinking about these sorts of negotiations. Guests who walk its length encounter a kind of modern-day Potemkin-village, certainly not on the grand scale of the Russian original, but a tremendously effective piece of entertainment and foolery nonetheless that suggests they have entered an older, simpler, less problematic world. However, its carefully scaled facades and forced perspectives hide no impoverished peasantry or backward culture; nor is the illusion here ever more than momentary and at times even quick to reveal itself, as guests who opt to tour the utilidors find. And as Eleanor Byrne and Martin McQuillan have observed, while for many the Disney text is "synonymous with a certain conservative, patriarchal, heterosexual ideology" and an aggressively capitalist stance, it is often and surprisingly almost "self-evidently" so (1–2), or, as I might suggest, rather *self-consciously* so. In any case, they believe that "the blatantness of Disney is what makes it so resistant" to much of the dominant contemporary critical agenda (3). And indeed, the results of several reception studies support this notion. Drotner, for example, finds in her audience surveys that "Disney products have not been accepted wholeheartedly and without reservation, nor have they promoted a uniform acceptance of American values and norms"; in fact, the Disney products have often "served as eye-openers about [local] cultural identity" (115). Yet while we continue to dissect the company's obvious weaknesses, and while the company itself, understanding that political correctness sells, has increasingly sought to counter those perceptions through the release of gender conscious and cross-culturally focused films like *Pocahontas* (1995), *Mulan* (1998), and *Holes* (2003), what continues to slide all too easily from view on Main Street and elsewhere, save for when the company chooses to *sell* that very view through one of its special tours, is the mechanism at their base, as well as the mechanistic attitude—one that emphasizes machine-like formulas, careful regularity, and efficient output—that drives Disney's worlds.

We might begin our walk, then, by noting that there is a theme to the Disney Main Streets: Technological Progress. The various shops and buildings we first encounter suggest gas-lit and rather conventional structures recalling the late nineteenth century, but as we move down the street, we find increasingly elaborate facades and interiors, depicting an electrified and prosperous early twentieth-century America.[7] Moreover, wherever they are located, the Disney Main Streets all share one quite striking, readily evident feature of this technological progress, one that identifies them as part of the larger Disney entertainment machine. Each one contains—or rather, depicts—an old-fashioned motion picture theater, often running a bill of classic Disney cartoons, but sometimes simply showing promotional films for other Disney efforts. That theater represents the ur-technology out of which the entire Disney universe—a multicultural, media-informed, and media-driven realm—has come into being. For the movies, and the mouse within those movies, the mouse that, as Walt Disney was fond of noting, made it all possible, *represent* the machine where Disney began, a key point of origin and connection, although just one segment of the larger Mouse Machine, as we might term it. While this depicted technology is small and unprepossessing, simply part of the varied cultural landscape offered to park-goers and a sort of technology that is meant to make them feel comfortable—if for no other reason than the fact that it offers a shady rest stop amid a sea of concrete—it begins to point us in an important direction. It suggests a level on which all that follows in the parks, all that branches off from Main Street, is designed as a cinematic experience, even a rather reflexive one. But more significantly, it hints of a level on which the entire Disney enterprise is linked to the development of what Virilio has described as "an entirely cinematic vision of the world" (*War and Cinema* 66)—a vision enabled by this technological progress, one that is part of contemporary technological culture, yet one that often goes unremarked.

In keeping with this linkage, Main Street appropriately occupies a sort of cusp position in the Disney worlds that signals its various technological functions and frames the many "narratives" that follow. Leading away from its theater, the street directs park visitors into both the past (Frontierland) and the technologically driven future (Tomorrowland), into an idealized America, along with its European roots (Fantasyland) and its unspoken imperialist aspirations (Adventureland). The trip down, and through, any Disney Main Street is thus a bit like boarding a machine that, like the movies themselves, allows for both space and time travel, taking visitors both backward and forward, to Disney's early media origins and along the varied cultural paths it has staked out with its commitment to an assortment of evolving media technologies. Main Street is, very simply, a terminus for multiple connections—even a site of contradictions—and an emblem of how the many technologies at work in the Disney enterprise all serve to "transport" audiences in a variety of ways. Even more specifically, it reminds us that the Disney worlds are driven by various technologies (and technological attitudes), that they deploy those technologies in carefully calculated ways, sometimes disguising their actual functioning, but often, disingenuously, presenting technology as their focus or subject matter, thereby helping to shape our perceptions of the very forces through which the Disney texts work so effectively on us.

In describing the impact of technology on our world, on what he tellingly describes as "the cinematic landscape" of contemporary life (*War and Cinema* 79), Virilio notes how, in the common experience, "geographical space has been shrinking," so much so that "technological development has carried us into a realm of fictitious topology in which all the surfaces of the globe are directly present to one another" (46)—or at least, in our everyday routine, might seem so. This effect, underscored by the rapid proliferation of video cell phones, global positioning tools, and Blackberry-type gear, can be, by turns, promising and rather disorienting. It hardly requires much prodding as we walk the Disney Main Street to see it and the entirety of the Disney theme parks, as symptomatic of that "shrinking" and as part of this new, technologically constructed "topology." In fact, one might argue that the original Disneyland is the real prototype of such topologies, and the proliferation of Disney parks, along with the company's increasing cross-cultural emphasis, points up its ongoing role in fostering this newly intimate topology, or what some have termed a "global culturalism."[8] Obviously, Main Street leads into Disney's own geography, that of Tomorrowland, Fantasyland, Frontierland, and Adventureland, all preexisting in the imaginary of the original *Disneyland* television show[9] and, we might suppose, in the imagination of Walt Disney himself. This special topology also points toward the final destiny of the Epcot theme park's design. For here a proposed "Experimental Prototype Community of Tomorrow" would, when it was reconceived and constructed sixteen years after its announcement, give way to those two strangely contiguous lands: the technology-intensive Future World at the front of the park, and at the rear the World Showcase, a series of international exhibits centered around a detailed and reduced-scale simulacrum of a country's signature and pointedly traditional architecture—e.g., an English pub, an Italian palazzo, a Norwegian stave church, a replica of France's Eiffel tower. As the pathways through Future World inevitably lead audiences into this ersatz old world crafted from the latest materials, Epcot demonstrates how the technological future can serve to neatly package and offer an easy, if questionably satisfying, connection to a traditional cultural past.

In fact, Disney has repeatedly and proudly boasted of how it painstakingly creates the sort of imaginary topology that branches off from Main Street as the basis for its various rides and attractions. Thanks to the transforming power of modern technology, the company has been able to carve out for each of its theme parks an amazing yet carefully planned *physical* landscape, marked by a series of arresting monuments: Space Mountain, Splash Mountain, the Matterhorn, Animal Kingdom's massive Tree of Life and Expedition Everest's 200–foot tall version of the Asian peak, Epcot's trademark geodesic dome, World Showcase Lagoon, and, most obviously, the European-style fairy-tale castles that mark all of its theme parks. These are landmarks that, with great technological effort, at massive cost, and with a keen appreciation for the visual power of the monumental, Disney has carefully constructed from the natural world—the orange groves of California, the swamplands of Florida, the marshes near Tokyo Bay—to serve not just as spectacles and attractions, but as living testimony to the power of technology and a technological mind-set. It is an attitude that, as Schickel suggests, seems intent on reshaping nature, on creating a new and very real world, partially populated by technological (Audio-Animatronic) figures and well-rehearsed performers, placed within carefully fashioned cultural contexts, and always waiting for guests to appreciate its perfection, to participate in and thus complete the illusion. The result is a world in which Disney guests can feel comfortable and safe, can experience the various geographies and cultures of the globe, albeit on a reduced scale, without the obvious importunings of politics and within the pleasant confines of a new sort of media landscape, one that artfully passes off that mediascape as a part of the natural world of the imagination. In short, it is a landscape that helps Disney to advertise and sell the broad-based cultural experience it has to offer, including that of technology and technological progress.

This description already begins to suggest where Main Street ultimately leads us. With its Audio-Animatronic denizens, its movie theater, its carefully disguised surround-sound audio environment (with speakers practically everywhere, piping in appropriate mood, theme, or culturally appropriate music), its cinematic lighting, its images of the past cinematized by the very latest technological developments, Main Street attests to the Disney partnership with technology that has allowed the company, like a kind of embodiment of the media itself, to grow, to branch out, to spread to other territories—Paris, Tokyo, Hong Kong—and, in the process, to redefine itself as the model of the postmodern international media enterprise. For the Disney Company has grown from a small cartoon advertising enterprise (Laugh-O-gram Films of Kansas City) to its current status as media monolith not only by negotiating links for us with the past and with other cultures, but also by constantly making deals for or striking compromises with the latest developments in entertainment technology, often in the face of rather difficult economic circumstances or significant shifts in the cultural or industrial landscape. It is a tendency that Steven Watts especially appreciates as he describes how, under Walt and Roy's original leadership, the company would periodically assert itself "with a remarkable burst of activity" that would almost invariably prove "both psychologically revitalizing and financially profitable" (285). And it is a note that Walt himself often struck, as when addressing the Society of Motion Picture Engineers, he remarked, "There is no knowing how far steady growth will take the medium, if only the technicians continue to give us new and better tools" (142).

III

Of course, our prime concern here is not with the parks, but with Disney's crucial place in the entertainment world and especially within the film industry. Thus I want to extend the implicit path of Main Street along a temporal line into a rather different sort of studio history, to describe how, at certain crucial moments in the company's development, Disney has innovated, adopted, and exploited a variety of key technological innovations. The following chapters, then, will look in detail at a long line of those developments. Among them, we shall note how the studio explored hybrid animation with its early "Alice" films and resurrected this technique with increasing technological sophistication at various points in its history, culminating in the critical and popular success of a film like *Who Framed Roger Rabbit* (1988). The studio also helped innovate sound into animation with the Mickey Mouse cartoon *Steamboat Willie* (1928), in the process creating one of the most popular and enduring "stars" in world film. It blazed a trail into three-strip color filming through its 1932 agreement with the Technicolor Corporation, which granted it a two-year monopoly on the use of the new technology. Disney added a greater illusion of depth to animation with its award-winning development and application of the multiplane camera, certainly a key ingredient in the success of its first animated feature, *Snow White and the Seven Dwarfs* (1937). To showcase its experimental animation of musical themes, *Fantasia* (1940), it created a stereophonic and surround-sound system that anticipated industry developments in this area by more than two decades. At a crucial point in the history of the film industry it helped open the way to cooperation between the studios and the new technology of television through its 1954 deal with ABC to produce the *Disneyland* television series; and by leveraging this deal for financial support, Disney was able to innovate a new and increasingly powerful form of entertainment with its development of the similarly named theme park in 1955. Further pursuing that media path, Disney established its own cable television network in 1980, eventually acquired ABC's television and radio affiliates in 1995, and through a series of partnerships with such media powerhouses as the Hearst Corporation, GE, and NBC gained access to a variety of highly successful outlets, such as ESPN, Lifetime, and the A&E Network. Through its partnership with and eventual purchase of

Pixar Animation, it committed itself to state-of-the-art digital animation, a technology that has had ramifications not only for the future of the company's animated offerings, but also for the whole range of feature film production, as Disney's digitally rich, live-action features of recent years, such as *Armageddon* (1998), *Pearl Harbor* (2001), *Pirates of the Caribbean* (2003, 2006, 2007), and *The Chronicles of Narnia: The Lion, the Witch, and the Wardrobe* (2005), clearly demonstrate. And Disney has also developed an effective internet presence that it uses, with growing sophistication, to entertain, to inform audiences about its latest productions, and, of course, to sell all things Disney, including artifacts from its theme parks, hotels, and movie productions. Through these many initiatives, it has become one of the world's largest and most powerful media and entertainment companies, a giant that today largely stakes out the technological path that other entertainment companies follow.

With these various and ongoing moves, chronicled in the following chapters, the Walt Disney Company has also done something more. Under the guidance of Walt and Roy Disney, later of Card Walker and Walt's son-in-law Ron Miller, and more recently of figures like Frank Wells and Michael Eisner, and today Bob Iger, it has gradually come to recognize that its province is not simply the animation that brought the company into being or even the larger field of the movies. In fact, acknowledging this broadening purpose, as well as the changing nature of the entertainment industry, in 2004 the company terminated most of its traditional animation staff and closed the animation facilities in several of its locales, practically abandoning the company's original function. In its place we find a more focused emphasis on creating those fictitious topologies, as we have termed them—or, at any rate, on what they *represent.* Todd Gitlin has characterized the contemporary media as "occasions for and conduits of a way of life identified with rationality, technological achievement, and the quest for wealth, but also for something else entirely, something we call *fun, comfort, convenience,* or *pleasure*" (5). And Disney, as a corporate entity, has come to understand that its real province is the entirety of this "something else," that ultimately it sells *entertainment itself* (thus Walt's description of Disneyland as "The Happiest Kingdom on Earth"). The many technologies the company has pioneered and/or embraced over the years have simply provided various innovative opportunities for it to constantly expand that product line— not only to reach out to audiences in different ways, but to offer them new connections, new experiences, new versions of their world.

Here, then, is where the Disney Main Street, in fact, the whole of those amusement parks and all the other products that make up the Disney enterprise today, invariably leads. For with its embrace of the various media technologies that form today's international cultural topology, that of the movies, television, the new media emerging from the computer, and the core mechanical, electronic, and cybernetic technologies that drive its amusement parks, the Walt Disney Company demonstrates, and speaks to, a larger cultural effort at coming to grips with a thoroughly technologized environment, an environment that is not simply the world in which we live and work, but one that, in its very fictitiousness, often seems to function as "entertainment," as the place of the cultural imaginary with its implicit connections to our past and to other cultures. In keeping with a postmodern spirit, the many Disney worlds—of film, television, theme park, and so on—thus emphasize, even call our attention to, a level on which our whole world seems constructed, Potemkinized for our entertainment, or perhaps for our distraction, while also suggesting both a certain inevitability to this condition and our very real and continuing need to negotiate with this mediated environment.

IV

The various case studies that follow and that describe what I have termed negotiations all proceed from two rather simple assumptions, one a factual observation and the other a critical guideline. The first of these is that Disney, as one of the largest and most influential media/entertainment conglomerates today, offers a key model for the application of cutting-edge technologies to the world of entertainment. In fact, its very reach largely derives from its investment at key moments in company, cinematic, and, more generally, entertainment history in a variety of significant new or emerging technologies at which we have already pointed: synchronized sound, color cinematography, three-dimensional imaging, stereophonic sound, Audio-Animatronics, broadcast television, the cable industry, CGI (computer-generated imagery), and so on. That acceptance of various technologies, as we shall see, has repeatedly helped the company to innovate new dimensions in entertainment, while furthering one of the most fundamental of business strategies: differentiating its products from those of its rivals. It also marks Disney as a potential model for studying the rest of the film and entertainment industry, as its ability to innovate or respond to the most significant technologies, those that promise—or even threaten—to alter the course or nature of the industry, has allowed it to grow, prosper, and ultimately to assume a leading international role in the world of entertainment and in the marketing of that utopian sense that entertainment conventionally generates.

This investment also shows up in the company's increasingly frequent focus on science and technology in its films, television programs, and theme parks, resulting in a substantial number of science fiction films, what the company at one time termed "science factual" television shows and theatrical documentaries, and technologically themed rides or other park attractions, such as Disneyland's original "Rocket to the Moon" ride, Disney-MGM Studio's "Backlot Tour," or the Magic Kingdom's "Carousel of Progress," all of which foreground Disney's corporate attitude towards the technological and even *celebrate* its technological achievements, rather uncritically suggesting what our own attitudes towards the technological might be. In this repeated focus, the company has sought to draw science and technology into the realm of entertainment by locating in the mechanisms that enable its work the very stuff of entertainment. And in the process it has managed a rather remarkable paradox: rendering those mechanisms and their cultural impingements nearly invisible even as they *are* being celebrated.

The second assumption behind this study derives from Neil Postman's analysis of technology's impact on contemporary culture. Observing American culture's eager acceptance of all things technological, he describes the emergence of what he terms a "technopoly" in our recent history, that is, the subordination or "submission of all forms of cultural life to the sovereignty of technique and technology" (52). That obvious impact—one that is hardly limited to America—prompts his warning that, "It is inescapable that every culture must negotiate with technology, whether it does so intelligently or not. A bargain is struck in which technology giveth and technology taketh away" (5). Disney's success in its technological investments and commitments, as I have implied, follows precisely from the sort of "bargains" it has, through the years and across various media, managed to strike with those different technologies, with the practices of the larger entertainment industry, and with the technological mindedness of its audience, from the sort of balance it has found in what technology gives and what it takes—or as some of the company's more skeptical critics would contend, what the technology has allowed *it* to *take*. By walking the technological path suggested by the Disney Main Streets through a variety of Disney texts, both classic and contemporary, this study aims to map some of the negotiations that have effectively created the Mouse Machine and helped it prosper.

This mapping should help us not only to better understand Disney as a cultural institution, but also to look beyond the Disney context. For as I have suggested, that Disney negotiation, thanks to its historical importance, ongoing development, and enormous success, models similar developments in the entertainment industry and in some instances pointedly parallels other studios' approaches to technological innovation and adoption. Certainly, Disney's technological history, particularly its embrace of sound film, its early involvement with television, and its profitable partnership with other media outlets, suggests some similarities to the industrial path followed by rival studio Warner Bros.[10] As a consequence, this study might also allow us a glimpse inside the box where entertainment and technology have effected their partnership, one that has come to typify the contemporary media and entertainment landscape, and to inform so much of our lives and condition the negotiations in which we are involved on a daily basis.

A further benefit of staking out this company and industry path is that through it we might better understand the central role Disney has played in a larger cultural trajectory at which we have hinted. Virilio, whose analyses are woven throughout this study, describes how we have come to inhabit a thoroughly "cinematized" realm today—an environment in which we often see our world as if it were a kind of movie set and ourselves as if we are players within a larger, technologically impelled narrative over which we have little real control. As he allusively puts it, today we are all in some way "victims of the set" (*Art and Fear* 79) and of a kind of totalitarianism that seems built into our various communications and entertainment technologies. Consequently, instead of confronting—and perhaps effectively dealing with—the real world, he suggests, we increasingly find ourselves encountering a "reality effect," a situation in which we are hard put to determine not so much what is *real,* as Jean Baudrillard might suggest, but rather *how* and *if* we can effect any change in a world that has become so obviously elusive/illusive. Yet what we can do, as Virilio reminds us, is to recognize the fact of this "cinematic derealization," try to map its shifting dimensions, and engage it, on both personal and cultural levels, "in a struggle, like Jacob with the angel" (Armitage 159).

On one level, we might think of the work of Disney, as many ideological assessments presume, simply as symptomatic of this situation and as another agent of manipulation and repression. It may be that Disney has achieved its prominent status in both the entertainment industry and in the world mainly because it so fully captures this spirit, works so easily and congruently with this broad cultural trajectory, and has labored throughout its history to link its name with notions of fun, family, and fantasy. Certainly, the Disney theme parks *are* like Potemkin-villages, and in walking through them we do find a postmodern pleasure in their very artifice, especially their naturalized vision of life-as-a-movie-set. For

the sort of cinematically derealized world they offer us just corroborates—
while also rather sanitizing—our everyday experience. This vantage, at
any rate, might help explain why today many think of Disney as, first and
foremost, a creator and operator of such parks, of "Lands" and "Worlds"
into which vacationers happily cast(away) themselves, becoming part
of the various fantasy narratives that the company, in all of its forms,
"tells." Yet on another level, Disney, thanks to the various channels
through which it speaks to a worldwide public—television, cable, film,
internet sites, company stores, vacation resorts, and so on—also begs to
be considered as more than just a symptomatic manifestation. Through
its various technological negotiations, Disney has itself become a powerful driving force that contributes to this "derealization" effect, as well as
a site that, somewhat surprisingly, at times makes its effects practically
transparent and, in the process, also helps us to recognize and deal with
them.

For such reasons, Byrne and McQuillan pause early on in their cultural study of Disney to raise a question. Acknowledging—and effectively satirizing—that long recent fashion of cultural critiques of Disney,
analyses that have accused the company of a staggering range of ills,
including "sexism, racism, conservatism, heterosexism, andro-centrism,
imperialism (cultural), imperialism (economic), literary vandalism, jingo-
ism, aberrant sexuality, censorship, propaganda, paranoia, homophobia,
exploitation, ecological devastation, anti-union repression, FBI collabo-
ration, corporate raiding, and stereotyping" (1), they wonder if there is
anything left to say about Disney or even any point to say it within this
common climate of vilification. Certainly, that litany, with its strange
mix of well-documented historical problems and every manner of more
trendy accusations, might give anyone pause, particularly if one were
trying to stake out some alternative territory. Yet they also wonder if,
perhaps, the very nature of the various Disney texts is in some way responsible for both the persistence of these often extreme attacks and their
almost inexplicable resistance to such challenges. In the face of numerous deconstructions and demythologizings, Disney simply continues
to grow in popularity and profitability. Part of that strength may derive
from the way in which the Disney name has become a rather slippery
signifier, one that, like our constantly changing technology, suggests "a
set of contradictory and unstable ideological codes" (5). But another part
is that Disney has become so much like the very fabric of our modern
technological culture.

Again, I would take our constant need to negotiate with the technological as a lead. For the Disney texts not only grow out of a corporate/

industrial negotiation that involves constant change, but in their depictions of a thoroughly technological world, they also provide audiences with changing narrative models of that activity, whether effective or ineffective, ranging from Mickey's all-too-eager embrace of the Lindbergian gospel of the air in *Plane Crazy* (1929), to Captain Nemo's abjuring of 1950s-era nuclear technology in 20,000 *Leagues Under the Sea*, to *Tron's* (1982) demystification of the world of the computer by equating it with game playing. These and many other Disney texts, including, as we shall see, an increasing number of the theme park rides, are pointedly narratives *about* our relationship to technology—narratives that dramatize key cultural concerns or anxieties, suggest possible terms for responding to those concerns, and invite audiences to project themselves into those circumstances, albeit often from the generally passive vantage of rider or audience. In the process, they grant audiences a certain satisfaction not simply from the sort of imaginary solutions offered—indeed, some Disney texts sketch far-fetched solutions to the concerns they foreground—but more from that sense of participation in or, more precisely, witnessing of a dialogue about those concerns. It is a dialogue that carries little immediate cultural guilt since, at least in recent times, it tends to be scrupulously politically correct, as a film like *Atlantis: The Lost Empire* (2001) particularly demonstrates in its defeat of early twentieth-century technology by a superior and far older nature-based technology. Yet it is also a dialogue—and this is part of its fascination—that seldom seems to make heavy demands on its audience. Thus, Byrne and McQuillan deftly describe the typical Disney text of today as projecting an "aporia of undecidability" (55), as in its efforts at addressing a family audience it also slips away from controversy and extends those negotiations within the narrative to the realm of the audience, as it prompts us to work out *our* attitude towards the real as well. It is as if the Disney text has simply become our own magic mirror, one compelled by our *desire* to strike deals with that technological world, to confirm our most widely held feelings.

Leonard Maltin has pointed out how, for Disney's most recent executive regimes, "embracing new technology is now a way of life" (*Disney* 351). In fact, Al Weiss, president of the Walt Disney World complex of parks, recently announced that while the company plans on "adding new shows, new attractions, and new lands" in all of its parks, the larger corporate strategy is "to look at technology as a way to continue to grow our business" (Schneider). What this study should demonstrate is that this attitude and the resulting corporate growth are not new; they have always been "a way of life" at Disney, even if that way often grew out of the conflicting impulses of Walt to pursue the latest technological developments and Roy to resist their inevitable costs. The manner of this embrace, the constant round of negotiations that always require trade-offs and concessions for every element of gain, has become part of the studio's corporate identity and of the cultural partnership it enjoys. For the Mouse Machine has, from the start, helped innovate and effectively deploy the latest developments in film and entertainment technology, and the negotiations involved in their adoption and employment have produced a wealth of texts that have fashioned a successful working— and entertaining—relationship with the technological, even pleasurably depicting such a relationship for Disney's family audience. The result is, like a walk down any Disney Main Street, typically a pleasant enough experience, one that makes few real demands, that prods us to admire and perhaps to discuss some of the effects we experience, even as it also, like the larger machinery of culture, impels our movement in a generally agreeable direction, one carefully and promisingly laid out for us. The technological "exploitation" that Schickel noted only follows from an ongoing struggle with and in terms of the technological—a struggle that has become a constant of the entertainment industry and part of our modern way of life. Yet Disney has proven itself quite capable of negotiating this struggle and even of finding ways to integrate it into its diverse texts, so that the Mouse Machine can continue, profitably, to work, to grow, and to produce its many pleasures.

1   Sound Fantasy

> The great satisfaction in the first animated cartoons
> was that they used sound properly—the sound was as
> unreal as the action; the eye and the ear were not at war
> with each other, one observing a fantasy, the other an
> actuality.
>
> —Gilbert Seldes (in Leonard Maltin, *Of Mice and Magic*)

In his commentary on early sound film, the noted critic Gilbert Seldes lavishes an ostensible praise on those pioneers like Walt and Roy Disney who embraced the potential of the new technology. It is, of course, something of a backhanded compliment, alluding, on the one hand, to some of the misbegotten efforts at sound narrative readily found among the live-action feature films during the rush to sound in the 1927–28 period, while also implying that the first sound cartoons, such as those produced by the Disney Company starting in 1928, were quite limited in scope, and that Disney especially had elected to use sound, as Alexander Walker also concludes, "non-realistically" (189). Certainly, in many of the early sound films—a situation lampooned in a movie like *Singin' in the Rain* (1952)—image and sound often seem at odds with each other, particularly as the *imperative* to talk combined with the era's bulky and sensitive sound equipment to stultify action in many live-action films. That account, however, along with the critical assessment that has often followed it, hardly does justice to early Disney efforts. For it seems to suggest that we see them all simply as part of a natural aesthetic trajectory that would culminate in a feature film like *Fantasia* (1940), a work that does in many ways seem designed to see just how closely fantasy images might be matched with fantastic sounds.

Certainly, the first Disney sound cartoons do demonstrate a level of fantastic aural imagery that at times hints that, in its early usage, sound existed largely for the purpose of furnishing additional gags, that is, simply for comic effect. As an example, we need only consider the scene in Disney's first sound cartoon, *Steamboat Willie* (1928), in which screen newcomer Mickey Mouse finds that a goat has swallowed Minnie's sheet music. After twisting its tail into the shape of a hand crank, Mickey and Minnie quickly turn the goat into a phonograph to reproduce that music, playing "Turkey in the Straw." Even in the midst of various other such transformative turns, though, we can also see Disney trying to work out more naturalistic applications of the new sound technology, as if already mindful of what would come to be known as the "illusion-of-life" aesthetic that would increasingly become an informing principle for the studio's productions. In fact, we might describe the use of sound technology in early Disney cartoons as less focused on producing fantastic sounds, as Seldes suggests, than on creating a kind of sound fantasy, an aural environment in which real and expressive sound imagery easily merge, where they are constantly in narrative negotiation, constructing a kind of in-between world that is, I would offer, one of their key attractions.

As is so often the case in early film history, the sort of complementary activity I am suggesting follows from a variety of influences, one of them the pointedly economic decision to invest fully, as a studio, in the nascent sound technology. Douglas Gomery has convincingly argued that Disney's embrace of the new technology resulted from a fundamentally sound business sense, the recognition that this very small studio, often on the verge of bankruptcy, needed "to find an appropriate business niche" in an increasingly competitive animation market (72). Fortunately, it was an understanding that worked to keep Disney from going under at a crucial moment in its history. Having just lost control of his modestly successful cartoon character Oswald the Lucky Rabbit, Walt Disney, together with his top animator Ub Iwerks, had managed to fashion a new potential "star," Mickey Mouse, around whom they hoped to build another cartoon series. The mouse, however, originally differed little from the rabbit: the body looked similar, but with circles for ears; backgrounds were again simplistic; the action and gags were much the same, and in some cases were simply copied from the Oswald shorts.[1] In fact, Richard Schickel suggests that, at this stage, the overall style of the mouse was hardly distinctive, but was rather "very much a product of the then-current conventions of animation" (95). Given this general similarity, the first vehicle for Disney's new star, the silent cartoon *Plane*

Crazy (1928), predictably met with a lukewarm reception from potential exhibitors, one that initially seemed to destine Mickey, as Schickel adds, for "a life no longer than many of his competitors" (95). Yet as would so often become the story for the Disney Company, innovation, and with it the needed level of product differentiation, would come not simply from the character but from the technology behind it, in this instance, from a technology that would give both voice and character to Mickey, and sound to his animated world.

Getting access to that technology, however, involved a variety of additional business negotiations and compromises—between the Disneys and the various vendors of the new technology, and even between the Disney brothers themselves, as they weighed the consequences of fully staking their personal futures and that of their company on sound technology. Having tested out the possibility by projecting a cartoon while ad-libbing sound effects and comments, Walt announced that the result "was terrible, but it was wonderful!" (107), and both Disneys agreed that sound could prove a valuable addition to their films. They then worked out a method for adding it, by timing the action to be animated to a metronome that was set to the measure of the music and sound effects they wanted to use.[2] Having established a crude but workable procedure for simply adding a sound increment to their films, Walt then set off for New York, where he hoped to arrange for sound accompaniment for their latest effort, *Steamboat Willie.* Along the way, he stopped in Kansas City to contract with old friend Carl Stalling to compose a simple score for the film. The next step was to decide which of the competing sound technologies to employ—a decision that largely depended on which of the new technologies the small company could afford.

An added difficulty in making this decision came from the fact that there was, as yet, no industry-wide consensus on the best technology, and many of the various sound devices relied on shared or similar patents. As Bob Thomas recounts, Walt rejected the sound-on-disc approach of the Warners-Vitaphone system for some of the same reasons others in the industry hesitated to embrace it: because of its fragility and the ease with which sound and image could lose synchronization. While he found the Fox-Movietone sound-on film system more attractive, largely because of its reliable synchronization and lower follow-up costs (e.g., no need to constantly replace worn-out or broken discs), Fox "was too busy . . . to bother with a small cartoon maker from the Coast" (*Walt* 91). And the other leading sound-on-film vendor, RCA, essentially priced its system beyond the Disneys' modest capacities. Pat Powers, often described in film histories as a "con man" and a "wheeler-dealer," offered an alternative.[3] He was at the time marketing the Powers Cinephone System, a sound-on-film technology created by R. R. Halpenny and William Garity, based on—and, some have suggested, pirated from—the RCA Phonofilm system (Geduld 228). As Schickel offers, Powers saw "in the Mouse exactly the sort of gimmick he needed" to help promote the questionably legitimate Cinephone (101), and so he was quite eager to strike a deal with the Disneys.

Initially, though, finances still stood in the way of this marriage of mutual convenience. A ten-year contract with Powers would cost the Disneys $26,000 per year plus the cost of the Cinephone equipment—a rather substantial investment when they had only been receiving $2,250 from the distributor for each of their Oswald cartoons, which they had been producing at a rate of slightly more than one per month (Merritt and Kaufman 99). As recompense, Powers agreed to distribute the new sound cartoons nationally and pay production costs (underestimated at approximately $2,500 per cartoon), while taking only 10 percent of the gross receipts (Watts 30). Roy's reluctance to proceed with this contract and to begin production on another Mickey cartoon met with pleadings from his brother; in a letter Walt implored, "Why should we let a few dollars jeopardize our chances? I think this is Old Man Opportunity rapping at our door. Let's don't let the jingle of a few pennies drown out his knock" (Thomas, *Walt* 94). To seal this familial side of the negotiations, though, Walt himself had to compromise, agreeing to sell his prized Moon roadster: "I had them send the pink slip to me. I signed it, I sent it back. They sold my car to meet payrolls before I ever got out of New York" (Thomas, *Building* 62).

However, the product that resulted more than repaid these various negotiations, as the Mickey Mouse cartoons quickly caught on and would, in short order, prompt Disney to consider creating another series of cartoons, the Silly Symphonies, designed expressly to capitalize on sound's possibilities as something more than simply an aural complement. In order to assess that accomplishment, and particularly to determine how it is that the Disneys managed to strike the public fancy with their use of this new technology, we need to look in some detail at a few of these early sound cartoons, particularly the groundbreaking *Steamboat Willie* and the first of the Silly Symphony efforts, *The Skeleton Dance* (1929). And as a gauge of the Disney Company's rapid development of what might be described as a characteristic sound aesthetic, I also want to consider a later effort, *Mickey's Trailer* (1938). Coming a decade after *Steamboat Willie,* this cartoon suggests the subordination of that early "sound fantasy," as I have termed it, to the imperatives of the "illusion-of-life" aesthetic that was gradually developed during the 1930s and that had become a dominant influence on the Disney films by the time of *Mickey's Trailer.*

While *Steamboat Willie* was not, as we have noted, the first Mickey Mouse cartoon—or even the first cartoon to employ sound—it is clearly the initial effort at designing a Mickey narrative with a consciousness of the various possibilities sound afforded. Certainly, Walt and Ub Iwerks already had a sense of their new character Mickey, after creating *Plane Crazy* and *Gallopin' Gaucho* (1928). He was, as the very first scene of *Plane Crazy* makes explicit, an embodiment of the Machine Age and its spirit, for we see Mickey admiring a magazine picture of the ultimate Machine Age hero, Charles Lindbergh, and arranging his "hair" and smile to match the figure in the photograph. Mickey's energetic nature is drawn from another key figure of the era, Douglas Fairbanks Sr., whose films obviously inspired the second cartoon *Gallopin' Gaucho.* And *Steamboat Willie,* the third Mickey film, echoed yet another iconic figure of the era, Buster Keaton, by recalling his recently released *Steamboat Bill, Jr.* (1928), and evoking not only his athletic persona, but also what Miles Orvell has described as "the essential Keaton fantasy," an inherent capacity for "transformation" (29). What makes this first true sound cartoon especially interesting, though, is the extent to which that power of transformation is bound up in the film's aural dimension, as Mickey emerges not simply as an embodiment of change, but, almost literally and far more importantly, as a *conductor* of change, as would become most obvious in a later work like *The Band Concert* (1935), wherein he conducts a local orchestra in a successful concert despite a variety of interruptions, including a tornado that destroys practically everything around him.

What makes *Steamboat Willie* particularly striking is the extent to which Disney was able to build that capacity to orchestrate change into the film's soundtrack, even as the company was obviously still struggling to determine how best to use this new technology. One of those uses, of course, is simply to emphasize the reality of the images by selectively giving them voice—or as Paul Virilio has put it, by overcoming the moviegoer's seeming "deafness" (85) in the face of early film. Here, sound provides an aural context for the typical cartoon action, as chickens cluck, a duck quacks, a cow moos, and a boat winch makes a realistically mechanical winding sound. When Mickey's steamboat approaches the landing, we hear the chug of its engine, if not the sound of the water splashed by its paddlewheel, and when Minnie Mouse runs to catch the boat, her shoes provide a pronounced clopping noise. More significantly, other sound effects serve to build a sense of spatial reality by suturing off-screen space to on-screen. Thus when Mickey moves from the steamboat's deck on which the goat/phonograph is playing "Turkey in the Straw" to the ship's interior, we continue to hear the tune, as if through a window, and when at the end Mickey throws a potato at a mocking parrot and knocks it out of a porthole, a splash is clearly audible, indicating that the parrot has fallen into the river. Moreover, that same sound motivates Mickey's impish smile of satisfaction on which the film concludes. These and similar sounds essentially function to help construct the traditional reality illusion in a variety of ways: denoting an action, announcing a presence, suggesting contiguous space, and motivating character response.

Yet at the same time, they also underscore their function as part of a larger aesthetic construction, for the animals make their specific identifying sounds only on cue, with silence following each cluck, quack, or moo, so that we never get the sort of barnyard cacophony reality might actually demand. While the winch contributes its mechanical noise, the boom of which it is part silently swings into action. And as the steamboat approaches the landing and Minnie chases after the boat, the sounds of the boat engine and of Minnie's feet remain constant in volume; there is no hint of sound perspective to suggest changing distance, only indexical sounds to denote presence or action. In fact, it quickly becomes apparent that the sounds we do hear are all carefully selected, and that others we might well expect to hear—such as the splash of the ship's paddlewheel— remain absences just as in a silent film. The result is clear evidence of the soundtrack's general divorce from the image track, or of the extent to which Disney was already adopting what Rick Altman has described as "Hollywood's habit of *constructing* reality (as opposed to *observing* it)" at the level of sound, just as at the more obvious level of the image (47).

What we see in this first Mickey Mouse cartoon is not just the development of a new character, then, but also an effort to sort out some of the narrative possibilities afforded by the new sound technology and ultimately to link those possibilities to character. Sound's potential obviously offered some support for that "illusion-of-life" aesthetic, insofar as it helped to build a realistic mise en scène and motivate character actions and reactions. Yet it also opened onto a transformative potential, as we not only have a goat becoming a phonograph, but each animal on board the steamboat, in turn, proving an effective musical instrument in Mickey's hands. It is as if the goat's eating of the music—literally *internalizing* the potential for sound—inspires Mickey to then *externalize* it, to recognize and then release the potential for music everywhere he sees it. Thus, to join in with the music he pulls a cat's tail to provide a high note and then swings the animal by its tail to produce a continuous siren-like sound. A goose becomes a bagpipe, a pig proves another sort of wind instrument as he plays on its teats, and a cow's mouth becomes an effective xylophone. In fact, the various animals Mickey uses—and clearly abuses in the common fashion of early cartoons—easily mesh with the other "found" instruments he plays—a washboard, pots, pans, a wooden tub—to suggest a world of unexpected potential, marked by its fantastic sounds, that Mickey doesn't simply *produce* but *discovers* and *discloses* to the delight of both Minnie and the audience. And with this demonstration, we also see sound helping to produce—and disclose to the audience—Mickey's basic character.

It is in this same context that we might read the effect that is most commonly cited, rather slightingly, in descriptions of the early Disney talkies—"mickey mousing." Supposedly coined by David O. Selznick, the term describes "the close synchronization of music to action" (Handzo 409), such that the action is continuously punctuated by a specific musical tempo or motif. Sometimes seen as an unfortunate influence of the exaggerations found in the early Mickey cartoons, the term is typically used pejoratively, to suggest overscoring and a pointedly manipulative or intrusive use of the soundtrack that violates the reality illusion. However, that effect most commonly works in conjunction with realistic sound effects—and, in fact, it largely gained that negative implication *because of* this conjunction and the rather difficult narrative negotiation it imposes on the audience. It is, consequently, also in some ways the essence, perhaps even the glory of the early Mickey Mouse and Silly Symphony cartoons, because of the way it suggests the very spirit that moves in them. For "mickey mousing" shows us how the world of these films adapts itself to sound, moves to the beat of the new sound environment, finds its full aural/musical potential, thanks to the energetic intervention of the mouse or some other figure or force.

It is also important here that we recognize that Mickey holds no monopoly on the transformative or conductive potential that is played out in the early Disney talkies. Designed expressly to foreground music and supposedly inspired by Carl Stalling's suggestion of "finding music that was evocative of some mood and building a cartoon around the theme,"[4] the Silly Symphony shorts were inaugurated in 1929 with an eye to, as Steven Watts suggests, being "more experimental in their techniques and structure . . . and full of free-flowing fantasy" (31), without the conventional reliance upon recurring characters to anchor their stories and denote their series status. Robert Haas hits upon one of the main reasons for the success of this new series, as he relates it to the then-popular musical genre and notes how, "unhampered by the restrictions of early sound-filming procedures . . . , Disney combined sound and image in an expressive manner impossible for live-action narrative cinema" (75). That "expressive manner" largely follows from the foregrounding of the soundtrack in these films—a foregrounding that would shortly produce the first hit song for the Disney studio with 1933's "Who's Afraid of the Big, Bad Wolf" from *The Three Little Pigs*—and would eventuate in the studio's ambitious experiment in *illustrating* classical music, *Fantasia*. That expressiveness, though, is also vested in the narratives themselves, carefully chosen to allow for the sort of sound fantasy we have previously described.

The first of these efforts, *The Skeleton Dance,* neatly demonstrates a major form that this expressiveness would take. Scored in part to Edvard Grieg's classical composition "March of the Dwarfs" and set in a graveyard one night, the film describes a transformation in the natural world, as dusk surrenders to deep night and morning eventually dispels the darkness. Marking that shift is a change in the very "music of the night," as a medley of natural sounds gives way to those produced by a host of skeletons, which are, in turn, replaced by the natural sounds associated with dawn's breaking. As the film opens, we hear a variety of natural sounds, all set in time to a musical accompaniment: an owl hoots, the wind whistles, a church bell sounds, wind-blown reeds beat on logs, bats flap their wings, dogs howl, and cats screech. It is a kind of natural cacophony—or symphony—and one that underscores its naturalness by having sounds bridge from one shot to another and by effectively using sound perspective: the bell seen in the deep background sounds as if from a distance, while the bats that emerge from the church steeple make louder noises as they fly into the foreground. While these effects demonstrate how much (and how quickly) Disney had developed in the melding of sound and animation since *Steamboat Willie,* particularly in creating what we might describe as a normal sound environment, they also pointedly serve to build the eerie atmosphere of the scene, in fact, to turn it into something of a mood piece. That eerie mood prepares for the film's key transformation, as a skeleton appears from behind a gravestone, hears the owl's hooting off-screen, and throws his skull at the bird, effectively dispelling the natural sounds in favor of the fantastic sounds of the skeleton dance that follows.

A comic danse macabre then develops as four skeleton heads appear from behind another tombstone, all at different heights, so that the heads and necks form a kind of stylized musical chord, as if visualizing the music that then takes over the soundtrack. That music both announces the start of the skeletons' frolicking and partly emerges from them, since it includes the syncopated sounds of their rattling bones, the chattering of their teeth, the clip-clopping of their feet, and their own musical efforts, such as when one skeleton plays another like a xylophone or when a skeleton, taking a cue from Mickey in *Steamboat Willie*, stretches a cat by its tail and turns it into a bass fiddle. The music simply seems part of the larger spirit of transformation that rules here, as the skeletons freely change shape, stretching and contracting with the music, as they become objects such as a pogo stick or a wheel, and as they all fall, clattering, into a heap of bones, only then to become reanimated and to reconfigure themselves as one larger skeleton. Under the sway of the spirit of the night, this world seems ruled by fantastic sounds and empowered to change at will—or at least at the will of its own sort of "mickey mousing."

However, the film ends on a note of balance, as a natural sound heralds the end of the dance and of this skeleton fantasy. For as dawn breaks, we see a rooster crowing nearby, and a cut to a skeleton offers a reaction shot, as the soundtrack repeats the crowing, only more faintly to suggest distance, to realistically link the two scenes within a contiguous space, and to underscore the sound effect as motivation. Using these naturalistic sound effects not only for structural ends but also in such a *dramatic* way, to signal an end to the night's transformations and its aural fantasies and a return to normalcy, to everyday reality, clearly illustrates Disney's developing sense of sound's narrative potential—and its very rapid placement within a more realistic register. We might note that, earlier in the film, in the middle of the dance, one skeleton moves directly into the camera until the skull completely fills the frame, and as it does so, its teeth chatter in time to the Grieg music, becoming louder as it nears us. This very dramatic use of sound perspective pointedly serves a fantastic effect, underscoring a kind of transgression as the skeleton moves beyond the proscenium-like situation in which the dance has occurred, as if it were coming into our world. Yet in the conclusion, that same perspectival effect, lodged in the rooster's crowing, serves to tame events, to mark the end of the night's transformations, sending the skeletons scurrying back to their graves. This use of a similar aural effect to serve very different ends suggests the successful negotiation with the new sound technology that Disney had managed, a harnessing of its potential in part by tying it to the conventions of realist narrative while retaining some of the transformative character that marked the best early animation.

To better frame that development, though, we might consider a later film like *Mickey's Trailer*, a work that marks a decade of Mickey Mouse cartoons and of Disney's sound work, and one that appears as the Silly Symphony series is essentially being replaced by feature-length cartoons, such as *Snow White and the Seven Dwarfs*.[5] It is a film that, in fact, illustrates the extent to which, within a decade, sound had become a naturalizing influence, helping to ground even the most outlandish visual ideas in a real-world, rather than a fantastic, context. While the film offers a fairly simple story of three Disney friends, Mickey, Donald Duck, and Goofy, who live and travel in a car-drawn trailer, the trailer itself is a fantastic projection of Machine Age ideas, embodying that spirit of transformation we observed in the previous cartoons in the trailer's various mechanical features—its artificial landscape, swiveling walls, collapsing bathtub, disappearing kitchen, and so on. However, sound here consistently helps to reel-in (or real-in) those features, to anchor them and the trailer's three occupants in the natural world, albeit without losing its contributions to the film's more fantastic gags.

Seen in this context, the film's opening is particularly revealing, for it visually announces, through a trompe l'oeil effect, the problematic nature of the real. As Mickey emerges from the trailer, apparently early in the morning, he looks around and offers what should strike viewers as a quite accurate and obvious assessment: "Oh boy! What a day!" Throwing a lever, though, produces the sounds of a motor, grinding gears, and unseen moving mechanisms, as the bright sunny backdrop behind the trailer collapses like a fan, revealing the trailer situated amid the gray, smoke-draped City Dump, as a sign informs us. Then the grass, fence, and other landscaping roll up, and a car emerges from the trailer's side with its engine running. The sounds, in short, reveal reality here, showing that the idyllic illusion on which the film began was—as is the case in most films—simply a construct, the product of a machine. And as the trailer—and the film—moves along, this principle is repeatedly played out. As Mickey pushes a button in the trailer's kitchen, we hear gears and machinery move into action and continue into the next shot, as the bedroom in which Donald has been sleeping turns into a bathroom. Another button push produces similar sounds that forecast the next transformation, as the bathroom turns into a dining room where Mickey serves breakfast. What all of these sounds emphasize is an unseen motive force, a transformative power, lodged not in the mouse but in the "machinery" of this world, always ready to reveal something new.

If the surprise effects of these repeated transformations suggest another sort of fantastic dimension in Disney's use of sound, they also readily link to the more realistic use of sound that had become a standard of

Disney animation. For these rather mysterious off-screen sounds—the sounds of the Machine Age itself, one might suggest—function in much the same way as do the naturalistic sound patterns we have already observed, that is, to suture off-screen space to on-screen, to link scenes, to suggest depth or distance, and to indicate causality or effect. Here, for example, we see Goofy driving the car that pulls the trailer and singing "She'll be Coming 'Round the Mountain," and when the narrative cuts to the interior of the trailer and Mickey fixing breakfast, we still hear Goofy's song, although faintly to suggest the distance. And when Mickey is interrupted by a distant call of "Hey, Mickey!" from off-screen, a cut to the car shows Goofy calling to him. When Goofy accidentally releases the trailer and it goes careening down a mountain road by itself, the narrative branches in several directions, while sound bridges serve to parallel those segments, link them, and even resolve their branchings. For off-screen sounds of, first, a truck, and second, a train announce other vehicles dangerously approaching the trailer and motivate cuts to the truck coming in the opposite direction, or to the train as it races toward a railroad crossing and then reappears shortly after at another crossing. Those same sounds also form narrative rhymes as they recur and motivate repeated reaction shots of Mickey and Donald as they respond to a series of apparent impending disasters. And having avoided multiple collisions, the trailer appears "coming 'round the mountain" just as, from another direction, Goofy appears in the car, singing that same verse, unwittingly and ironically announcing another potential collision.

The narrative is, very simply, masterfully organized around a series of sounds that support and structure its illusion of life. Yet they are also sounds that contribute a measure of suspense, surprise, and even a fantastic irony, as when, in the final image, the trailer bounces on a rock instead of hitting Goofy in the approaching car and then reattaches itself to the car, while we hear Goofy calmly reassuring Mickey and Donald that he did, as promised, "bring you down, safe and sound" from the mountain. Certainly, *Mickey's Trailer* has its share of fantastic if conventionally humorous sound effects, such as when Donald opens a collapsible bathtub and we hear a zipper noise, when Mickey and Donald eat ears of corn and produce a typewriter racket, and when Donald shaves and a scraping sandpaper sound results. Yet those effects, much like the "mickey mousing" of other sounds that accompanies the trailer's wild ride, sit easily within the larger, more naturalistic aural environment of the film, forming a narrative context that is, like the visual illusion that begins *Mickey's Trailer*, a most effective construct, produced not by a lever, of course, but by what had become by this time a complex if somewhat conventional mechanism for combining realistic and fantastic sound features within an animated world.

What all of these cartoons suggest is, on the one hand, a pattern of sound development largely in line with the illusion-of-life aesthetic that was coming to dominate Disney animation, and, on the other, a continuation of exaggerated or surprising sound effects that would still lend a fantastic dimension to the narratives. While *Steamboat Willie* shows at least some mindfulness of how sound might help suggest a level of reality, *Mickey's Trailer*, a decade later, demonstrates how important sound had become to constructing the qualified reality illusion of classical narrative—to suggesting three-dimensional space, linking scenes, establishing narrative parallelism, motivating action and reaction, and so on. By this point, of course, sound itself had become for audiences something less than a new feature or special attraction and was instead a natural part of the film world, including the world of animation. Yet, as these cartoons show, a key import of sound, the transformative potential it almost literally announces, would linger in those fantastic sound elements that still provide jokes, help build a comic atmosphere, inject irony, and ultimately contribute part of that "great satisfaction" Gilbert Seldes, like throngs of others, found in these films.

Virilio has suggested that this introduction of sound technology had a profound impact on life not only within but also outside the confines of the movie theater. As he offers, "Once you have the talkies up and running, you can get walls, any old animated image whatever to talk. The *dead* too, though, and *all who remain silent*. And not just people or beings, either, but things to boot!" Yet along with that seemingly exaggerated observation, he sounds a warning: "You do not lend speech to walls or screens with impunity" (*Art and Fear* 75). In referring to "any old animated image," he might well have had Disney's early cartoons in mind, for as we have seen, Disney took great delight in suddenly bringing the inanimate to life, even giving it speech, such as with the laundry in Mickey's *The Jazz Fool* (1929) or a pack of matches in *The Whoopee Party* (1932); and "the dead too," as evidenced by that first Silly Symphony cartoon, *Skeleton Dance*, with its skeletons that come to life in the moonlight in order to play music and dance, or the quartet of mummies in *Egyptian Melodies* (1931) that emerge from their sarcophagi to dance to a Middle Eastern tune. With speech—or music and song—possible, a most silent world, like the graveyard of *Skeleton Dance* or the pyramid tomb of *Egyptian Melodies*, seems readily to become a noised-filled one, propelled by its own rhythms, suddenly endowed with a new power, and with that power suggesting a world that is always open to change, one that contains, as Cecelia Tichi finds reflected in the literature of this era, constant hints of an "uncontrolled, destabilizing power" (52) that we have been allowed to glimpse—or overhear. Through their capacity for sound, these cartoons had provided audiences with a new sense of connection to their world, a new awareness of its possibilities.

We might say that these melodies were simply meant to be merry, and that they most fundamentally demonstrate the talent and imagination of their creators, combined with the yearnings of their audience for simple entertainment. Thus Steven Watts suggests that we see in them evidence of Disney's fine "instinct for the rhythms and emotions of mass culture" (33). However, they also prompt an interesting question about these cartoons' mixture of the fantastic and the real. For to "lend speech" to objects in this unreserved way starts us to wondering not what they can say or say next, but when they might be silent once more. Does a goat turned into a Victrola ever become a goat again? Thus a staid party in *The Whoopee Party* quickly becomes a raucous musical embodiment of the song that Mickey keeps playing, "Runnin' Wild (Lost Control)." In *The Band Concert* Donald Duck *compulsively* interrupts Mickey's orchestra with his crude tooting of "Turkey in the Straw" on one flute after another, and even a force of nature, a cyclone, is only able to quiet him momentarily. In these instances of what we might term a sound compulsion we can see at work a kind of "impunity," a display of the power of sound that has been unleashed, that had quickly become tied to the character of Mickey Mouse especially—although it would soon transfer to Donald thanks to his tendency for loud and demonstrative comic tantrums—and that suggests how an element of the fantastic might linger at the core of the Disney films. It is a power that is clearly central to these cartoons' fun, and also one that can, pleasurably, bring us up short, as it opens onto an unpredictable, even fantastic dimension of our world, something a bit beyond those realistic "rhythms . . . of mass culture."

While synchronized sound had quite quickly transformed the movie industry—making and destroying careers, bringing a modest studio like Warner Bros. to prominence, dictating the development of new narrative formulae—it also broadcast a message of transformation, and in the case of Disney a hint of what this small, Poverty Row studio might achieve through that technology. However, the Disney films would have to talk more and better. Donald Duck would soon succeed Mickey Mouse as the studio's "star," with his persona largely defined by his verbal sparring with practically everyone and everything he runs up against, and his dialogue constantly taking his character over the top, revving up to a comically unintelligible combination of words and quacks. Feature-length animations like *Snow White* and *Pinocchio* (1940) would develop not as stretched cartoons, but as full-fledged musicals, succeeding in that form even at a time when the live version of the genre was beginning to wane. And Walt Disney, perhaps with a mind to reclaiming a bit more of the fantastic dimension of sound, would push for what David Bordwell has termed "the most famous experiment in stereophonic sound" of early film history (Bordwell, Staiger, and Thompson 359) with *Fantasia*, or as Walt himself would describe this work, an experiment at *"seeing* a concert" (141).

In fact, as a conclusion to this discussion of sound technology, we should briefly consider the case of *Fantasia* and its pioneering stereo system, particularly since the rhetoric surrounding its technology hints of this same tension between the real and the fantastic that underlies the studio's early use of sound, and its problematic reception suggests another dimension of that process of negotiation at Disney—that is, what happens when the studio stumbles or fails in its efforts at technological bargaining. Richard Schickel offers a rather simplistic personal explanation for the creation of *Fantasia*'s special Fantasound system, as he suggests that it was just another instance of Walt Disney wanting to have "his customary technological pleasures" (207). With a more intimate knowledge of its creation, though, William Garity and J. N. A. Hawkins, two Disney engineers involved in developing this technology, describe two very different impulses that impelled their work on the Fantasound system. On the one hand, they suggest a straightforward economic imperative, noting that the studio was hoping for an enhanced level of realism and felt that a simple "improvement of sound-picture quality" would be "reflected at the box-office" (127). Yet on the other hand, they admit to a more ambitious agenda, noting that "perfect simulation of live entertainment is not our objective," and they describe their hope that a technology like Fantasound might allow film to "evolve far beyond the inherent limitations of live entertainment" by exploiting the system's ability to construct and manipulate sounds. As one example, they note how multiple-channel recording might allow a "point-source of sound" to stand out while surrounding sounds could be muted. For another, they suggest that while live sounds "are fixed in space," and that "any movements that do occur, occur slowly," "artificially causing the source of sound to move rapidly in space . . . can be highly dramatic and desirable" (127, 128). Both those "highly dramatic" (or fantastic) effects and a desire for greater aural fidelity (or realism) would come into play in creating a film that, as Steven Watts offers, "took both the realistic naturalism and the fluid fantasy of the Disney style to new levels" (115).

While in some ways little more than an experiment, the *Fantasia* initiative obviously grew out of the earlier short cartoons, which were marked, as we have seen, by their own amalgam of real and fantastic sounds. Indeed, we might term *Fantasia* the ultimate Silly Symphony, since it was originally envisioned as a one-reel cartoon and appeared the year after the last film in that series, *The Ugly Duckling*. However, it grew in length and ultimately in ambition beyond the other feature films the studio was producing, presenting Disney with problems that, for a variety of reasons, simply could not be worked out as easily as had earlier issues surrounding the studio's short cartoons. The primary controversy that initially swirled about this film had to do with another sort of negotiation, the manner in which it tried to bring together classical music with popular cartooning, seen most flamboyantly in the "Dance of the Hours" sequence, with its ballet of hippos, ostriches, elephants, and crocodiles. In fact, some critics would attack the film simply on the basis that the music was not meant to be visualized, and in probably the most extreme of these attacks—one obviously colored by the political climate of the time—Dorothy Thompson in the *New York Herald Tribune* described the film as a "Nazi" effort for its desecration of high art and saw it as symptomatic of "the collapse of the civilized world" (13). But many cartoons, both Disney's and others', had previously offered visual interpretations of both classical and popular music, typically in the service of visual punning, and in this instance Walt Disney had pointedly directed his staff to be sensitive to their classical material, avoiding "broad gags for subtle touches of humor and elaborate forms of fantasy" (Watts 114). As Esther Leslie convincingly argues, though, Disney had been seen, both by the critical establishment and by other filmmakers (such as Sergei Eisenstein), as different from the general run of cartoon producers. His films had often been linked to the world of avant-garde art, particularly in the way they offered audiences a "modernistic dissolution of conventional reality" that politically conscious commentators had much appreciated throughout the 1930s (149). Yet with works like *Snow White* and *Pinocchio,* and their increasing emphasis on a more conventional sense of realism, those opinions had begun to change, and *Fantasia,* in linking this style to a rather middlebrow musical sense, suffered the brunt of this political recoil, which saw the film as an instance of "vulgarization and enchantment through sound" and as part of a cultural "process of making audiences immature and dependent" (Leslie 180).

While this debate on content and treatment lingered in the popular press and intellectual community, an equally significant accomplishment—and equally difficult negotiation—received scant attention. For a significant part of the project of *Fantasia* was this effort to reproduce the *quality* of a live musical experience, particularly to offer audiences in movie theaters throughout the country an aural experience akin to that enjoyed in a sophisticated sound environment, such as that of the Philadelphia Academy of Music. Prior to the development of workable sound systems like Vitaphone and Movietone, this notion had been on the minds of many in the film industry, who hoped to replace expensive orchestras with film sound and to provide audiences with concert-like cinematic performances, as some of the early Vitaphone shorts featuring famous musicians and opera stars attest. The sound quality produced by these first-generation systems, however, easily frustrated such hopes, and the rush to adopt an industry-wide standard, along with the costs of the new equipment, undercut the rapid development of a more capable system.

Begun with somewhat more limited ambitions, as an effort at using stereophonic sound technology in a Silly Symphony–type cartoon, *Fantasia* started with *The Sorcerer's Apprentice* sequence, recorded on a specially modified sound stage at the Pathé Studio in California. It employed new sound equipment co-designed by Disney and RCA engineers and an orchestra of one hundred musicians conducted by Leopold Stokowski. Arranged in a semicircular orchestra shell, the musicians were divided into five sections, separated by double-plywood partitions, each of which contained its own microphone, so that a multiple-channel recording could be obtained that would allow for any desired dynamic balance when the music was eventually fitted to the animation. In a technical report on this initial effort, Garity and RCA engineer Watson Jones explain that a major goal of this approach was "the reproduction in the theater of a full symphony orchestra with its normal volume range and acoustic output as well as the illusion that would ordinarily be obtained with a real orchestra" (Garity and Jones 7). That first attempt, though, produced less than satisfactory results, especially because of the poor low-frequency separation and impaired tempo due to the absolute separation of the musicians within their confining plywood partitions. As this elaborate Silly Symphony cartoon developed into a more complex project, growing into Disney's "concert film," as it would eventually become known around the studio, a decision was made to use the Philadelphia Symphony Orchestra in place of Hollywood musicians and to record them in the Academy of Music, which would provide excellent acoustical properties and which already contained some of the RCA multiple-channel recording equipment that had recently been used for Universal Pictures' production of *100 Men and a Girl.*

Throughout the spring of 1939, Garity and Jones supervised the set-up of the Fantasound system in the basement of the Academy. The basic scheme for Fantasound involved four optical-film sound tracks—a control track, screen left, screen right, and screen center—all recorded on standard 35mm film and then printed side-by-side across the useful area of another 35mm reel (Garity and Hawkins 135). These tracks were mixed from eight recording channels that, in the case of *Fantasia,* were focused on 1) violins, 2) cellos and bass, 3) violas, 4) brass, 5) woodwinds, 6) tympani, 7) a mix of the first six channels, and 8) "a distant pickup of the entire orchestra," capturing its general balance and the room's reverberations (Garity and Hawkins 144). Later, a ninth channel was added, which recorded a "beat" or tempo to aid the animators in timing the various sequences. All of the microphones were channeled to a central switching panel next to the conductor's position, and there an operator, following the score, would mute those microphones not then in use "to minimize noise and leakage" (Klapholz 67). A key feature, or as Garity and Hawkins offer, "the brain" of the Fantasound system (131), was its tone-operated gain-adjusting device, or Togad, which controlled each of the three sound-track levels through variable gain amplifiers and which could be used to customize the system for ambient noise in a particular theater, to create the illusion of a sound moving across the screen, and even to isolate specific tracks while muting other sounds, as in the case of the choir rendition of "Ave Maria" at the film's conclusion, wherein the "sacred" music of the hymn gradually takes over from the dark melody of Mussorgsky's "Night on Bald Mountain." With the Togad device applied to each of the channels, Fantasound was able to produce both a more naturalistic sound experience than in other sound films and fantastic aural effects through its capacity for isolating and manipulating individual sounds.

These achievements, however, were destined never to reach a large audience, thanks in part to Disney's status as a minor, under-capitalized studio, and thus to a bottom-line business sense that, under Roy Disney's guidance, ultimately ruled many of these negotiations. Unlike the major movie studios, such as Paramount and MGM, Disney owned no theaters of its own in which to set up the new equipment, and because of the bulkiness of the Fantasound playback system, the expense of installing it, and the limited number of units then available, the stereo version of *Fantasia* could only be exhibited with its designed soundtrack on a limited road-show basis. Installing the equipment in participating theaters was a most difficult fit. Garity and Jones note that the complete Fantasound package, which weighed approximately fifteen thousand pounds, required forty-five packing cases, and took up one-half of a standard freight car space. Of the theaters in which it was eventually installed, six had to have new power lines run, three needed the projection room enlarged, and in every case some of the equipment, particularly some of the eleven racks of amplifiers, had to be placed outside of the projection booth. The initial installations at New York's Broadway Theater and Los Angeles's Carthey Circle Theater, the only theaters to actually purchase the system outright, cost $85,000 apiece. That expense prompted Disney to scale back the elaborate fifty-four-speaker system used in these two theaters and to offer for the subsequent road-show appearances a leasing arrangement that ran to $45,000—still a very expensive proposition for 1940. And while Garity and Jones suggest that further efforts at "developing mobile units . . . would have lessened installation time and costs" (15) and perhaps would have made the system a more attractive proposition for high-end venues, diminishing returns from the road-show distribution and the scarcity of electronic equipment due to growing defense needs, or what they allusively describe as "wartime conditions" (15), effectively ended those efforts.

The relative failure of the Fantasound system does remind us that the development and embrace of a new technology are not always easy, automatic, or profitable, even when the technology itself proves workable. While Disney had been quite successful with its early adoption of sound and, as the next chapter will detail, with its early move into the latest color technology, in the case of Fantasound there were simply too many factors to be easily negotiated, some of them unconnected to either the studio or the technology itself.[6] If the film's relative failure—or at least lukewarm public reception—proved a financial disappointment to the Disneys, it was also an important lesson in the limitations, and potential pitfalls, of that technological embrace.

And yet, like so many other technological developments to which the studio would commit itself over the years, Fantasound did offer great potential. Addressing the Society of Motion Picture Engineers, Walt Disney announced that "fully exploited, Fantasound should prove a startling novelty" (142). And as Garity and Jones observe, those who used the system quickly recognized that, "no matter in what form, ordinary sound-track reproduction is flat and dull by comparison" (15). Consequently, even after *Fantasia*'s disappointment at the box office, Disney continued to experiment with the system. E. H. Plumb of Disney's music department recounts that by 1942 the studio had recorded orchestral performances of five additional compositions for possible use in future Fantasound films, concentrating in these efforts on "two qualities of Fantasound that seem to us to be important—the illusion of 'size,' possible to attain by proper use of a multiple-speaker system, and recognizable placement of orchestral colors important to the dramatic presentation of the picture" (18). Plumb held out the hope that has often buoyed the film industry as it introduced a new technology, that "it is within the power of Fantasound, as an idea, to revitalize the industry" (21). Yet the recognition that this system, because of its still experimental status, remained largely an "idea," a technology that lingered, as Plumb puts it, "at the wandering stage of its development" (21), is noteworthy. It suggests that Fantasound, on another level, was still perceived as something of a fantastic or futuristic conception that could not be squared with the realities of a prewar and wartime film industry. Despite Seldes's observation, it was a technology that, for all of Disney's pioneering experience with sound, would remain caught somewhere between fantasy and actuality. Its successful negotiation would remain in the far future for both Disney and the entire film industry.[7]

2 Minor Hazards:
Disney and the Color Adventure

Acquiring a tool, any new piece of equipment, industrial
or otherwise, means also acquiring a particular danger; it
means opening your door and exposing your private world
to minor or major hazards.

—Paul Virilio, *A Landscape of Events*

In discussing the sort of "accidents" that typically accompany
what he terms "technical evolution," Paul Virilio traces them back to
a kind of compromise or bargain we typically have to strike, much like
those varied bargains we have been describing in the previous sections.
To pursue the advantages offered by any new technological development, we also have to accept the fact that problems will accompany it;
as Virilio puts it, we must expose ourselves to a potential "symmetry
between substance and accident" (54). To an extent, he is reformulating
an idea that has received increasing notice in our technological culture,
that every technical leap involves dangers or trade-offs. Edward Tenner,
for example, makes a similar point, as he describes how our technological
developments invariably seem to "bite back," confronting us with "the
ironic unintended consequences" of our own ingenuity (6). Yet Virilio
goes a step further, as he tries to describe how we should respond to those
hazards, try to accommodate this almost predictable "symmetry" in our
modern media environment. One common strategy is simply to repress
the dangers, that is, to deny their existence or assert that we have effectively guarded against them—a common political expediency at all levels.
Another approach is to ward them off or render them less threatening by

foregrounding or exploiting them; as he puts it, "to expose the accident so as no longer to expose oneself to the accident" (55). I note these different strategies, these discourses of denial and of exposure, as we might term them, because they offer a useful way of describing another of those negotiations in which the Disney studio was involved, in this case, one of the most significant technological advances in film, the introduction of the three-strip Technicolor process in the 1930s. Already well chronicled from the standpoint of the economic and technical issues surrounding its introduction, the history of Technicolor's appearance, particularly when the Disney studio adopted it in 1932, is marked, aesthetically, by an interplay of these two responses—of denial and exposure—that seems particularly characteristic of the studio and its developing approach to new technologies. And it is an approach that the studio would use again when it moved into color television broadcasting in the 1960s.

From the first, the three-strip Technicolor process was offered to the film industry with an understanding that certain "dangers" attended its adoption. Other color technologies had already appeared and disappeared, including two-color Kinemacolor, two-color Prizmacolor, three-color Chronochrome, Technicolor's own two-color system, and numerous others (Neale 114–28). But these and many similar processes all failed after producing less than satisfactory color, requiring substantial technological investment, and generally increasing print costs far more than rentals could be expected to recoup. As a result, the film industry in the early 1930s was leery of embracing yet another process that produced potentially unsatisfactory results and less than eager audience response, especially following hard on the expensive conversion to sound and the dwindling box office receipts that had accompanied the deepening Depression. As a response, and as another way of differentiating its new product from these previous processes, the Technicolor company, as Richard Neupert has chronicled, adopted a public discourse about "natural" color, one that specifically targeted criticisms that its prior color process had produced unnatural or "artificial and distracting" ("Painting" 110) colors. Neupert further recounts how Natalie Kalmus, chief of the company's Color Advisory Service and its top "Color Consultant," also tried to reassure the film industry that the newly developed three-strip Technicolor format would produce no such "accidents." Deploying this discourse of denial, Technicolor claimed that, by combining its new three-strip technology with the careful supervision of its use by the company's trained color advisors and adherence to accepted aesthetic conventions of color use, it had "taken the aesthetic risks out of shooting" in color (Neupert, "Exercising" 22).

And yet, for many in the industry, questions had to remain, partly because the industry itself seemed unsure precisely what it wanted from—and indeed whether it wanted or even *needed* to pursue—color cinematography. Robert Edmond Jones, a top Broadway stage designer, had come to Hollywood during this period precisely to assist in developing color films; he served as production and costume designer on several of the first live-action three-strip Technicolor films, including the short *La Cucaracha* (1934) and the feature *Becky Sharp* (1935). Writing about that experience, he described his dissatisfaction with those productions, complaining that "color and Hollywood's idea of color are two different things" (206). The few early two-strip films that had found some measure of success and audience acceptance, he argued, were effective largely because they had managed to capitalize on two rather different appeals: "the color gratifies our desire for novelty . . . and it appeals to our sense of recognition" (207). A sense of the unusual and a sense of the natural, he believed, had worked hand in hand. And yet both Hollywood and the Technicolor Corporation seemed at some pains to dismiss the element of the unusual. The novelty effect, it was felt, would quickly wear off, and Jones saw both the industry and Technicolor in the mid-1930s as concentrating largely on the ability of the new process to so match the natural world that "the audience would forget [the film] was colored" (207).

Yet what was missing, Jones suggested, was another sort of novelty— a clear sense of color's own narrative power and a freedom to employ it in an almost expressionistic way. In fact, he advocated a discourse of exposure, an approach to the new process that would tout and exploit the three-strip capacity not simply to make the filmed world look natural, but to function much more like it did on the stage, as "a dramatic agent of real value" (209), as an aesthetic component that could bring a new source of meaning to the film narrative. However, he believed that the desire to avoid what, because of past failings, might seem to some audiences little more than an "accident"—a misuse or distracting misregistration of nature's colors—would work against developing this sort of "dramatic" color value and thus achieving the full promise of the new process.

Kalmus had tried, a bit cautiously, to frame the company's product more in this context. While emphasizing the "natural" use of color, she also suggested employing "color's cultural connotations" or traditional "symbolic associations," and using these links for "delivering essential story information" (Neupert, "Exercising" 24–25). These steps were all consistent with her larger policy, one that emphasized applying "the laws of art properly in relation to color" (Kalmus, "Color" 25). Of course, this approach was hardly unconventional or challenging, but rooted in a rather customary, even conventional sensibility. Ultimately, it represented another sort of naturalness; as Neupert explains, Kalmus's policy simply followed "a long line of color practitioners who accept as fairly natural that color's meanings are fixed and definable" ("Exercising" 26). Comparing color to sound, Kalmus described color as the next logical step in film's historical trajectory, "tending towards complete realism." While helping to mold film's vision "according to the basic principles of art," her approach ultimately aimed to produce what she termed an "enhanced realism" (Kalmus, "Colour" 116).

And even as Technicolor offered a rhetoric that tried to rule out the accident, that which might in some way further put off viewers, it also had to confront several aesthetic concerns within the industry. As Bordwell, Staiger, and Thompson note, while the company sought "to stress that color was simply an increase in realism applicable to any film," many in the film industry and even in the movie-going public from the start linked such processes to notions of "stylization and spectacle" (355). Despite Technicolor's claims of offering "a 'lifelike' rendition of the visible spectrum," cinematographers expressed little confidence that the three-strip process could adequately accommodate "classical" cinematography, particularly the practice of creative photography that "conformed to norms of softness, low contrast, and diffusion" (355), allowing especially for the creative presentation of that centerpiece of classical narrative, character. A truly creative cinematography, it was felt, required something other than that "lifelike" promise inherent in Technicolor's supposedly "natural" discourse.[1]

Of course, with animation, and especially cartoons, the question of naturalness was not necessarily a restrictive concern, and the relative ease with which even established cartoon characters could evolve over the years suggests that another order of creativity typically ruled their development. Even though the Disney studio had already established a reputation for realistic animation, thanks in part to Walt's insistence on the natural, illusion-of-life style to which we have previously referred, as well as on his efforts to assist his animators in achieving this look by providing in-studio art classes, that level of realism, even in black and white, ultimately served a more complex strategy. It represented a kind of compromise that Steven Watts, describing the structure of later Disney films, has termed an "aesthetic hybrid." For Watts this sort of compromise simply reflects the vein of "sentimental modernism" that he sees running through most of the Disney narratives, an attitude "in which visual verisimilitude and a free-flowing modernist sensibility supported each other with a kind of tensile strength" (104). Yet that balance was even more fundamental than just a component of narrative structure. In a memo to Don Graham, the art instructor Walt brought in to tutor his animators, Disney sought to clarify a basic animation aesthetic that he had in mind: "The point must be made clear to the men that our study of the actual is not so that we may be able to accomplish the actual, but so that we may have a basis upon which to go into the fantastic, the unreal, the imaginative" (quoted in Watts 108). A compromise, one that served both the realistic and the spectacular or fantastic impulses, was thus built into Disney animation from early on, rendering it potentially more accommodating to the various concerns that surrounded the new color process, and making the company a suitably flexible fit for the new technology.

Conventional wisdom has suggested that the Technicolor Corporation approached Disney largely because the major film studios showed little enthusiasm for the new technology, thanks to industrial and social conditions, as well as their prior unsatisfactory experiences with other color processes. In the early 1930s, as Gorham Kindem explains, "audiences were declining, production budgets were being cut, and musicals, the genre with which two-strip Technicolor had become closely associated, were suddenly considered box-office poison" (150). Disney, while a small studio and reliant on the majors to distribute its product, for several reasons seemed a useful, even a most appropriate client for Technicolor. One of the most important of these reasons was, as Kindem suggests, that "innovators of one feature-film technology often innovate another" (152), and this small independent studio had already established a reputation for technological innovation, particularly with its quick embrace of sound. With the coming of talking pictures, Disney did not, like many of the majors, wait for a format on which the entire industry would standardize, but instead quickly moved production to sound, using the still experimental Cinephone system, and in the process pioneering the sound cartoon. Based on the great success of that effort—which arguably saved the studio by making Mickey Mouse a "star"—Walt and Roy Disney had committed the company to sound, even creating the new Silly Symphonies series, based on musical themes, to exploit the new technology and diversify their product line. And sound was not the only studio innovation, for as we shall see in subsequent chapters, Disney was quickly developing a reputation as a studio pointedly open to technological development, and one that saw such innovation as important to its success in a niche market.

I would add, though, that the very nature of the Disney product was almost equally important in establishing the atmosphere for a partnership with color. For Disney's approach to animation must have seemed a welcome way around some of those aesthetic qualms noted above, a way of allowing Technicolor to continue its industry-oriented discourse of "natural" color, while also exposing the separate narrative influence that color might wield. By their very nature, cartoons *were* an exaggeration of the real, yet a large measure of their pleasure resided in their ability to *approach* the natural world, to make their constructions suggest a recognizable reality, while also offering an interpretation of that reality. In effect, the Disney style was most accommodating to the sort of double discourse that seemed to swirl around discussions of color cinematography. As a result, with Disney Technicolor had a client that not only was sympathetic to innovation, but also had a product, the animated cartoon, that might show its technology to maximum effect.

However, before Disney could officially commit to the Technicolor Corporation and its process, one further bargain had to be struck, an economic one. As many have noted, at the heart of Disney's success was a kind of dynamic tension between Walt, the creative genius, and his brother Roy, the careful financial manager, with the former constantly proposing new ideas, initiating new projects, and the latter always attempting to hold the budgetary line and rein in his brother's flights of fancy. As had been the case with sound, Roy opposed altering the status quo by committing their struggling studio to an expensive and still unproven technology. According to his biographer, Bob Thomas, Roy told his brother, "We'd be crazy to take on the expense of color" (*Walt* 114). Roy had, after all, just finished negotiating a new deal with United Artists to distribute their films, and he well knew that, while the color films would cost far more to produce, UA would not advance them any additional money to offset that expense. He also feared—and rightly so, as later experience would prove—that the paints then in use might not adhere to the animators' cells or would fade under the hot lights required for color photography. Moreover, Walt's enthusiasm for the new technology promised to have an immediate negative impact on the studio's production schedule, since he proposed scrapping much of the work that had been done on a current Silly Symphonies production, *Flowers and Trees,* in order to redo it in color and so that they might rush the first Technicolor cartoon into theaters.[2] In a variation on that discourse of exposure, though, Walt used Roy's opposition for leverage. By announcing his brother's misgivings, Walt gained a concession from Technicolor that, in turn, finally won Roy's approval—a two-year exclusive-use contract that would guarantee the sort of product differentiation that most of the studios typically tried to claim for their films.[3] And in an increasingly crowded animation market, one that included not only the well-established Fleischer brothers and Warners' cartoon unit, but also Disney defectors like Ub Iwerks, that differentiation could prove very important.

To make this bargain work, the still-developing Disney illusion-of-life aesthetic quickly had to accommodate more "exposed" color applications. As a result, the Disney artists seem from the outset committed not just to adding color or to using it to create a more convincing and impressive sense of reality, but to exploring the possibilities of using color creatively. Even the studio's first Technicolor effort, *Flowers and Trees*, a work, as we have noted, originally conceived as a black-and-white production, demonstrates how quickly the animators began experimenting with highly atmospheric and even symbolic uses of color, uses that fit right in with the more ambitious trajectory that Disney was starting to lay out for the studio's animation (as would become obvious in a pointedly experimental work like *Fantasia* [1940]), and uses that could hardly escape some of those early qualms about "stylization and spectacle."

With its release in late 1932, *Flowers and Trees* quickly rewarded Walt's enthusiasm, since it proved extremely popular. As Bob Thomas points out, the first color Silly Symphonies cartoon "got as many bookings as the hottest Mickey Mouse cartoon" of that time, thereby prompting Walt's decree to produce all future films in this series in color (*Walt* 115). However, this first effort still suggests some caution about deploying the new technology in an overtly "stylized" way. For much of its story, the colors seem to operate primarily on a naturalistic scale, with greens and browns naturally dominating the forest setting. The plot is a simple love triangle, involving slender boy and girl trees whose happy dancing is spoiled by an old, gnarled, and mean-spirited tree. The young trees are a light brown with green leaves serving as "hair." In contrast, the older tree is a dark gray, suggesting its age and recalling a figure from a black-and-white Silly Symphony, with its only hint of color a green "tongue"— actually a lizard that repeatedly pops, lasciviously, from its mouth. The other major elements of the story also have pointedly "natural" color correspondences—the yellow and white daisies that dance around the younger trees, the orange and brown mushrooms that spring up from the ground and form a kind of appreciative audience for the dancing trees, the black birds whose nests and hatchlings suggest the proper goal of the young trees' romantic dance, and the golden caterpillar that also joins in their dance. These colors are all clearly appropriate to the figures and help paint a recognizably natural world.

And yet *Flowers and Trees* manages to draw specific thematic resonances from these colors, illustrating a pattern that would continue as the Silly Symphonies developed into more complex narratives and as the Disney animators became more accustomed to what the new Technicolor technology would permit. Certainly, the near absence of color in the older tree serves a minimally symbolic function, its gray lending it a deathly pall and bracketing it off from the warm shades of the natural world, while the green lizard it sports contrasts sharply with the leafy green of the other trees, imparts a menacing tone to what should be a sign of life and vitality, and hints of its motivating jealousy. When the older tree's effort to seize the young girl tree is rebuffed, he uses dried gray twigs to produce fire, the small red tongues of which are pointedly juxtaposed with the oranges and browns of the mushrooms, and the effect of which is to remove color from all that the fire touches, reducing elements of the forest to black ashes, complementary in color to the old tree's gray. And the defeat of the old tree and its fires is marked by the return of a variety of colors—the flowers reappearing to form a garland for the girl tree, the mushrooms resurfacing as a colorful audience, and the golden caterpillar rolling into a circle, becoming a ring to mark the union of the girl and boy trees. In this last effect especially, *Flowers and Trees* at least verges on a discourse of exposure.

Since *Flowers and Trees* had not been from the start designed with color in mind, it could hardly be expected to fully exploit the technology's possibilities, but within the year and after a number of other color Silly Symphonies had been produced, we see a more complex use of color begin to surface, as a film like *Babes in the Woods* (1932) illustrates. A variation on the Hansel and Gretel fairy tale, *Babes* begins with a rather stylized image, as flowers and birds, all in highly saturated colors, dominate the frame and surround a black rock, roughly shaped like a witch. They create an almost festive atmosphere for the narrative that follows, essentially a flashback to an earlier time, prior to the witch-rock's appearance, and they anticipate another element of color, two gaily dressed Dutch children walking through the woods. The colors, in fact, create an effective atmosphere and largely tell the story here, for as the children move through the forest, its colors gradually change, from greens to browns to grays, suggesting movement deeper into this world, while also obviously developing an ominous atmosphere. A clearing, however, introduces the unexpected, as the children come upon an elf village, with the elves all dressed in bright shades of red, sporting stark white beards, and going about their daily work as if it were play. With the elves' appearance, the dark woods become bright again, as if their darkness only disguised a bright, colorful, and happy realm, one of perpetual childhood in which the brightly dressed Dutch children seem at home and happy.

The second stage in this story, though, twists this vision by playing upon the children's—and our own—*colored* expectations. From the dark edges of the forest appears an old woman, the witch, dressed in gray and black and surrounded by black birds. This dark extension of the woods frightens off the elves, but after taking the children for a ride on her broom, she reintroduces a riot of color, landing them in another clearing where they find her house, one made of brightly colored candies, cakes, and pies—or as she offers, "sugar, spice, and everything nice." When they are lured inside, though, the children find the interior of this colorful location to be dull, colored in grays and browns, and containing cages full of black creatures: bats, spiders, rats, and cats. As the children quickly learn, when the witch pours an elixir from a black vial on the boy and turns him into another black spider, these captive "pets" are simply children like themselves, similarly lured to the witch's lair by its attractive and colorful appearance. When the elves reappear and distract the witch, though, the girl discovers a green bottle (a color of vitality), pours its contents on her brother, and restores him; she then pours the liquid on the witch's other pets, transforming them all back to brightly dressed children. Together, the elves and children then defeat the witch and drop her into a vat of another of her concoctions, from which she emerges and turns red, then brown, and finally a dark gray as the material hardens. She becomes that witch-shaped black rock on which the narrative opened, and bright color returns to the narrative, as a dissolve restores the opening scene—the black rock surrounded by flowers, vines, and brightly colored birds. It is the triumph of life, vitality, and variety—of color—over the dark, stifling, and monochromatic vision that she represented, a kind of trial run for the more ambitious story of *The Three Little Pigs* that followed the next year.

With a film like *Babes in the Woods,* color took on such a thematic resonance at least in part because the narrative could not rely on developed characters to help convey the story. When the studio decided in 1935 to extend the use of Technicolor to the films of its "star," Mickey Mouse,[4] color could easily have taken a back seat and become more "natural," since it would have to be subordinated to an established character. Yet *The Band Concert*—the first Mickey cartoon shot in Technicolor and one that, as Steven Watts notes, many critics consider "to be Disney's masterpiece among his animated shorts" (65)—strikes a medium ground between denial and exposure. Its color scheme is clearly designed not only for a naturalistic effect, but also to advance the principle of carica-

ture. In fact, the setting—a rural scene of a small bandstand in a clearing, surrounded by trees, fields, and a few farmhouses—is indistinct for
much of the film, with the backgrounds just broadly suggestive of the
setting and done in pastel shades of blue (the sky) and green (nature).
Against this sparsely detailed and vaguely naturalistic backdrop, the
film repeatedly centers Mickey, the bandleader, or other music-playing
anthropomorphs (Goofy, Horace Horsecollar, Clarabelle the Cow, etc.)
in the foreground wearing uniforms in the highly saturated Technicolor
primaries—red, blue, and green—that make them stand out against the
muted backgrounds and argue for the heightened importance in which
these characters see themselves and their actions. Mickey's long red
military-style coat with gold buttons and epaulets seems to comment
particularly on his status, since it is many sizes too big for him: dwarf-
ing him, slipping over his arms as he leads the band, so that one arm
constantly seems much longer than the other, and causing him to trip
over its tails and fall on his face as he tries to fend off a pestering Donald
Duck. If the bright red coat signals his status as leader, it is also practically a character itself insofar as, much like the Duck, it repeatedly seems
to mock him, to point up the disparity between his slightness and his
persistent sense of self-importance. And it is a point underscored when
a storm comes up and undresses several of the band members, stripping
them even of their red long underwear, while also, in two cases, inflating
the underwear to suggest animated figures—like themselves.

The other key color motif consistently highlighted here is that of
gold or brass, the color of the trim on all the band uniforms, of the music stands, and especially of the instruments that, as the brief narrative
unfolds, increasingly become comic props or foils for the action. By the
way it stands out against the muted pastels used to represent nature,
the gold imagery quickly suggests another order of things, an intrusion
that predicts the later appearance of the cyclone. Mickey's gold epaulets
flip-flop as he waves his arms, almost as if they had a life of their own;
the gold and red caps of each band member repeatedly lift off their heads
as they play their instruments, as if propelled by the force of the sounds
they produce; and a yellow and black bee (another sort of "accident"),
stirred up by the music, proceeds to harass each of the band members,
while also anticipating the arrival of the cyclone that seems to have been
evoked by their rendition of "The Storm." The sense of vitality linked
to this color carries over to the instruments, which not only produce
the music, but often seem to produce the characters themselves, as they
precipitate key actions. For example, the slide of a trombone accidentally
snares the Duck and releases a golden shower—myriad flutes he has been

using to bedevil Mickey by joining in with the band's playing. Horace's cymbals become a way of swatting the bee that is interfering with their playing—but also another sort of interference, as he accidentally claps Goofy's head between them, producing a truly goofy-looking Goofy. And a bright tuba, picked up by the storm, lands in center frame to cover up and at last shut up the Duck, practically literalizing the notion that silence is golden. Finally, the flutes that Donald keeps producing, and that Mickey repeatedly confiscates and breaks, seem to appear as if by magic—in fact, the Duck several times poses as if he were a magician as he materializes them—becoming the golden emblem of his persistence and of another sort of storm that can simply take things off on its own course, hijacking the music and the musicians, shifting their tunes from classical to popular styles (from gold to brass).

Of course, such uses of color hardly deserve to be called accidents, but they did constitute a kind of "accidenting" of the new color technology, much as in another film from the same year, the Academy Award winner *The Tortoise and the Hare*, in which the Hare, after stepping out of his training robe, emblazoned with his nickname "The Blue Streak," begins running and becomes, quite literally, a *blue* streak on the film. Such cases pointedly drew out from or revealed in the Technicolor process a potential that the company was at some pains to disguise, deny, or simply compromise. Caricature, particularly through the use of color, as we see in the case of both the Hare and Mickey in *The Band Concert*, does not quite lend itself to the sort of transparent reality that was a hallmark of classical film narrative. And consistent color motifs, such as the gold that attaches to every sort of "music" in *The Band Concert*, even the buzzing bee, were not, on the surface, consistent with the aesthetic that the Disney studio, at least *publicly*, tended to emphasize—that of the illusion of life.

Ultimately, the Silly Symphonies, the Mickey Mouse cartoons, and even the feature-length *Snow White* did not radically alter the film industry's pace in switching over to color production. While they established the quality of Technicolor's three-strip product and demonstrated that there was an audience for color films, they were, after all, simply cartoons, mainly program support for the serious business of the feature film. And indeed, the first major Technicolor feature, *Becky Sharp*, probably had little more effect, thanks to its rather awkward efforts at a dramatic color usage.[5] It was only in the latter stages of the Depression, as David O. Selznick released three successive Technicolor features—*A Star Is Born* (1937), *The Adventures of Tom Sawyer* (1938), and *Gone with the*

Wind (1939)—all of which had strong box offices, that the industry finally began serioiusly to consider regular color production. Although it was at this point too that color was most self-consciously "accidented." For in 1939 *The Wizard of Oz* clearly demonstrated that color need not be bound to realistic reproduction in order to be effective. And it was a point hardly lost on Disney, for in the following year *Fantasia* appeared, a feature that was obviously color keyed for maximum narrative effect. Esther Leslie's analysis of the film begins from precisely this point, as she argues that "Colour harmony went beyond aesthetic stylization into the near ideological, as the centaurs and 'centaurettes' paired up in matching colour casts. All the colours were keyed psychologically, matching the changes in emotions being expressed by the actions" (286). However, with the advent of World War II, with its attendant restrictions and box office uncertainties—with its own sort of imperative of compromise— such color experiments were destined to have little industry impact. In fact, color production would represent less than 10 percent of major studio output until after the war's end (Izod 136).

Fittingly, with the rapid spread of television in that post-war period, Disney again took the lead in the use of color, demonstrating a very similar color strategy for working in this new medium. After the initial success of the *Disneyland* television series from 1954 to 1961, and an increasing number of disputes with their home network, ABC, the Disney brothers began to consider a new home for their flagship anthology show. Walt had from the start, and despite ABC's veto, wanted to present the series in color, even shooting all of the show's new material in color, despite the fact that it was being broadcast in black and white, since he felt that, as Bill Cotter notes, "color was essential to making the best use of his products" (67), allowing them to connect with the audience, while supporting the possibility of later theatrical releases. As the leader in color television broadcasting, NBC loomed as a promising alternative, and further strengthening the possibility of a fit, NBC was engaged in its own effort at product differentiation. At this time it was heavily promoting color programming, partly because the network had the largest number of national affiliates equipped for color broadcasting, but also because its parent company, RCA, was the major American producer of color televisions. When RCA agreed to sponsor half of the episodes if the Disneys would agree to move their anthology show to NBC,[6] a deal was quickly struck, with the program changing its name to *Walt Disney's The Wonderful World of Color*—a title that underscored the new partnership between Disney's fantasy perspective, RCA's color

technology, and the natural (or *Wonderful*) world, while also suggesting
a kind of "industrialization of vision" at work in the new program, as
well as in the larger entertainment industry.

A remarkable first show for NBC on September 24, 1961, underscored
these links, as well as the new color-ful identity for the series. Instead of
the original *Disneyland*'s animated depiction of the different thematic
worlds on which the series had focused—Fantasyland, Frontierland, Adventureland, and Tomorrowland, all presented in black and white on
ABC—the newly titled *The Wonderful World of Color* opened with ka-
leidoscoping images of the world done in brilliant color, accompanied
by a new theme song, reminding viewers that "the world is a carousel
of color, wonderful, wonderful color." This beginning would, over the
next twenty years, become the series' familiar signature, linking it simultaneously to television's developing color technology, to the colors
of nature, *and* to the technological construction of color. The following
"Adventure in Color," as the initial NBC episode was titled, emphasized
each of these links, while also promoting Disney's new network and its
chief sponsor. Against a black-and-white background, Walt Disney, the
series' host, appears in full color—a clever visual negotiation and a most
obvious accidenting of color. Holding a painter's palette, he recounts some
of his studio's technological milestones, recalling what "a very important
breakthrough" *Steamboat Willie*'s use of sound represented, and noting
how the studio had also "made quite a splash" by being the first in Hollywood to adopt three-strip Technicolor. In a variation on earlier episodes
of the series that had offered studio tours or an insider's glimpse of animation being created, the scene then shifts to a room Walt describes as the
paint laboratory, the place "where the whole *magic* of color begins," but
ironically, here too people and objects in black and white surround him.
In response, Walt resorts to the sort of "accidenting" we have previously
noted in the studio's move to Technicolor, as he attempts to conjure up
a uniformly lifelike color by trying out various "magic" incantations
drawn from familiar Disney films, such as "bibbidi bobbidi boo." When
he finally hits on the appropriate term, "NBC Color TV"—denoting the
magic of technology—the image shifts to full color. With that shift complete, he then offers several reminders of the audience's need for a color
television to fully appreciate what was being offered, of NBC's leadership
role in color broadcasting, and—again—of the Disney studio's similarly
pioneering efforts in this and other technical areas. The effect is to make
the entire program seem like an advertisement for RCA, for NBC's color
broadcasts, and for Disney's own productions, and to remind audiences of

how these companies, as technological leaders, have all worked together to produce this new level of entertainment.

Yet like many other episodes of the series, the rest of "Adventure in Color" does try to establish a pointedly "educational" and even "natural" atmosphere, using the color technology to provide audiences with a new appreciation of and connection to that "Wonderful World of Color." Thus it devotes time to describing the importance of color in nature, to demonstrating how the colors of the spectrum work together, and to explaining the scientific principles behind color television cameras and receivers. Of course, this elaborately developed scientific background never quite disguises the industrial-business context that has produced this color effect, particularly when, as if it were just another Disney cartoon character, an animated color peacock, the NBC trademark, *accidentally* wanders into one of Walt's scenes and has to be shooed away by the host. The message this episode repeatedly sounds is of color's importance to both the entertainment industry and to life itself, and of the significance of this new partnership between Disney and NBC, which would enable them to bring viewers this simultaneously "natural" and "magical" vision of the world. By exposing the industrial mechanism behind color photography and broadcasting, as well as the role of fantasy or even whimsy in constructing that color experience, though, Disney here helped to ease the transition to both color and the new network venue for its successful series.

By almost literally, as Virilio says, "opening" the "door" of the studio and the color process, once again employing a discourse of disclosure, almost hand-in-hand with a discourse of denial—the constructed alongside the natural—the studio made it easier for audiences to embrace its latest incarnation, as well as the other color shows on which its new partner NBC would increasingly depend for its ratings. Of course, it here did so without the difficulty of brother Roy resisting this latest innovation as he had with the initial move into television, of trying to convince others at the studio that this development might prove, as Bob Thomas offers, a "disastrous course" for the studio (*Walt Disney* 114). For the studio had by this point firmly established its technological credentials; both Disneys recognized that color broadcasting would only show the studio's product in its best light, and they had a well-developed strategy for deploying the technology, as this behind-the-scenes introduction attests. In again balancing the natural world with an "accident" strategy, they demonstrated that television's color technology—like Technicolor before it—was nothing more than a minor hazard that they could easily and quite profitably negotiate.

3 Three-Dimensional Animation and the Illusion of Life

The trick in the early days was just to make [the characters]
move—make 'em walk, make 'em run, make 'em turn
around, make 'em talk to each other, in pantomime, of
course.
—Friz Freleng (in Merritt and Kaufman,
Walt in Wonderland)

As veteran animator Friz Freleng recalls, the essential "trick"
of early film animation was simple character movement and action, with
little sense of the world in which those characters functioned. But like so
many other "attractions" of early cinema, these simplistic images, emphasizing motion for the sake of motion, offering audiences the minimal
excitement of seeing something seemingly come alive, soon wore thin.[1]
As Leonard Maltin in his history of the animated cartoon describes this
situation, "A treadmill effect started to set in until sound lifted animation out of the doldrums" (*Mice* 1). Sound, however, was only one of a
number of effects that would eventually be added as animators turned
their art to ever more complex purposes, aiming not just for those simple
but intriguing signs of life that drew early audiences, but for a standard
that would allow cartoons to approach the verisimilitude that modern art
demanded, that was a particular hallmark of classical film narrative, and

that would ultimately pave the way for cartoons to transition into feature-length narratives. This standard is what Walt Disney himself would term "the illusion of life," or what might more accurately be described as an illusion of a *version* of life that audiences would readily recognize, accept, and even find comforting, as cartoons increasingly came to resemble the real world and to begin to touch on its concerns.

Of course, this trajectory, especially as it was laid out at the Disney studio, was hardly novel. It simply reminds us that the historical pattern of popular animation, that which, just like the conventional cinema, was abetted by a variety of technological innovations and often described as demonstrating a pattern of technological evolution, closely followed the path that we usually associate with the broad history of film itself. The classical touchstone for such discussions is the work of André Bazin, particularly his evolutionary version of film history, famously codified in his notion of the "myth of total cinema" (Bazin 22). Bazin saw the development of the film apparatus as essentially a response to a "deep need," a human "obsession with realism." And at the core of that obsession, he argued, is humankind's dream of "the reconstruction of a perfect illusion of the outside world in sound, color, and relief," of "the world in its own image" (20, 21). That image, it was thought, could provide us with "the power to lay bare the realities" (15) of our world, to better understand it, even to awaken a political consciousness of that world so that we might gain a kind of control over it and the forces that often invisibly work on the individual. From this vantage, the landmarks in the film apparatus's evolution are naturally seen to be the technological developments that most clearly serve cinema's ur-myth: the mobile camera, the long-take technique, the various lenses, lights, and film stocks that promoted depth of field. This approach further recognizes that the development and supposed perfection of animation corresponds to its increasing ability to imitate the effects, especially the depth effects, achieved through those technological developments and deployed for rather similar ends in live-action classical narrative.

In tracing the developments leading to today's efforts in digital animation, Lev Manovich underscores Bazin's importance, but also reminds us that this evolutionary account is only one version of the history of film realism, and he suggests that we might balance it with the more pointedly "materialist" history offered by critics like Jean-Louis Comolli (Manovich 6–7). In describing the development of deep-focus photography, Comolli simply asserts that, "It is not possible to postulate a continuous chain of connections running through the history of the cinema" (430). Thus his account argues that depth effects, for example, are less telling than ideology, since an ideological understanding better explains how various technical, aesthetic, and social influences constellate in different eras or cultural situations to construct "the social 'real'—rather than the 'invisible' to the eye relations of productions" (Manovich 7). This perspective, then, suggests that the concept of film realism depends on a variety of "reality effects" that are constantly in flux, constantly being renegotiated in order to sustain the proper ideological relations between the film and its historically and culturally situated viewers. As an example, Manovich notes how a technological development like the introduction of panchromatic film stock in the late 1920s altered film style by undermining that very depth of field prized by Bazin, even as, in recompense, it allowed the cinema to keep pace with the latest standards in "photographic realism" of the time (7), and thus, in another manner and with some irony, to reaffirm its status as an apparently reliable mirror of the real.

Of course, either account, as Manovich allows, can claim some validity, especially when we focus on the *effects* of technological change. For example, if we simply compare the flat, two-dimensional, broadly representational images from the early days of animation to those produced by modern, three-dimensional computer graphics, we can easily demonstrate how "images progress towards the fuller and fuller illusion of reality," culminating in such effects as "smooth shadows, intricate textures, aerial perspective." Furthermore, this observable "progress" readily suggests that, on a broad scale, Bazin's "evolutionary narrative appears to be confirmed" (9), and at least it provides a highly useful version of film history. Yet at the same time, the history of animation, and particularly of that produced by Disney, also demonstrates a constant trade-off in *codes* of realism. Thus, if early animation often compensated for its flat characters by emphasizing perspective and movement in depth, recent work, particularly in digital animation, as Manovich observes, more often employs "shading, texture mapping, and cast shadows" to build its reality illusion (9). Either account, then, presents us with a *version* of film history, of animation history, and of the history of a cinematic realism, and together they suggest there may well be other accounts that could also effectively argue for their validity.[2]

Following Manovich's lead, this chapter attempts to draw on both sorts of accounts in order to describe several of Disney's technological efforts at approaching and furthering its illusion-of-life aesthetic, and to suggest another variation on that larger process of negotiation that informs the studio's products. Andy Darley's contention that Disney's animated films have always demonstrated a "preoccupation with heightened realism" (19), if taken at face value, suggests that we might easily situate the company's innovation of technologies to enhance the reality illusion, particularly one of its most heralded devices, the multiplane camera, within a historical line of such developments in early animation history. Seen from this vantage, Disney's introduction of this device in the Silly Symphony cartoon *The Old Mill* (1937) signals an effort not simply to imitate the codes of classical Hollywood cinema, as other efforts in this direction seem to do, but also to locate and exploit the narrative potentials in it, to develop the various dramatic possibilities that this device made available. Yet in only a few years Disney was employing that same technology not so much to underscore and further exploit the reality illusion as to fashion a new sort of *fantasy* vision, one in which the very *difference* between live-action and illusion-of-life animation would be foregrounded and become the very stuff of narrative.

Of course, as early cartoons readily suggest with their simplistic figures, flat backgrounds, and horizontally oriented action, the reality illusion was not easily achieved, in large part because of the very process of animation, as well as the labor involved. Typically, animation cels were placed in layers directly on top of a background as each frame of film was exposed. This process created various challenges, such as in the production of appropriate shadow and lighting effects, shifts in shade or color to suggest dimensionality or distance, and an emphasis on vanishing points to create the illusion of distance, particularly in those instances when a character would move or action would be staged between foreground and background. Given these challenges, some animators simply chose to exploit the possibilities of difference between the real and the animated worlds. For example, Otto Messmer's Felix the Cat cartoons, beginning in 1919, increasingly played off of what has often been described as a surrealist sensibility. We might note in this context Felix's trademark transformation of his tail into any device narrative circumstances or possibilities might require—a baseball bat, a telescope, a cane, a car crank—along with his ability to burst the boundaries of the narrative, as when a question mark above his head becomes a hook for his use or when he interacts with the cartoonist, as we find in the conclusion of *Comicalities* (1928), when he confronts his animator and prevents him from iris-ing out the film. The nature of the Felix cartoons is such that, as Esther Leslie neatly describes it, "everything in the drawn world is of the same stuff" (23). In effect, there is a kind of flattening or evening out of all that constitutes the cartoon world, as if to match the form's essentially flat nature. And this very playfulness with reality was often seen as a key to the attraction of such early animation, as Creighton Peet's contemporary praises for Felix underscore:

"Unhampered by any such classical limitations as dramatic unities, or even such customary necessities as the laws of gravity, common sense, and possibility, the animated drawing is the only artistic medium ever discovered which is really 'free'" (quoted in Maltin, *Mice* 26). It is an assessment we also find echoed in William Kozlenko's early appreciation of Disney cartoons, which he saw as exemplifying the strongest appeal of animation. He notes that, "The uniqueness of the animated cartoon lies in the fact that, of all film forms, it is the only one that has freed itself almost entirely from the restrictions of an oppressive reality" in favor of "the logic of fantasy" (246).

Yet at the core of all early animation there was always a tension between reality and the freedom implicit in that "logic of fantasy"—a tension that would necessitate both theoretical and technological negotiations. Leslie's study of the relationship between animation and the avant-garde nicely sketches the theoretical context behind these considerations, particularly the rather problematic attitude towards the real that largely guided critical responses to early animation. With its fundamental elasticity, its bending of the laws of physics, its plastic characters, and so on, early animation appealed to the avant-garde precisely because of the ways it rejected a "once-and-forever allotted form," proposing instead "freedom from ossification, and the ability to assume any form" (232). And that ability was linked to a kind of revolutionary spirit, as it analogously suggested the plasticity of our own world, the possibility of and an openness to new political/social constructions. But as animation approached a more realistic practice, it was increasingly seen as abandoning this spirit. Thus Leslie describes how many critics reacted negatively to the new "movie-style technique" manifested in a film like *Snow White.* It was seen as employing an approach that "negates flat space and the self-referentiality of the drawn cartoon and substitutes a deep cartoon space" analogous to that found in classical Hollywood narratives. For those who found early animation's chief value to be its potential for political/social commentary, this effect was nothing less than a "sell-out of the quintessence of cartoons" (148, 149).

For many years Disney's chief competitor in the animation industry, the Fleischer brothers, had heavily capitalized on the sort of freedom the avant-garde so prized by pushing a surreal dimension in their "Out of the Inkwell" cartoon series. In fact, Leslie argues that for the Fleischers, "consciousness of the medium was part of the entertainment" (14), and animation historian Michael Barrier emphasizes this point as well, suggesting that, "whatever their ostensible subject," the Fleischer films "were always cartoons about what it was like to be a cartoon"

(25). Certainly, many of their early efforts draw out what little plot they have precisely from such a reflexive foundation. Thus their first "star," KoKo the Clown, in film after film interacts with both his animator and the ostensible audience, and in a cartoon like *Bedtime* (1923) KoKo, like a nightmare come to life, grows to monstrous proportions as he stalks through the streets of New York, visualized through still photographs of the city, in search of his creator Max Fleischer. Yet the Fleischers hardly saw themselves as avant-garde artists or their work as particularly political in aim. While Max had studied at the Art Students League and Cooper Union in New York, much of his initial fascination with animation seems to have come at least as much from his interest in mechanics as in his concern with art, as his stint as art editor at *Popular Science* magazine might suggest. We can easily see these multiple concerns at work in the Fleischer brothers' own development of an aesthetic for this relatively young form, for even as their work explored the great imaginative possibilities of cartooning, it also increasingly demonstrated a pronounced realist impulse, as is illustrated in the frequent use of photographs as backgrounds for their animated action (seen in *Bedtime*), in the hybrid animation techniques used in both the KoKo the Clown and Betty Boop cartoons, and especially in their development of the rotoscoping technique, which allowed the Fleischer animators to trace photographed live action in order to achieve smoother, more naturalistic movements.[3]

In keeping with that Bazinian realist trajectory, the Fleischers would eventually develop this dimension of their cartoons in the direction of a technology for increasing the illusion of depth. One product of Max Fleischer's abiding fascination with various mechanical innovations was the "turntable camera," a horizontal device that consisted of a camera attached to a twelve-foot diameter pie-wedge platform on which were placed miniature sets, props, and figures, as well as frames to hold their animation cels. When suspended and photographed in front of the three-dimensional images, the animation cels would gain a three-dimensional quality of their own—a characteristic that was further enhanced by turning the tabletop so that the camera would seem to pan across the scene or track with character movement. While used for brief scenes in a number of Betty Boop cartoons, the turntable camera was probably most effectively employed in the Fleischers' more ambitious two-reel efforts, such as *Popeye the Sailor Meets Sindbad the Sailor* (1936) and *Popeye the Sailor Meets Ali Baba's Forty Thieves* (1937). In both of these films the action is keyed to make maximum use of the depth illusion, with interaction between foreground and background or movement of the characters within (actually *between*) the three-dimensional sets. However, as Leonard Maltin notes, the construction of the miniature sets and the tricky alignment of the animated action with the substantial sets and props were both difficult and time-consuming activities, and ultimately made for a process that never proved to be "economically feasible," given the always limited Fleischer staff and the usual rush to produce cartoons on a short regular deadline (*Mice* 110).

A somewhat similar development would emerge from another small studio, that of Disney's former top animator and later chief technical consultant, Ub Iwerks. Shortly after forming his own animation company in 1930, Iwerks also began experimenting with a mechanism for increasing the illusion of depth in his cartoons. The result was his version of a multiplane camera, which, as fellow animator Jimmie Culhane describes it, was "built out of parts from an old Chevy that he had bought for $350" (Iwerks and Kenworthy 130). Horizontally oriented, like the Fleischer brothers' mechanism, and with a fixed focus, it allowed the primary animation cel to be posed against variously layered background images, but it limited the camera itself to a panning motion across the images. It was used for a series of 1934 cartoons, such as *The Cave Man, The Headless Horseman, The Valiant Tailor,* and *Don Quixote,* and it was also adapted for experiments in stop-motion animation with Iwerks's unreleased film *The Toy Parade.* However, the depth illusion that resulted from Iwerks's device ultimately added little to the cartoons, in part because it was used rather sparingly in each case, but also because it was never really integrated into the narratives themselves, usually serving as little more than an interesting optical effect. In both *The Valiant Tailor* and *Don Quixote,* for example, the multiplane process primarily serves to add depth to scenes in which the title characters ride *across* three-dimensional landscapes, but it is not in evidence in any of the scenes involving interaction between characters, nor do the characters ever move *into* those three-dimensional views. It is as if Iwerks simply found the technology interesting in itself, as a technological response to one of animation's irritating limitations, and it became, as his biographers offer, simply one of many illustrations of how his fascination with "technical experimentation often superseded his interest in creating cohesive story lines for his cartoons" (Iwerks and Kenworthy 131), resulting in technical explorations that produced appealing visual punctuations but finally had little narrative impact.

In 1937, with the release of *The Old Mill,* Disney would demonstrate its own approach to these efforts at creating three-dimensional effects in animation. The studio had experimented with several early versions of a multiplane camera, most of them, like the Fleischer and Iwerks models, drawing on the techniques of live theatrical staging, and as old-time Disney animators Frank Thomas and Ollie Johnston describe them, for the most part rather crudely and cheaply fashioned "of wood and glue and tape" (264). However, as it was eventually developed by William Garity, then head of the camera department, and Roger Broggie of the studio's machine shop, the Disney multiplane camera—or the "control device for animation," as it was termed in U.S. patent 2,198,006—was a far more elegant, complex, and pointedly cinematic device, which cost approximately $70,000. And its success was quickly measured in the industry, as it brought the studio an Academy Award for technical achievement, enabled *The Old Mill* to win a similar award for Best Animated Short Subject, and added effective dramatic touches throughout Disney's first feature, *Snow White and the Seven Dwarfs* (1937), such as when, early in the film, Snow White runs *into* and *through* the dark and menacing forest, while the camera seems to move with her.

The key to the success of the Disney multiplane camera lay at least partly in its shift from the horizontal conception of earlier efforts to a vertical design that allowed for more complex effects. It consisted of a frame formed by four vertical posts into which a series of horizontal planes were inserted, each of which could move independently between the posts. The camera stood above these planes, 11' 4" above the ground, photographing downward through the various planes. With gear tracks running the entire length of the posts, the planes attached to the gears could be moved in very precise increments towards or away from the fixed camera. The two uppermost planes received the basic animation cels, the next two were used for various elements of a scene's background or setting, and the final, unmoving plane typically supplied sky or neutral backgrounds. To further enhance the reality illusion, each plane had its own light sources, placed along the sides, with individual controls to balance independently the light level for each image. As the opening images of *Bambi* (1941) effectively demonstrate as they take viewers ever deeper into the forest setting, through the careful orchestration of these planes and their lighting levels, an essentially static camera could seem to track across, crane up and down, or dolly into a scene, just as might a camera photographing any live-action scene.

Yet the effectiveness of the multiplane camera was not due simply to its ability to simulate complex camera movements. Certainly, in traditional animation a camera might well have been moved toward the cels being photographed, but any such movement would only have resulted in all objects becoming larger at the same rate—an effect contrary to real-life experience, to what we term parallax. Through the independent movement of its planes, Disney's device simulated that elusive parallax effect. Moreover, the multiplane camera allowed animators to avoid one of the constant pitfalls of creating heavily detailed images, which were usually produced by stacking multiple animation cels on top of each other. That stacking could at times produce a silhouette effect for a character or object and problematize correct shading. There were also problems with lighting differing parts of a scene and a "color shift" of cels in the lower layers of an animation stack, resulting from the lesser levels of light they received. With the multiplane's separation of layers and individualized lighting effects, these problems essentially disappeared, resulting in crisper and brighter images.

Another key to the success of the Disney multiplane camera was that, even given the studio's illusion-of-life aesthetic, it ultimately was used not just to support a conventional realist aesthetic. Certainly this technology to some extent allowed the animators to produce more realistic looking films, although, as Timothy White observes, that tendency shows up "mostly in the studio's feature-length animation, not the cartoon shorts" (8). Still, it was a tendency that was noted and criticized by many who, as we have already noted, saw it as a move away from animation's main province, as well as a kind of non-artistry produced from simply duplicating live action—which was similar to the criticism leveled against the Fleischer brothers for their use of the rotoscoping technology. Yet we need to qualify that effect, since Walt Disney himself had a rather problematic attitude towards realism. Thomas and Johnston recount how there was "some confusion among the animators when Walt first asked for more realism and then criticized the result because it was not exaggerated enough." The reason, they explain, is that "when Walt asked for realism, he wanted a caricature of realism," a combination of "believability" and "exaggeration" (65–66). To better understand this "caricature of realism," we need a more precise assessment of the multiplane technology's use and impact. What that assessment will show is that the multiplane camera actually opened up a key point of negotiation in the developing Disney studio style, precisely because of the way it foregrounded realist issues and thus helped bring into focus the need to work out a relationship between the real and the fantastic. For in practice the multiplane camera did not alter the fantastic elements in a narrative or make the images themselves more lifelike; it simply enabled Disney's artists to set those elements against more realistic backgrounds, while also allowing them to more readily approach their subjects—much in the way that today's digital animators do—*as if* they were real and living within a three-dimensional environment. It thus helped the animators to maintain their subjects' fantastic dimensions *and* their fantastic *ap-*

peal, as we see most obviously in the cases of the caricatured figures of the dwarfs and the witch in *Snow White.* And thanks to that seemingly mobile camera, audiences too could more easily sustain their fascination with those images by moving in and around them, by physically exploring that fantasy world, and by seeing its characters as linked to yet extending beyond the real world, thereby even allowing for an interrogation of the real in a manner that Disney's critics in this period seldom recognized.[4]

And perhaps even more important, the effects of the multiplane camera created an analogue for the world Disney's audiences inhabited, a world that could be examined more carefully, and one whose fantastic dimensions could be explored if one only looked carefully. This effect is precisely the point of Disney's initial effort in multiplane photography, *The Old Mill.* Walt Disney himself once described this film as "an experimental short subject, incorporating many of the problems that we expected to encounter in the making of *Snow White,*"[5] but since *Snow White* had been in production long before *The Old Mill* was begun and the short was released just a month prior to the feature's world premiere, we have to be a bit skeptical about Walt's comment. However, Richard Schickel followed this lead, describing the cartoon as essentially a test piece for the new technology and arguing that, "It had no real plot, and it consisted, not unnaturally, of a succession of trucking shots that showed the activities of the animal inhabitants of a deserted windmill" (165). That description, largely seeing its camera movements as showy effects, simply sells the film short, for it is a far more ambitious effort than Schickel's comments allow. Michael Barrier gives the film a bit more credit when he describes it rather as a trial run for the flower ballet in *Fantasia* (1940) and indeed for the complex "pictorial effects" found throughout that later film (249). Certainly the visual style and the relation between music track and image look toward *Fantasia,* but even that link shows little real sense of what the film is up to. For ultimately *The Old Mill* is not just putting some of the technical possibilities of the multiplane camera on display; it is also effectively mining that technology's stylistic enhancements for both narrative and thematic capital, something only a few sequences in *Fantasia* so effectively demonstrate and that no other animation of this period approaches.

The Old Mill opens with an intricate composition in depth, an image that prepares us for an interplay between the natural world that dominates the scene and the dilapidated human structure that we see centered in the deep background of the first shot. Yet even as it seems to invite movement into the frame, this low-angle shot also confronts the viewer with barriers—tall weeds, a spiderweb, a marshy area—that separate fore-ground from background, and a variety of motions that draw the eye in different directions, as a spider climbs up the web, the marsh water clearly ripples towards the background, ducks move along the surface from left to right, and in the deep background a line of cattle slowly moves from right to left beyond the windmill. This intimate view of nature suggests that it is a complex and even busy world, which the camera then allows us to explore by tracking in, past the spider and its web, over the marsh, and following the ducks as they turn towards the mill in the background, and then to an opening in the mill itself as a bird approaches and flies in. A dissolve then exploits another dimension of this technology by allowing the camera to seem to slowly crane up to show the variety of life now sheltered in the apparently abandoned mill: on the lowest level a family of bluebirds nesting in a hollow of the millwheel's base, above a group of mice in the old mechanism, higher up two doves on a beam, above them an owl, and in the highest rafters a flock of bats that awakens and flies out into the darkening sky. By using this craning motion rather than the sort of crowded long shot that typifies many of the early Silly Symphony cartoons, the film has carefully marked off the narrative space for each group, engaged viewers in a kind of cognitive mapping of the mill's interior, typical of classical film narrative, and allowed us the pleasure of discovery, as the camera slowly reveals each animal grouping and suggests the importance of this physical space.

While the ostensible subject of this film is the old mill, that humanly crafted structure occupying the deep background of the opening shot, the multiple planes of action, the deliberate tracking in to the structure, and the slow, lingering crane shot moving into its various precincts point us in several additional directions. These effects all emphasize a teeming life, nature in great variety and—in a typically Disney vein—even harmony, with the abandoned human structure simply another sort of shelter that these creatures have made their own. The other subject is this natural world and its ability to adapt and to persist, despite such perils as the violent storm that suddenly arises, threatening both the mill and all the creatures sheltered there. Through its ability to move into the action and to track across it, the multiplane camera has not only supported an illusion of depth, but has allowed us to move intimately into what we come to recognize not as a *human* realm but as the *animals'* world—a world that normally we just do not perceive—and then to discover an empathy with those creatures. By putting that "ecosystem" in danger, the storm that occupies the dramatic center of this brief narrative plays effectively upon that new sense of intimacy or connection, particularly when its power threatens to unleash the human mechanism of the mill-wheel and to crush the bluebird nest, along with the mother bird that refuses to leave her eggs. The sense of depth then enhances the danger as the millwheel breaks free from its rotted rope restraints and lurches forward, toward the bluebird nest, which is providentially spared only because a missing cog allows mother and nest, in their slot in the base, to go untouched. With this family drama played out, the storm can pass off, leaving this world battered but relatively intact, while also allowing audiences to see in this drama of endurance, as was the case with another Academy Award-winning Silly Symphony cartoon, *The Three Little Pigs* (1933), another reassuring fable about America and its similar weathering of that cultural storm, the Great Depression.

With the coming of dawn, the film's opening patterns, all of which showcased the possibilities of the multiplane camera, are essentially reversed. From the foreground the bats fly back into the mill, with the camera following and then craning down to survey the structure's various inhabitants—owl, doves, mice, bluebirds, now with their eggs hatched—and to show that all have safely endured the storm. As in the initial sequence, a dissolve then allows the camera to move outside and begin a slow track back, as it again follows the family of ducks, pulls back through the marsh, and passes beyond the spider's web. Glistening and still wet from the storm, the web provides narrative closure here, not only by signaling that we have returned to the cartoon's visual starting point, but by leaving us with what we now recognize as a kind of metaphor for the "web" of nature that we have, thanks to this film's technological advances, been permitted to glimpse, to understand, and almost to *feel*.

With the aid of the multiplane camera, Disney's artists could certainly fashion a more compelling illusion of depth for their nature fantasy. But just as significantly, the camera helped bind together the two stories we have described, the fable of cultural endurance along with the technologically enabled insight into the natural world that would later become one of the studio's staples with its "True-Life Adventure" documentaries.[6] More than just a technical experiment in adding *visual* depth, then, *The Old Mill* supplements a by-now-familiar tale with *narrative* depth by dramatizing the notion that there is more to the natural world than immediately meets the eye, and creating a sense that we have enjoyed a privileged view of that "more." Of course, it was just the sort of view that audiences had come to expect from the best live-action films of the era—from the sort of complex narratives that Disney was at that very moment preparing to release, starting with *Sleeping Beauty,* and that would significantly expand the field of narrative cinema.

II

In the midst of Disney's 1945 release *The Three Caballeros*, we find a close-up of Donald Duck, staring wide-eyed at a pretty Mexican woman, the singer Dora Luz, who is reflected in each of his eyes as a sign of the duck's enchantment. It is a brief but telling shot in a film that has attracted a range of historical and cultural commentary on the various relationships it suggests, in part because the film here and elsewhere seems to transgress so surprisingly, crossing historical and cultural boundaries. It marks a point, quickly noted by reviewers of the era, at which Disney animation becomes overtly sexualized, by depicting the animated duck as a possible suitor for a real, live woman, demonstrating what a reviewer in *Time* described as "an alarmingly incongruous case of hot pants" that probably discomfited some viewers expecting the usual Disney family experience ("*Three Caballeros*" 92). For contemporary critics it has also evoked, in its treatment of Luz and other figures in the film, a complex image of American imperialism of the time, or what Julianne Burton-Carvajal terms "an allegory of . . . colonialism par excellence" (142), as Donald acts out America's all-too-eager courtship of its South American neighbors during World War II. Yet it also implicates another border crossing that supports these depictions: the aesthetic one built into Donald's gaze that both parallels and to some extent qualifies these other effects. For the duck's eyes mix animated and live-action images, offering audiences a hybrid experience that also speaks to the film's other border crossings in the way it blatantly frames the real as part of a larger fantastic cinematic construct. In effect, it suggests an evolving aesthetic in Disney animation, resulting from a continuing negotiation between real and fantastic elements, as well as a rather different application of those possibilities that, as we have seen, were to be found in the multiplane camera.

Michel Foucault has described a curious fallout—some possibly unexpected effects—that typically follows from the sort of transgressions that we see acted out in *The Three Caballeros*. As he offers, "The play of limits and transgression seems to be regulated by a simple obstinacy: transgression incessantly crosses and recrosses a line which closes behind it . . . and thus it is made to return once more right to the horizon of the uncrossable" (34). Whether we are considering the literal movement across Central and South American borders, a violation of typical audience expectations, or the sudden appearance of animated characters in the human world, those transgressions, as he suggests, all reveal a kind of "obstinacy," an abiding frustration or elusiveness. All boundaries, it seems, tend to be fugitive, since every crossing always opens onto another boundary just beyond, a border still uncrossed that makes us acutely aware of how those boundaries are always being fashioned—and refashioned—by culture, circumstance, and perhaps technology. For Foucault, the real impact of such boundary crossing thus lies in what it might reveal, how it can "immediately upset" all of our previous "certainties" (34), or call into question the very notion of boundary. In the case of *The Three Caballeros* and its formal transgression into hybrid animation, that sense of "upset" pervades the narrative, undermining the film's supposed ideological project and producing a compound of frustrations that can help us better understand both its mixed effects and the technologically influenced trajectory of Disney animation, particularly in the post–World War II cra.

One thing that is fairly certain about the film is that there has never been a clear certainty about it, other than that it in various ways missed its supposed mark. James Agee, for example, simply dismissed the film as "intricately wrong" (187). For some, such as Otis Guernsey, the problem was precisely its hybrid approach, as it seemed "a variety show with the accent on trick photography and oddities of line and color" (quoted in Schickel 233). Drawn by its element of "trick photography," *Popular Science* did a feature article on the film in which it praised and elaborately described the technology involved, particularly its new application for the multiplane camera, but also wondered whether the "mystification" bound up in the film's technique might ultimately "outweigh story interest" ("How Disney" 110). *The Saturday Review*, though, saw *The Three Caballeros'* adult elements as at fault, as a sign that Walt Disney was having "audience trouble, that he could not make up his mind whether he was appealing to the young or the old" (Brown 23). Recent commentators, as we have noted, are more prone to see the film as an indication of how the Disney studio was beginning to go *culturally* wrong with a stereotypical treatment of South America and its people that supported unflattering cultural and ethnic clichés (more pointedly the case in a film like *Dumbo* [1942]). This broader social context is what Eric Smoodin points to as he notes the impact of "changing cultural attitudes toward such disparate subjects as genre, cartoon style, audience, representations of female sexuality and race" (*Animating* 104). Curiously, Barbara Deming sidestepped all of these vantages. In her contemporaneous commentary she found most intriguing the film's vision of a "nightmare realm . . . where visions tantalize but deceive, what seems substantial may prove insubstantial" (121). She saw in *The Three Caballeros* a "violent caricature" of "the painful visions" (120) found throughout films of the wartime era, which repeatedly played out stories of the elusive American dream, of frustrated hopes, of characters who, like Donald Duck here, are largely victims in a world where "nothing is sure" (121). It is an interesting perspective, not only because she treats the duck as if he *were* a human character, but because her emphasis on the unsure and the "insubstantial" echoes Foucault's comments about "uncertainties." That point might help us sort out the film's accomplishments and its failures, even see it as a film, perhaps unwittingly, *about* failure.

As we have noted, the film implicates several border crossings—sexual, cultural, aesthetic—and apparently with the hope that, together, these transgressions would help build an effective narrative. Like an earlier Disney effort in this vein, *Saludos Amigos* (1943), *The Three Caballeros* was intended as a goodwill effort, as part of a larger political strategy set out by the Office of Inter-American Affairs to build a cultural bulwark against Axis intrusions at a time when, as Eric Smoodin notes, "Argentina and Brazil had become major battlegrounds" of political influence (*Animating* 139). And the Disney team's various trips to research the film, which specifically targeted these two countries, suggest how serious their effort was.[7] Moreover, the film's advertising stressed its unexpectedly adult aspects, perhaps because, as Smoodin offers, Disney was looking "to expand his viewership" (115) at a crucial point in the studio's history. Tellingly, one poster for the film offers no hint of animated content, instead showing a bathing beauty posed provocatively next to ad copy that gives the film's title and trumpets: "Yes! She's real! Alive and Lovely in a Walt Disney Picture! It's amazing, wonderful, and thrilling!" Just what that "it" referred to—the girl, the film, or the *appearance* of a sexy figure in a Disney film—though, is another sort of uncertainty left for prospective viewers to ponder. Meanwhile, the film's theatrical trailer emphasized its hybrid character, lauding its mix of live action and animation as "the newest thing to hit the movies since talking pictures came in." Yet all of these efforts, hinting of new directions for Disney, for animated film, and even for American culture—directions that recall Disney's experiment at creating a new kind of animated film with *Fantasia* and an abortive effort to involve Salvador Dali in studio projects—met with various sorts of frustration.[8] For while the notion of inter-American relationships might well have been coded as a kind of courtship or even a sexual pursuit—indeed, some South American countries might have seen aggressive male overtures as accurately describing America's attitude to its neighbors—working those elements into a hybrid style of narrative rendered them all too transparent, too obviously part of an insubstantial world being constructed by the American cinema.

What I want to suggest is that the hybrid approach, through the way it pointedly reconstructs cinematic reality, cast into relief the difficult negotiations between ideology and aesthetics that Lev Manovich discusses—an effect that also exposed the deeper uncertainties that mark this film and larger cultural relationships of the era. Of course, hybrid animation was hardly new either to the American film industry or the Disney Company as it set about making *The Three Caballeros.* Disney's first success in animation involved precisely this technique with the studio's Alice comedies. Between 1923 and 1927 Disney produced fifty-eight shorts that, drawing on the inspiration of Lewis Carroll's *Alice in Wonderland,* typically placed a young girl in an amazing cartoon world where, along with her animated cat Julius, she would go through various reality-defying adventures.[9] While the Disney studio abandoned this technique with subsequent series, such as Oswald the Lucky Rabbit, and especially the Mickey Mouse and Silly Symphony cartoons on which it would largely build its reputation, it has resurrected this approach throughout its history, especially in the World War II and immediate post-war eras when the economies of production and new stylistic possibilities it provided, including a new approach to the question of realism, proved attractive.

One of the initial reasons for adopting the hybrid approach was that it allowed the studio to reduce the amount of animation that was needed. And given the simple lack of animating talent available when Walt and Roy Disney began their company and the need for speedy production to meet their distributor's demands, it was a logical response. Incorporating live-action footage meant fewer animators were needed, simple backgrounds could be used for the live action, the live actors provided useful scaling and timing measures for the animated figures, and, ultimately, films could be produced more rapidly. These economies, as well as various stylistic options to which this approach lent itself, also explain why several other early animators employed it, including such pioneers as Winsor McCay and Earl Hurd. And even as cartoon production became more sophisticated, some competing animators retained that hybrid approach. Among them we might note Walter Lantz, who in the 1920s appeared in his own Dinky Doodle cartoons, and especially the Fleischer brothers, for many years Disney's chief competitor in the animation industry, who, as we have already noted, freely mixed live action with animation in a variety of cartoons, most notably with KoKo the Clown in the "Out of the Inkwell" series and in a number of Betty Boop films throughout the 1930s.

Yet that approach had its drawbacks, both for an increasingly sophisticated audience that began to recognize when shortcuts were being taken, and for animators, particularly those at Disney, who were being guided by the concerns of that illusion-of-life aesthetic. Properly synchronizing the actions of the live actors with the animated figures was, of course, always difficult, and the three-dimensional presence of live actors usually cast the two dimensionality of their animated counterparts and contexts into unflattering relief.[10] As animation became more realistic, that three dimensionality also necessitated a greater concern with composition, since live actors operating primarily on a two-dimensional axis only underscored the technique's limitations and the artifice of the animated elements. As a result, perspective had to receive more attention and action had to be constructed in depth. Additionally, any contact between the live actors and the animated figures proved difficult and increasingly unconvincing. As veteran animators Frank Thomas and Ollie Johnston admit, they always found it "difficult to know how the final pieces would all fit together and to judge how anyone should act" (525). In fact, the Alice cartoons had at times only accomplished this effect by emphasizing those "pieces," that is, by actually posing cut-out photographs of Alice and animating them along with the drawn characters along the frame's horizontal axis.[11] This approach, however, only reinforced her two dimensionality and thus the very constructed nature of the image. In general, this inability to get away from a two-dimensional, constructed look and to fashion a convincing level of interaction proved consistently troublesome and resulted in the most successful animators eventually abandoning this approach as audiences and industry alike came to expect more realistic cartooning.

With the advent of World War II and the attendant drain on manpower and talent, though, hybrid animation found a new lease on life at Disney. At the start of the war the army occupied the Disney Studio and seized many of its facilities for war work, and at the same time, like most American industries, Disney began losing manpower to the armed forces. To maintain a level of productivity and to retain as many of the company's trained artists as possible, Disney agreed to produce training films for the military at cost, while also trying to sustain a lower but regular level of cartoon production. However, as Steven Watts notes, the resulting "budget constraints, stifled creativity, and depleted ranks of artists were visible to anyone who peered behind the scenes" (234). While initially conceived as a series of shorts, a film like *The Three Caballeros* offered Disney other options: to support the country by furthering its official "good neighbor" policy, to provide his artists with a new creative challenge, and to produce a feature-length film with limited resources. And the formula proved serviceable enough so that even after the war it figured in a string of hybrid features, including *Song of the South* (1946), *Fun and Fancy Free* (1947), and *Melody Time* (1948).

But there was something inevitably frustrating about the hybrid films: how they troubled both that "illusion of life" and our sense of the real, especially as they situated the human in a world of uncertainty where all borders are clearly arbitrary and constructed to serve an effect or narrative end, and as they, almost in spite of themselves, rendered interaction not as natural, not as a seamless element of the reality illusion, but as a pivot-point of curiosity, and thus, ultimately, as a kind of *hole* in that illusion. This sensibility was basically foreign to Disney, whose stories generally adhered to the conventions of classical narrative and the certainties that attended those conventions. In fact, *The Three Caballeros* seems particularly mindful of this effect in the way it initially establishes an exotic context that its live-action elements might then demystify. The result, though, is an abiding sense of uncertainty, as the narrative repeatedly draws towards this "other" world and then pulls back, as if the very project were haunted by an air of frustration, and its border crossings had proved far more complex than anticipated. In this instance, no simple negotiation of technology would suffice, for too many other factors, especially those ideological ones, would qualify this film's reality effects.

Certainly, by this point in its history, Disney had acquired a justified reputation for technological innovation—one that might have made an effort like *The Three Caballeros* seem like little more than an interesting aesthetic challenge. That challenge, however, did necessitate the combination of three separate photographic processes to produce this "newest thing to hit the movies." As we have noted, integrating live action with animated characters or scenes essentially meant mixing two worlds, one three-dimensional and the other flat. But thanks to the multiplane camera, the animated elements of this project, such as Panchito the rooster riding atop his magic serape, could be photographed in what looked to be a three-dimensional context, constructing a far more substantial—or realistic—figure that could then be mixed with the live action, potentially producing a more convincing hybrid result.

But two additional processes then had to be employed to effect that mixing of live and animated elements. One involved a special "process projection" technology to combine animated foreground action with background live action. Using the lower sections of the vertical multiplane camera, this process necessitated first projecting live-action footage onto a mirror in the base of the multiplane rig, which then reflected the images upward onto a small screen. Above the screen on other levels the animation cels were put in place, carefully lit for the combination effect, and photographed one frame at a time by the Technicolor camera mounted over these planes. Reversing this mix, that is, combining live foreground with animated background scenes, required a third process, the more commonplace rear projection. In this case the cartoon action was created using the multiplane camera to provide a sense of depth, and that material was projected onto a fourteen-by-twenty-foot translucent screen, in front of which the live action was staged. Set twenty-five feet in front of the action, the Technicolor camera then recorded the combination, producing an effective hybrid scene.[12] While this complex process still allowed some savings in time and labor over the traditional animated film, the ultimate effect was hardly a seamless realism; rather, the result was a somewhat self-conscious production that almost invites viewers to examine the manner of its construction.

The original working title for the film was *Surprise Package* (Barrier 372), and that is precisely the note struck in the opening, as Donald Duck happens upon several brightly wrapped boxes "from his friends in Latin America." That start suggests both uncertainty and possibility, and links those effects to film itself, since the first box Donald opens holds a movie projector and several films—films that, apparently, are meant to bring those new friends to life. Yet the two films he then watches, one about Pablo the penguin and the other about the Argentine boy Gauchito and his donkey-bird, are rather conventional. Both are fully animated and done in classical Disney style: with soft, rounded figures, set in a recognizably realistic context, and with the exaggeration of specific traits or features that emphasize personality. Yet in a hint of what is to come, the subjects, while done in the *style* of previous Disney creations, seem pointedly other, almost unbelievably different—a penguin whose only wish is to be warm and a donkey with wings—as if to suggest Latin America's exotic nature. There is nothing sensual, no hybrid animation, not even a suggestion of a *real* South America to which North American viewers might be brought closer. Opening that first box just produces an amusing take on south-of-the-border folklore, done in the familiar Disney manner, with just a hint that the ensuing narrative will bring us more information about these sorts of strange birds.

While the following sequences begin similarly, with other boxes to be opened and other "surprises" awaiting Donald (and, by implication, the viewers), they also move away from this conventional and cute approach without ever dispelling the opening's exotic implications, even as they also introduce the film's hybrid elements. Opening a second box brings the Brazilian parrot Joe Carrioca and a pop-up book offering images of his country, initially presented in a very realistic style, showing doves flying around a church steeple and a highly detailed cityscape. Joe's urging to Donald, "Let's go" to Brazil, though, brings a shift in both style and content that prefigures more uncertainties. For Joe surrealistically multiplies and suddenly transforms into a row of images suggesting the popular "Brazilian Bombshell" Carmen Miranda, all beckoning alluringly to the duck. When Donald finally follows these fantastic images into the book, suggesting the sort of dimensional possibilities we might typically find in a hybrid film, the visual style changes to counter that movement. For as they literally hop onto a train depicted on one page, the images become flat and hard-edged and the color scheme over-saturated, all characteristics of Disney artist Mary Blair's distinctive style, which was also, as John Canemaker argues, "the polar opposite of the representational 'illusion of life' associated with Disney."[13] Consequently, a sequence that initially seemed to promise a more realistic view of South America, a kind of demythologizing of the film's opening cartoons, and certainly a "deeper" look, only becomes visually more exotic, employing almost nightmarish multiplication and shifts in scale, and hinting not of a real Brazil but of one constructed out of our current cinematic imagination, as described in films familiar to the audience, such as *Flying Down to Rio* (1933), *That Night in Rio* (1941), and *The Gang's All Here* (1943).

Fittingly, those implications are almost literally *fleshed* out with the first hybrid scenes. For as pages in the Brazil book flip by, they also bring a complex series of transformations, expanding upon Joe's easy gender shift to a Carmen Miranda look-alike. An animated shadow emerges from an animated street scene and then becomes a real woman, the Brazilian singer Aurora Miranda, representing a peasant girl musically selling cookies. That three-dimensional introduction, however, evokes another kind of cartoonish flatness. The sister of the better-known Carmen, Aurora obviously recalls the previous Miranda reference and quickly suggests some element of the patronizing attitude toward Latin Americans that was bound up in her caricature persona.[14] Joined by a group of live male admirers, she sings and dances, inspires Donald and Joe to imitate the group, and then they all become animated shadows, dancing against a darkly colored background, as if the spirit of the Brazilian town of Baia were, after all, simply the product of the Disney animators, and this mixture of animated and live action just another sort of pleasant exoticism. While this scene introduces one of those key border crossings, as Donald offers Aurora flowers and receives a kiss in return, that interaction has no narrative impact. In fact, the scene primarily demonstrates the ease with which animated images become real and the real images, in turn, quickly dissolve into animated ones, as all relationships prove only fleeting. It suggests a world where boundaries are fluid and as elusive as the girl who simply disappears after doing her number, as if she were just as insubstantial as the cartoon characters with whom she has apparently interacted.

The next unboxing introduces Panchito the Mexican rooster and his native country, and it offers a more elaborate hybrid effort, as if by opening boxes within boxes the film had finally discovered a surprising depth. It begins with conventional Disney animation, as Panchito emerges and leads Joe and Donald in the film's title song, showcasing its cultural agenda, particularly its affirmation of inter-American unity ("Through fair or stormy weather we're always together" is the song's refrain). And as in the previous sequence, that conventional imagery gives way to stylized animation, a montage of Mary Blair's flat sketches depicting Mexican Christmas traditions (which, in their images of small children, anticipate her design scheme for the famous Disney theme park attraction "It's a Small World"). Another animated book, this one about Mexico, then opens to show live images of the Mexican countryside and to allow the "three caballeros" to fly into this real world on a "magic serape," to move in depth here, as they visit three apparently representative cities: Vera Cruz, Acapulco, and Mexico City. Done like postcards come to life, these live-action scenes marginalize the animation and suggest a more complex, even contemporary Mexico, showing paved highways, automobiles, and modern cities. Yet they also evoke another kind of exoticism, by recalling travelogue footage of the era, such as MGM's "FitzPatrick Traveltalks," eight episodes of which the staff had screened prior to the Mexico trip (Kaufman 266). In fact, John Mason Brown in his review pointed up this similarity, describing this part of the film as "a travelogue far lovelier in its shots than most" (24).

An elaborate series of interactions between the animated characters and the live figures who "represent" these cities only furthers that sense of otherness. Representing Vera Cruz is a group of Mexican folk dancers who invite Donald to join in. When he finds he cannot do their dance—a clever narrative approach to negotiating the problem of hybrid interaction—he offers an American-style jitterbug and dominates the scene. It is a performance that, while graciously received, only underscores cultural difference and marks the folk dance as quaint and exotic. Acapulco is represented by a beach scene that Donald readily identifies for viewers, looking through a telescope at what he terms "hot stuff," young girls sunbathing on the beach. Yet as Disney director Jack Kinney has revealed, the "beach" was actually constructed in a parking lot at Disney's Burbank studio,[15] and the bathing beauties were American girls, standing in for Mexican women who consistently elude Donald's advances, laugh at him, and eventually toss him into a pool of water. Also presented as a postcard that comes to life, Mexico City introduces the singer Dora Luz and the dancer Carmen Molina, each of whom Donald pursues, only to have his romantic overtures again rebuffed, further painting him as the sort of "frustrated" character Barbara Deming described.

Perhaps more telling is the series of rapid and dizzying transformations that attend these last two interactions and lead into the narrative's conclusion. For the live subjects of Donald's infatuations—Dora Luz and Carmen Molina—repeatedly shift appearance, like the boundaries they signify, constantly moving away and mocking every effort by the duck to interact with them. Singing "You Belong to My Heart," Luz first appears as an animated star in an animated sky, then a real person in the animated sky, and finally a face within an animated star. Repeatedly she appears and disappears, and, as Aurora Miranda had earlier, increasingly becomes part of an animated world. As everything, even *character*, turns fluid, the sky becomes an abstract garden within which Donald becomes a flower. When she eventually disappears, Joe and Panchito suddenly appear in her place as another sort of hybrid, with their animated torsos joined to human legs, dancing, multiplying, and forming Busby Berkeley-like abstract designs, while her love song is speeded up and distorted in their voices. The result is a kind of nightmare in which depth disappears, construction is foregrounded, and interaction becomes impossible.

The next subject of Donald's pursuit is presented from the start in a fashion that predicts a similar result. Carmen Molina appears in a stylized Mexican cowboy costume, brandishing a riding crop as she dances. When she beckons to Donald, he rushes to join her but is almost immediately crowded out by the sudden appearance of several lines of animated cactuses. They then take his place in the dance, their emphatically phallic shapes mocking his apparent desire and, as they dominate the foreground, reducing him to a kind of visual irrelevance here. As Molina finally dances into the deep background of the frame and Donald again rushes after, she too becomes an animated cactus—the goal thus becoming yet another sort of boundary as he approaches. And that transformation leaves him with a most prickly embrace and yet another rebuff, in fact, a most fitting emblem of the fate of interaction here.

In these two instances when the live image interacts most extensively with the animated, it is presented as alluring yet also elusive, as a kind of empty promise. Both Luz singing her Circean love song and Molina brandishing her whip seem to invite contact, to promise a new dimension of hybrid interaction, much as the film itself, in keeping with its

Office of Inter-American Affairs origins, seems to aim at a new level of understanding and friendly relations between North and South America. Yet these are promises that simply cannot be kept, boxes that, when opened, only prove empty. And given the sort of characterizations the film has deployed—a Carmen-Miranda stand-in, American-style bathing beauties, a whip-wielding cowgirl—perhaps thankfully so. The live images keep turning into animated ones, into just the sort of exaggerations and caricatures that probably inspired their depictions. Ultimately they not only elude the duck's grasp but leave him frustrated, caught up in a variety of nightmarish and unpredictable shifts—such as when Donald himself becomes a flower—and even injured—in hugging the cactus or later being treated as a bull in a comic bullfight. Those shifts seem to mock the various overtures involved here and to suggest that we have, in effect, reached what Foucault terms "the horizon of the uncrossable," the point at which all of those efforts at border crossings simply reveal, like the hybrid style itself, their built-in "obstinacy" or frustration, leaving the duck in a world of comic uncertainty and audiences unsure of how to respond to the film's surreal shifts, much less its attitudes towards our "exotic" neighbors. Despite the film's announced intentions, it seems that closer relations—on a personal or a cultural level—must remain little more than the gleam in Donald's eyes, reflections of an otherness that, because of the technology employed or the attitude behind that technology, keeps avoiding his—and our—grasp.

Of course, the transformation of a beautiful woman into a prickly cactus also represents a kind of dirty trick, like many others Donald, a consistently unsuccessful lover and imperialist, endures during the film, and it is fully consistent with his character in other Disney cartoons. But here it not only frustrates the duck's manifest desires, but even punishes him for them, for trying to cross that cartoon/human border or for believing we could so easily unwrap another culture. At the same time this transformation has a somewhat similar effect for the audience. It frustrates the narrative trajectory the film seems to set out—the meeting of cultures and the meeting of cinematic styles—while revealing film's raw power: its ability to offer images and to withhold them, to construct pleasing images and to reconstruct them to manipulate our desires. Like animation intruded into live action, it only reminds us of the depthless nature of the film world, the *unreality* of its visions—a confrontation, as I have implied, that seems implicit in the hybrid style itself. This scene simply images the real import of the present to Donald that began the film, that first box that held a projector and several films. Both Donald and the audience, it seems, are in their own ways products of that cinematic construction and similarly subject to its powers.

On this note of disappointment, it seems appropriate that the film abandons its hybrid efforts, or tries weakly to recuperate them, by offering a completely animated conclusion, done in classic Disney style. Here too, though, that transformative spirit seems to rule, as Donald is himself trapped in an exaggerated image, a papier-mâché bull, another present from his "friends." In it he becomes the subject of a comic bullfight and is then stuffed with skyrockets and shot skyward, where he explodes, producing a fantastic fireworks display that spells out "The End" in English, Portuguese, and Spanish. It is a somewhat confusing conclusion, celebratory yet also punitive, leaving Donald, who has opened his last box, tricked, transformed, and frustrated, even as the fireworks seem to celebrate a kind of multicultural harmony and understanding. It may simply be, as Burton-Carvajal offers, that Disney "felt the need to reassure" our South American friends "that they need feel no threat from this North American neighbor" (143). But if so it is a rather one-sided reassurance, suggesting that crossing the border—stylistically, culturally, or sexually—has its pleasures and its perils, leaving us in a realm where the one certainty, as Foucault offers, is that all "certainties . . . are immediately upset," and where even images of joy and harmony come to seem strained and constructed.

What I would suggest, then, is that we see this film not, in a kind of knee-jerk fashion, simply as an instance of cultural hegemony, as one more trace of the ways in which cultural flow across the borders was carefully controlled and cultural thinking laid out for audiences during this era. While that is, of course, partly the case, the film also reminds us, through its narrative of frustration, surprise, and uncertainty, of just how difficult it was to control that cultural flow, and of how that flow was conditioned by a host of conventionalized images that seemed to have a life of their own. More tellingly, we might think of this film as symptomatic of a much more fundamental sort of boundary crossing, linked to the film's technological approach. Paul Virilio notes how during World War II the "vision machine," as he terms it, emerged as a significant, perhaps even the most important weapon for all combatants, opening the way for the ongoing "cinematization" of the contemporary world. The very fact that a film like *The Three Caballeros* was made already points in that direction, as does much of its imagery. Yet one symptom of that cinematization is often overlooked, what Virilio describes as a new crisis of depth, a lost sense of dimension, ultimately what he terms "the de-realization of the world" (*Lost* 42) to which all cultures were becoming subject. It is an effect just glimpsed here, as live images repeatedly turn into animated ones, South America becomes a cartoonish realm, and desire dissolves into pyrotechnic excess. That "de-realization," of course, would eventually make a hybrid or pointedly constructed world easier to depict and to accept, as evidence more recent films like *Who Framed Roger Rabbit* (1988), *Cool World* (1992), *Space Jam* (1996), *The Adventures of Rocky and Bullwinkle* (2000), and *Osmosis Jones* (2001). In fact, the Disney-produced *Who Framed Roger Rabbit* would make great capital out of foregrounding that construction, using its hybrid world to expose the nature of our contemporary world. But such depictions and acceptance are, as I have suggested, much easier for a postmodern world that has become accommodated to a different sort of reality, to the real's seeming dissolution amid a welter of constructs, to its competition with what Virilio terms "reality effects." In such a context we often seem, after all, simply less real ourselves, our world lacking in dimension, our relationships with others—and other cultures—all too appropriately defined in the most superficial and jingoistic ways, even as the borders that would divide us become ever more fluid and irrelevant.

Those who criticize *The Three Caballeros* for its cultural failings, of course, are partly responding from the vantage of this thoroughly cinematized culture, one that readily recognizes how the media help produce those superficial and jingoistic perceptions, constructing our world and our selves. But in trying to add depth to our understanding of our southern neighbors, this film faltered not just because it opted for culturally trite and superficial images, such as its Carmen Miranda or cowboy references, nor because it partially framed that encounter as a sexually charged meeting between a male North American and a Latin America often represented as female. The hybrid approach selected for this project, driven by Disney's technological efforts at constructing the real, also got very much in the way, with the result foreshadowing that postmodern context and letting viewers glimpse inside the box where cultures and cultural views are constructed. Simply put, the film failed to work out the difficult and competing claims of ideology and aesthetics, despite the seeming promise of its technology to do so. And, as critical reactions to the later *Song of the South* suggest, further following this path in the post-war period would only lead Disney into a world of uncertainties. Of course, it is a world with which we have since then become quite familiar, and that difficult hybrid technique, made all the easier by the multiplane camera and its various offshoots, simply marks *The Three Caballeros* as an early signpost on the path of our future cinematization—a path that Disney, despite its technological accomplishments, was not quite ready to negotiate.

4   A Monstrous Vision: Disney, Science Fiction, and CinemaScope

The post–World War II era would see the emergence of a new cinematic discourse *about* technology with the sudden popularity of the science fiction genre. While this formula had staked out a place in the cinematic imagination at a very early point in film history, as Georges Méliès' *A Trip to the Moon* (1902) attests, and while its subjects naturally resonated with the development of film technology itself, it had found only sporadic success and, in the late 1930s and 1940s had largely been relegated to the realm of the serials. When it did burst into popularity in the 1950s, it would manifest a rather remarkable character. As Susan Sontag notes in one of the most famous assessments of the genre, the science fiction cinema of the 1950s and early 1960s took the form of a kind of collective "imagination of disaster," wherein was forecast all of the cultural anxieties about science and technology that were the inevitable baggage of the Cold War and its constant specter of atomic annihilation— anxieties that were frequently taking the form of monstrous and destructive alien invaders, nuclear warfare, or atomic mutations.[1] And as Sontag further suggests, while those films were generally quite popular, in large part because of their efforts at visualizing the extraordinary, or what she terms their emphasis on "the aesthetics of destruction" (216), they typically demonstrated an "inadequate response" to "the most profound dilemmas of the contemporary situation" (227). For while they provided a thrilling technological vision, they offered little effective suggestion of how to cope with that looming new world.

This linked vision of technology and a monstrous imagery may seem an exaggerated way of approaching another significant technological turn for Disney, especially given the studio's customary family orientation. However, its less-than-satisfactory experience with the hybrid system in the 1940s, the technologically driven destruction brought by World War II, and a Cold War atmosphere that repeatedly evoked very unfamily-like visions of scientifically driven apocalypse must have given Disney some pause in its otherwise consistent embrace of the technological. As it moved into these relatively uncharted waters, the studio had to weigh a clear economic attraction, the fact that there was a large postwar audience that was in some measure thrilled by glimpsing the latest technological advances, which were quickly moving from scientific development to familiarity and home consumption, against a potential difficulty, the awareness that this audience was also increasingly worried by the forces—and the monsters—that these advances seemed to be unleashing. As a result, we find that as Disney sought to further diversify its offerings by moving into this popular—and generally quite profitable—genre, and as it began to shift into pure live-action filmmaking that would also inevitably engage it in a cultural discourse *about* technology, it did so in a rather ambivalent or qualified way that would clearly differentiate its product from most other science fiction films of the period.

Unlike most other science fiction efforts then being filmed, Disney's first offering in the genre was an adaptation of a classic novel, Jules Verne's 20,000 *Leagues Under the Sea* (1954). Of course, by telling that nineteenth-century story the studio would not have to *directly* address the mid-twentieth-century issues facing its audience. And yet Verne's novel already contained an ambivalent treatment of science and technology that would allow the film to sound its own cautionary note. Moreover, Disney decided to add an element of technological attraction, for 20,000 *Leagues Under the Sea* would also mark the studio's first foray into one of the latest developments in cinematic technology, the new widescreen CinemaScope process. The resulting adaptation deemphasized the extraordinary voyage aspect of Verne's work, placed at the narrative's center a monstrous encounter that, like the many other monsters, mutations, and suddenly awakened creatures that so filled our science fiction dreams of the period, spoke to the cultural anxieties about the world that our scientific and technological developments seemed to be constructing, and wrapped everything in an appealing new technological packaging. In sum, as Disney crafted its first foray into science fiction, we can see the traces of that widespread cultural anxiety, of the studio's desire to address the monstrous specter behind this anxiety, and of its hope to offer a technically thrilling package that would also therefore be less disturbing for the typical Disney audience.

Yet given the company's history of eagerly adopting the latest film technology and its preeminence in the realm of fantasy, the move towards science fiction at this time must also have seemed a quite natural and, indeed, economically sound one. In fact, following the popular trend, the studio determined to take on science fiction almost simultaneously in film, in its first television series (as we shall see in the following chapter), and in the Tomorrowland area of the new Disneyland theme park. However, the subjects of that genre represented just as much of a problem for Disney as for the other film studios and, indeed, for the rest of American culture, as if they marked a troubling site of unstable references or were terms in a negotiation that refused to be satisfactorily concluded. While few might have looked to Disney for something better than the sort of "inadequate response" Sontag describes, and while the choice of texts might have offered little promise in addressing the "contemporary situation," the political/ideological impingements of the subject matter seem to linger very near the surface of this film, as if inviting the sort of confrontation that a film like *The Three Caballeros* had largely sidestepped.

Certainly, by 1954, after a flood of sensationalistic titles like *The Thing from Another World* (1951); *Invasion, U.S.A.* (1952); and *The War of the Worlds* (1953), the studio's choice of 20,000 *Leagues Under the Sea* as its initial science fiction effort must have seemed a rather "safe" one for this typically forward-looking genre. For Verne's novel pointedly looks back, further back than any Disney Main Street, to the emerging industrial mindset of the nineteenth century, to a kind of naïve technological vantage that was typical of the various books in Verne's "Voyages Extraordinaires" series. Of course, Verne's works were usually set in his own present to better facilitate his negotiations with the emerging technological world. As Edward James offers, he wanted to emphasize to his readers "that scientific and technological changes were occurring in their own society, and that more were imminent" (17). But for this very reason, Disney's choice to keep that nineteenth-century context, thereby producing a kind of nostalgic narrative, seems noteworthy, especially given the studio's very contemporary efforts in this direction that were then underway for its *Disneyland* television show and its theme park. But this choice is at least partly explained by the fact that such present-tense narratives risked stirring those fears and anxieties that beset the contemporary world, evoking the sort of monsters that might not sit well with the traditional Disney family audience, and perhaps *too* closely linking the Disney product with that cinema of "disaster." And too, intimations of disaster simply went against the grain of that fundamental Disney approach to the technological we have earlier described. Hence, a nostalgic science, something that could frame present-day technoscience in a safely remote past, wherein the "references" were a bit clearer and less ambiguous, represented a useful start to negotiations, a compelling and somewhat sensible compromise given both the issues mentioned above and the great cost of this film adaptation.[2]

However, negotiations would hardly be that easy, given the cultural climate, and monsters would proliferate throughout the narrative—monsters imagined, real, and looming. In fact, Paul Virilio has described as "monstrous" one effect that shows up here, and one with which our scientific and technological developments have increasingly confronted us: "the loss of references, the loss of all distinctions" (*Crepuscular* 165), a level on which our very world can seem monstrous because it has become so confusing. The Verne novel actually looks toward this conception, for it begins by establishing the public's misperception of the submarine *Nautilus* as a sea monster—a misperception that was part of the ship's protection, since it resulted in a public discourse about monsters and the ocean's secrets rather than an outcry against a nineteenth-century terrorist, a discourse that looked back to the realm of legends instead of forward to the latest scientific developments. More importantly, this initial confusion of monster and technology allowed Verne an effective critical vantage, letting him contrast older fears of the unknown with a modern, rationalist attitude—a strategy, as we shall see, that the studio would appropriate for a number of its television episodes in this vein. But the Disney conception would more directly develop and exploit this monstrous aspect of Verne's narrative and the play of confusion that attends it, proliferating monsters as a central metaphor of the film and a key term for effecting its complex negotiations.

Even prior to shooting the film, though, Disney was already facing a rather unconventional sort of monster on this project. For 20,000 *Leagues Under the Sea* was, as we have noted, the studio's first foray into the new CinemaScope technology, which had just been introduced in 1953 by Twentieth Century-Fox. The product of a studio that was, as John Belton has described, "caught up in the turmoil of an industry-wide financial crisis and self-redefinition" (113), thanks to changing audience patterns, government regulation, and the new competition of television, CinemaScope was a technology the difficulties of which were still being understood and negotiated. In quickly adopting this new technology, Disney faced several limitations, among them the fact that, since Fox was heavily committed to pushing this new format for its own productions, which had first priority, it could only make a single CinemaScope lens available to Disney for much of the production schedule. Additionally, the aesthetics of wide-screen filmmaking—e.g., the problems of composing for a 2.35:1 aspect ratio rather than the conventional 1.33:1, of regulating camera movement, of compensating for a lack of depth of field, of appropriate editing rhythms—were just being explored. However, as Bordwell, Staiger, and Thompson note, the "new set of stylistic devices" that widescreen filming involved were relatively quickly "brought into line with the classical schemata" (361). As a kind of stylistic "monster," CinemaScope was, it seems, relatively easily tamed.

Helping in that process was the choice of director, for Richard Fleischer did have some experience with this sort of technological innovation. In 1953, for example, he had tackled the filming of a modern-day western, *Arena*, in a widescreen 3D process. In fact, contemporary accounts suggest that he was more troubled by and engrossed in the practical difficulties of underwater photography for *20,000 Leagues* than by the aesthetic issues associated with wide-screen shooting.[3] In practice, he seems to have let his subject matter largely dictate the film's compositional style. Thus, he used the CinemaScope frame to emphasize the long, stylized design of the narrative's principle visual attraction, the submarine *Nautilus*, to provide for dynamic shots by depicting the submarine advancing diagonally into the wide frame to attack another ship or to escape danger, and to place the ship in extreme long shot against the horizon, other craft, or land. Since the narrative generally shifts between empty expanses of ocean and the cramped quarters of the *Nautilus*, depth of field proved a relatively minor consideration. And the editing, save for in the climactic fight with a giant squid, is rather conventional. Long takes, along with frequent subjective shot/reaction shot pairings, for example, make maximum capital of the underwater and location scenes, producing effects similar to what we find in the popular Disney "True-Life Adventure" documentaries of the period. In effect, Fleischer seems to have rather easily coped with this technological monster and, in the process, probably encouraged the studio to release its next animated feature, *Lady and the Tramp* (1955), in CinemaScope as well.

While in this case the cinematic technology did not prove especially challenging, the effort at *talking about* technology would require a good deal more negotiation, as Disney tried to draw out of Verne's narrative a more appropriate-for-the-era emphasis on the monstrous. Thus, the film opens not with Verne's after-the-fact, journalistic account, stressing how "the human mind is always hankering after something to marvel at" (2), but with an image of a supposed page from Verne's novel, actually something written for the film to develop its concern with monsters. That page describes how "the shipping world was alarmed by rumours of an avenging monster on the loose"; it dissolves into a scene that offers a glimpse of such a monster, as a mysterious entity with a gleaming "eye" charges and sinks a ship; and then the narrative illustrates the public response to this attack in a typical seaport, San Francisco, as Old Billy, a survivor of the sinking, assures a crowd that "it was the monster alright—a cable's length long from beak to tail . . . with one big eye like a lighthouse." This opening context not only gives reason to the following naval expedition in search of the monster—an expedition involving the French scientist Professor Arronax, his apprentice Conseil, and the American harpooner Ned Land—but also establishes a public discourse about monsters that helps to structure the film's narrative and lend a frame to the film's precariously balanced discourse about the nature of modern technology.

The film further establishes the main terms in this discourse through the interplay between Professor Arronax and three reporters from the San Francisco newspapers, representatives of the nineteenth century's "yellow press." For while the professor describes his efforts to "gather facts," they try to prod him into saying something that might be turned into an arresting headline. His measured response, referring to "current scientific knowledge," is one of openness; while not acknowledging the existence of monsters, he allows that "If we could go deep enough, we would all be surprised at the creatures down there." This scientific assessment, though, simply serves to measure the sensationalistic attitude that has come to surround those "rumours," as the morning newspaper brings the headline, "Monster Exists, Says French Scientist," accompanied by a sketch of a giant sea monster, complete not only with "beak," "tail," and "eye," but even with wings. This lurid popular discourse that has paralyzed regular shipping is based in legends of the past, yet it is shown as all too easily emerging from and even obscuring the truly scientific, suggesting how easily the public mind can blur the difference between myth and science, and thus the various external pressures that can shape our sense of the scientific, effectively reframing it as what we today describe as technoscience.[4]

With the subsequent expedition to hunt down the monster or expose it as the stuff of such popular constructions or "rumours," the impact of this loss of reference takes on a more disturbing dimension. For it begins by further underscoring that, despite Arronax's view, science does not operate in a pure state, but that it is partly constructed by powerful cultural forces that can obscure its focus. While Arronax wants passage to the South Pacific so that he can shed some scientific light on these rumors, we see that he can only continue this research because the U.S. Navy and State Department, the military and the government, will back it in order to serve commercial motivations. Thus they invite him, as an internationally respected expert, to serve as an observer on an expedition whose objective is to dispel the fears and rumors that have interrupted normal shipping. And the expedition's leader, Captain Farragut, emphasizes this goal for the scientific expedition; as he pronounces, "In my considered opinion, no such monster exists or ever did." He further terms the subject of this search simply a "legend," but explains that the mission will "give the lie to those rumors" circulated by the newspapers. The one musical number in the film, Ned Land's "A Whale of a Tale," immediately follows this pronouncement and serves to further undermine the notion of a monster by framing it in the context of a series of comic tall tales of the sea. By this point in the narrative, the "monster," only briefly glimpsed at the film's beginning, has effectively disappeared into the realm of legend, rumor, and tall tale—all constructs of the human imagination and, finally, nothing really fearful. In its place we see emerging a number of other surprisingly disturbing—at least for a Disney film—menaces: big business and government that dislike disruptions, a military that serves the interests of business and government and tolerates no challenges to its presumed power, and a press that flourishes primarily by fostering fears and anxieties. This collection of critiques suggests at least an effort to create an ideological context for the narrative's eventual focus on both nostalgic and contemporary issues of science and technology.

However, with the monster's sudden reappearance the narrative moves in a rather different direction, offering another sort of transformation that shifts focus from such ideological issues to scientific ones, particularly to the difficult task of naming and categorization, of establishing limits or boundaries. For both before and after it attacks and cripples Farragut's frigate, the monster undergoes a series of misidentifications and alternate namings. A lookout initially describes it simply as "a floating object," suggesting debris from a sinking ship they have sighted and recalling a whale that had earlier been misidentified as the monster, while another sailor assures his shipmates that it is "the monster." Thrown overboard in the ensuing fight, Professor Arronax and Conseil come upon it enshrouded in fog, and initially think their landing is an island. Yet when Conseil determines that, rather, "it looks like a monster," Arronax after some deliberation corrects him, labeling it "a miracle," "a submarine boat," and foreshadowing another shift in identification. Offering that "there is great genius behind all of this," he is in turn cautioned by Conseil, "Yes, and great evil." Conseil's comment, of course, already suggests a kind of intellectual negotiation at work within the narrative, one that tries to frame this fantastic piece of technology in the context of the death and destruction it has wrought, while it also points to the key shift in the film, as the notion of "monster" comes to denote something else, something human and even individualistic: the creator of this extraordinary machine.

The subsequent sequence makes this shift explicit, as Captain Nemo reveals himself and exposes his own monstrous aspect, even as he directs his visitors to appreciate his "miracle" of fantastic technology, despite its menacing look, not as a monster but simply, as Arronax himself offers, "a craft of human invention." For over the next sequence, and in keeping with the pattern of Verne's novel, the ship and all of its working details are put on display for Nemo's "guests" as wonders of scientific achievement, largely removed from any cultural context, while Nemo himself becomes the narrative's monster. Thus, he soon informs Arronax that, despite the professor's assumptions, Nemo does not consider himself "a civilized man," and he orders the professor, Conseil, and Ned Land to be left on the *Nautilus*'s deck while it submerges, leaving them to drown. It is a monstrous act from which he relents at the last moment, but it establishes a pattern that recurs when he later threatens Ned with death and when he attacks a ship loaded with munitions, destroying it and all onboard. With that attack Ned underscores the narrative shift, describing how sailors just like him were being "slaughtered by that monster," and even Arronax, who at various points in the narrative expresses some sympathy for Nemo and an obviously detached admiration for his technological achievements, finally labels him "a murderer." Thanks to the effects of the CinemaScope lens, the extreme close-ups of Nemo as he plays his organ in anticipation of the attack only further this monstrous identification. For they distort his facial features, while also easily evoking a cinematic tradition of monstrous madmen, specifically recalling Lon Chaney's similar presentation at the organ in the classic horror film *The Phantom of the Opera* (1921).

And yet, the film never completely settles for such a traditional generic identification and strictly personal indictment. Despite these familiar images and Ned's repeated description of Nemo as "a madman," the monstrous appellation sits uneasily here, in part because we learn of the background that has turned Nemo into a self-professed "avenger" against humanity's own monstrous nature—thereby raising a note of sympathy—but also because the narrative inserts a series of other candidates to again shift and blur the "monster" reference. This blurring begins with the representatives of the unnamed nation that he blames for the torture and murder of his wife and child—military figures whom we see beating prisoners and loading their ships with the raw materials for war. It continues with the cannibals who nearly capture Ned and Conseil and attack the *Nautilus*, and whose nature is codified in the human skulls and bones that decorate their village. And it culminates in one of the most compelling monsters in the Disney canon, the giant squid that fulfills Arronax's earlier warning about the surprising "creatures down there" in the sea's depths, while also providing another elongated figure for effective wide-screen shot compositions. In its outsized nature, unreasoning assault, and nightmarish combination of features—as well as its dependence on what we generally term "special effects"—the squid quickly evokes more traditional cinematic monsters, and it mobilizes the sort of human response we often see in horror films, as everyone joins together—Nemo, his crew, his prisoners—to fight and defeat the creature in hand-to-tentacle combat. It becomes a familiar case of humans versus a *real* monster and, through their joint efforts against this creature, punctuated by Ned Land's saving of Nemo, helps to leaven the earlier indictment of humanity's own monstrous nature.

With the squid attack sequence, *20,000 Leagues Under the Sea* also manages to achieve the sort of retreat from present concerns that was always implied by its nostalgic narrative—and for which Disney films have often been scored. It has evoked a technological monster, only to shift that term to a traditional "mad scientist," then to various practically anonymous branches of the human family, and finally to arrive at a most suitable candidate, the sort of monstrous creature that audiences of the era were becoming quite familiar with thanks to films like *The Beast from 20,000 Fathoms* (1953), *Them* (1954), *The Monster from the Ocean Floor* (1954), and *It Came from Beneath the Sea* (1955). And yet, all of these mutant monsters of the science fiction genre were always just stand-ins, representatives of a larger monstrousness that had been unleashed on the world and that finally could not be avoided; they were just common players in a genre that, as Peter Biskind puts it, "was born with the atom and died in the late fifties when . . . we learned to love the bomb" (98). Mutants caused or creatures awakened by atomic testing, they invariably played out the terms of a larger cultural struggle with the monstrous forces of science and atomic technology that threatened to go out of all control, with their almost inevitable defeat reassuring us that such technologically born monsters might somehow be kept in check.

Yet, even given its satisfying narrative displacement of the monstrous onto the squid—which is just one more "beast" from "beneath the sea" literally and psychologically brought to the surface by the work of technology—the film cannot escape another level of easily shifting references, those bound up in modern American culture itself. For with the *Nautilus*'s return to its home base of Vulcania and Nemo's determination to destroy that base along with all of his discoveries, *20,000 Leagues Under the Sea* finally makes the same sort of connection as its generic brethren of the 1950s. The explosion Nemo sets off—"an explosion such as the world has never known," as he offers—destroys the island, kills the soldiers who have landed there, and eventually sinks the *Nautilus.* It is an ending quite unlike that envisioned by Verne's novel, which has the *Nautilus* defeated not by a technologically fashioned cataclysm, not hoist on its own scientific petard, but sunk by a natural force, a maelstrom in Arctic waters. More significantly, the Disney ending produces a familiar mushroom cloud, attesting to its nuclear nature and that of the secret power Nemo has discovered. It marks the final monster of the film, that of a scientific knowledge capable of producing, according to Nemo, "enough energy to lift mankind from the depths of hell into heaven, or destroy it." Yet, as a concluding voice-over intones, in a rhetoric that was unmistakable in the period, this knowledge is also one for which the world is not yet "ready"—a monster of the narrative's past that still haunted the film audience's present and that easily indicted all of the era's nuclear powers.

That image of the mushroom cloud provides a most sobering image for the film's conclusion, since despite Nemo's faint promise of "hope for the future," it invariably recalls American atomic testing in the same South Pacific, a location that did, after all, represent a pointed shift from the arctic setting of the novel's conclusion. Moreover, it opened onto another quite accidental present-day correspondence, since in 1954 and prior to the film's release the U.S.Navy had launched its first nuclear-powered submarine, fittingly naming it *Nautilus,* after Verne's technological monster. While reinserting Verne's vision into the public consciousness and thus providing something of a publicity windfall for the Disney film—one that would propel it to the position of third highest-grossing film in 1955 and Disney's top money-maker to that date[5]—this ship, as the first component of the new "nuclear navy" that was then being constructed, also brought with it some troublesome baggage, a reminder of how these technologies, the submarine and nuclear power, were being joined—and celebrated—as the latest weapons in the nation's arsenal. In short, it further established a connection to that dangerous real world and extended the lexicon of monstrous references by underscoring the link between atomic power and weaponry that Disney would be at some pains to counter over the coming years.[6]

But of what significance, finally, is this proliferation of monstrous figures in 20,000 *Leagues Under the Sea* and its various cultural kin, or the simple shifting of references that lets us all too easily play with this word "monster"? We have seen how rapidly the term surfaces and changes reference to finally include the era's atomic fears, even subtly—and surprisingly—indicting America and its new nuclear navy; but does this pattern do any more than reinforce, almost in spite of its nostalgic imagery, a sense of how embedded this film is in its 1950s context of science fiction, mutant creatures, and atomic paranoia? The great fallout from inhabiting a world bound by "new technologies," Virilio offers, is ultimately "a crisis of ethical and esthetic references, the inability to come to terms with events in an environment where the appearances are against us"; for in such circumstances, in a realm of "increased mediatization" of all knowledge, a *"reality effect* replaces immediate reality" (*Lost* 24). In short, inhabiting a technologized environment can fundamentally disorient us because of the way such an environment eliminates or replaces those references or horizons—"ethical and esthetic"—that help guide our lives and enable us to carry out the sort of negotiations in which we are always involved.

It is in this context especially that we might map this monster metaphor onto the Disney film, its own technological discourse, and its efforts at negotiating between scientific and ideological imperatives. We might recall how Virilio links the notion of the monstrous to the unsettling way in which terms easily seem to shift their meaning as we suffer a "loss of references," or simply feel we are at sea, somewhat like Ned Land trapped within the *Nautilus,* with all the customary points of reference shifted or lost, with a "reality effect," determined by this strange new habitat, the submarine, having replaced reality itself. Here, in fact, is a key link to the larger thrust of the film, for Ned and Conseil, as they try to figure out how to escape from this technological monster, find themselves frustrated, since, in another and most telling shift from Verne's narrative, all of the maps and charts on the submarine lack the conventional delineations of longitude and latitude, the appropriate points of reference that would let them situate themselves. Instead, they discover that Nemo has so rejected the normal world that he has created maps in which all markings and measurements extend out from a mysterious central point—his uncharted island base of Vulcania, the source of all his technological achievements—in effect, from his own subjective vantage that confirms him as a kind of master of this world.[7] This element stands in marked contrast to the novel, which is careful at every turn to cite place and position, latitude and longitude, even to have Nemo repeatedly mark for his "guests" the ship's position as a way of impressing them with its capabilities.[8] That conception of a subjective chart, then, in its own way stands as symbolic of the film's ultimate monstrous logic and of the real threat that Nemo and the new world he represents pose, as it shows how a "reality effect" might be mapped over our "immediate reality," and suggests, through the power latent in Vulcania—a power that could destroy the world—a grave danger that underlies such substitution.

Armed with this sudden insight, that the monster is the point of reference—or as we might interpret, that the arbitrariness of references is itself monstrous—Ned and Conseil manage their own sort of negotiation. They plot Nemo's charts against a normal map, literally find their place in the world once more, and send out messages noting their location, thus precipitating their eventual escape. They, in effect, act out the film's desire to escape from this modern dilemma, from this monstrous atomic and subjective disintegration, no less than from the disturbing concerns of modern technology, and to reassert a simple set of limits on and order in this world—an order that takes a casual form throughout the narrative in Arronax and Conseil's remarks on marine taxonomies. However, this escape is far from satisfying, not nearly as comforting as the conventional use of technology to defeat the technologically awakened mutants and monsters that we find in other science fiction films of the era. For it reminds us that the frightened populace we see early in the film indeed had reason to be scared. And it leaves audiences of the present, in that period when, as Nemo offers, "all this will someday come to pass," yet to cope with this power, to negotiate with our own technoscientific regime and the monsters it creates. It leaves us feeling rather like Ned, Arronax, and Conseil as the film ends, simply adrift in a small dinghy in a seemingly limitless ocean, with our horizons still threatened by an inescapably technological future.

Of course, this reading may seem rather somber for a film that many commentators have simply categorized as "fantasy at its best" (Maltin, *Disney* 121), or "spectacle" marked by "splendid special effects" (Gifford 38). But it also serves as a needed corrective to those who would sweepingly categorize all Disney texts, regardless of the era, as "carefully controlled" "fantasy," particularly marked by "escapist themes" (Wasko, *Understanding Disney* 118). Eleanor Byrne and Martin McQuillan, in trying to read Disney narratives like many other recent critics, primarily as "reactionary parables of the American right" (2), have also noted this interpretive problem. As they set about exploring what they assumed to be the simple "conservative values" of the Disney canon—values that seemed marked by a level of what they term "blatantness"—they also observed frequent challenges to those values, often finding in the films a pattern of contradictory, frequently shifting "ideological codes" (5) that they were unable to resolve. What the shifting notions of the monstrous in 20,000 *Leagues Under the Sea* point to is a version of that narrative instability—one that betokens an effort, both within the culture and in the Disney studio at this time, to negotiate different points of view on the technological. In this case, those unstable references trace out the Disney narrative's difficult confrontation with the psychological and cultural concerns surrounding the latest technological developments, which stubbornly resisted both conventional narrative resolution and a simple nostalgic relegation to the past.

More generally here, they point to what we might see as a recurrent Disney difficulty during this period in portraying the world of modern technoscience—or negotiating with its monstrous potential. As the studio first moved into the realm of science fiction, with such efforts as the Tomorrowland section of the Disneyland theme park, the To-morrowland episodes of the *Disneyland* television series, and 20,000 *Leagues Under the Sea*, it encountered various problems that defied easy resolution. Tomorrowland was simply not ready for the opening of Disneyland, and when the first guests arrived, a gas leak was discovered there. When confronted with Tomorrowland's problems, Walt is reported to have directed, "'Cover it up with balloons and pennants'" (Thomas, *Walt Disney* 268). When planning got underway for the television series, as Bill Cotter notes, the studio nearly "ignored the Tomorrowland section of the show," since "no one was sure exactly how to portray the future" (64). And here too the problem was "covered up" with other types of programming, such as the enormously popular Davy Crockett episodes. Ultimately, the fewest shows were devoted to this theme, and by the 1958 season, at the height of American space consciousness, no Tomorrowland shows were being offered. And 20,000 *Leagues Under the Sea* almost inevitably opened onto the more disturbing implications of 1950s technoscience, the simultaneous possibilities to, as Arronax offers, "revolutionize the world" and, as Nemo counters, "destroy it," as well as the disturbing recognition that our science and technology were largely guided by the interests of business, government, and the military. But these various possibilities are the same ones that we continue to try to negotiate today; for the monsters, as the Disney/Pixar film *Monsters, Inc.* (2001) humorously illustrates, remain in our dreams, in our cultural closets. To the credit of *20,000 Leagues Under the Sea,* and perhaps to the consternation of many of today's Disney critics, it does not, like many of its generic brethren of the 1950s, simply offer a formulaic solution to our technological concerns. In fact, this film seems to suggest that the satisfactory negotiation of technoscience's possibilities was simply more a fantasy than even a Disney narrative could easily visualize.

Yet *20,000 Leagues Under the Sea* did at least demonstrate one possible option, one way that the studio would, at several points in the future, manage to bargain with the troubling themes of technoscience. In 1959, for the first time in a decade Disney lost money, thanks largely to the cost of *Sleeping Beauty,* and to counter that situation the company again turned to a technologically themed story to restore their fortunes. They allocated the largest budget to date for a live-action feature— $4,500,000—to begin shooting *Swiss Family Robinson,* a film about a nineteenth-century Swiss family shipwrecked on their way to make a new life in New Zealand.[9] Salvaging all that they can from the ship— livestock, books, weapons, ropes and pulleys—the family creates on another South Seas island a thoroughly modern environment, in fact, one that, the father of the family brags, sports "all the latest conveniences." Through a variety of inventions and contraptions they even manage to defend their new and quite comfortable world from attacking pirates, as they effectively—thanks to the powers of science and technology— transform an interruption in their immigration into an acceptable end to their journey.

The narrative is, of course, essentially an adventure, much in the vein of *20,000 Leagues Under the Sea,* with few major developments in its plot. However, its central concern, as well as its chief attraction—as is especially attested to by the reappearance of the Swiss Family tree house as a theme park attraction first in Disneyland and later in Walt Disney World's Magic Kingdom—is the stranded family's technological ingenuity. For they almost eagerly apply the latest scientific lessons of modern European culture to their primitive island world, easily transforming its raw materials—palm trees, bamboo, vines, fresh flowing water—into the stuff of a technological society, and in the process providing audiences with a lesson in the advantages of modern technological culture at a time when technology had become all too closely linked to the contentions of the Cold War. And the film's box office easily measured the success of this nostalgic take on industry and ingenuity, as it earned more than $7,500,000 on its first release (Maltin, *Disney* 179). Here there are no monsters, apart from the human sort represented by the rather stock menace of pirates, and the family is quite at home with technology. In fact, through the Robinsons' *tree* house, we see how technology and nature might come to an accommodation, how a comfortable bargain might well be struck. Of course, that bargain works so easily in large part because culture itself has been removed from the equation, as the point of reference, just as with Nemo's Vulcania, becomes the Robinsons' island, while the rest of society is simply bracketed off. But *Swiss Family Robinson* is very much a wish-fulfillment fantasy, one that seems almost a reflection of Disneyland itself, and while not home to monsters, it is not the real world either.

5 Disney in Television Land

I

The new technology of television had loomed on the horizon of the film industry for a considerable time. It was talked about, demonstrated, and even depicted in films throughout the 1920s and 1930s. It was the subject of numerous spectacular demonstrations during the 1930s, most of them illustrating its ability to transmit images over ever greater distances: broadcasting from one city to another, from one country to another, from one continent to another, and in one instance from England to an ocean liner in the mid-Atlantic (Mosely 17). That ability to obliterate distance and bring visual entertainment into the home produced a variety of utopian predictions, such as the one offered by RCA head David Sarnoff, who promised that "television will finally bring to people . . . instantaneous participation in the sights and sounds of the entire world" (42). Thus, as Joseph Corn and Brian Horrigan suggest, throughout the pre–World War II decades "the idea of television in our future heated the popular imagination as few technologies ever have" (24). And yet in spite of some early experiments with using television to broadcast films directly into theaters, it remained a rather problematic, even troubling technology for the film industry, as the titles of such early films as *Murder by Television* (1935) and *Trapped by Television* (1936) might well hint. Adding to this attitude in the post–World War II era was the fact that television was perceived primarily as a delivery system at a time when the major studios were, thanks to the Supreme Court's Paramount Decision, finding themselves barred from involvement in product delivery. Consequently, the film industry generally saw television not so much as a sign of progress, as one more possible enhancement to or outlet for its work, but as a future competitor, even a potential replacement.

Because of that fear, which was only exacerbated by the downturn in attendance seen in the postwar era and the dismantling of the studio system that followed the Paramount Decision, the American film industry saw little possibility of negotiating an effective use of this new technology. In fact, as Fredric Stuart explains, the major Hollywood studios approached television in this period with an unofficial "policy of noncooperation" (302), buttressed by a series of internal moves—"reorganization, concentration on high-cost feature production, and technological development" (302)—designed to allow them to compete more effectively for audiences. And yet by the 1950s this new, potentially competing technology did have much to offer the film industry. Most obviously, it offered the studios a way of utilizing their excess production capacity; it might eventually provide another form of exhibition for companies that had been forced to divest themselves of their theater chains; it represented a powerful means of advertising the latest films to a wide audience; as had been the case with an earlier competitor, radio, television could provide a ground for developing talent that could be employed in feature films; and it might even prove an outlet for older films for which there was, under the old studio system, little use after their initial distribution. Moreover, since the studios also had much to offer the industry that was developing around television technology—and in great part fashioning itself after the film industry model—there was certainly room for bargains to be struck, in fact, bargains that would almost have to be struck as these industries moved into an ever more complex, mediatized environment, as it became increasingly clear that television was an unavoidable element of our technologized world.

As we have already suggested, recognizing such imperatives and responding to them had consistently been key strengths of the Disney Company. As far back as 1936, when Walt and Roy were in the process of renegotiating their distribution agreement with United Artists, the contract foundered on a clause assigning future television rights for the Disney films to UA. Disney biographer Bob Thomas cites a revealing comment Walt made at the time: "I don't know what television is, and I'm not going to sign away anything I don't know about" (*Walt* 141). It suggests an element of business acumen born in part of the various other financial negotiations in which the company had been engaged almost since its inception—negotiations, like that with Pat Powers for use of the

Cinephone system, that had made the Disney brothers justifiably wary. But it was also a response influenced by the business model that was quickly becoming a key to all of the company's activities, the pattern of synergy or integration of all corporate activities. In her *Understanding Disney*, Janet Wasko describes this pattern as a practice of "promoting . . . activities across a growing number of outlets, creating a synergy between individual units and producing immediately recognizable brands" (71), and she describes how this practice has become a fundamental tenet of all Disney operations today.

What often goes unremarked, though, is how early in Disney's history this practice developed, and thus how central it was to many of the studio's corporate moves, and ultimately to its start into television. As early as 1930, with their small animation studio desperate for cash to support its staple projects, as well as Walt's dreams of expansion, the Disneys were creating Mickey Mouse Clubs at theaters around the country and licensing the likeness of their "star" mouse to a variety of commercial vendors. Reflecting the fast-growing popularity of Disney's animated figures, sales for those licensed products—writing tablets, handkerchiefs, sleepwear, toys of every sort, even Mickey Mouse-embossed ice cream cones—quickly exceeded all expectations and led the studio to adopt such merchandising as a foundational part of company activity. Two spectacularly successful examples of this activity particularly stand out. One was Disney's contract with the Ingersoll-Waterbury Company, which, while executed at the height of the Depression, produced sales of two and a half million Mickey Mouse watches in just two years. In a second, almost equally successful agreement, Disney licensed the Lionel Corporation to produce a Mickey and Minnie Mouse handcar that ran on tracks. That product has been credited with helping Lionel not only to overcome bankruptcy, but also to gain the leading position in the American toy train market (Thomas, *Walt* 107–8). To facilitate such agreements, Disney set up a licensing office under the direction of advertising executive Herman (Kay) Kamen who, throughout the 1930s, negotiated agreements for the use of Mickey Mouse and other Disney characters to more than seventy-five manufacturers in the United States, forty-five in England, twenty in Canada, six in France, and six in Spain and Portugal, a move that, by the 1950s, was producing annual sales of over $100 million (Watts 148), thereby helping to sustain the parent company's traditional film activity. In fact, by the time of the release of *Snow White and the Seven Dwarfs* (1937), the first Disney feature film, this new strategy had already become, as Steven Watts notes, "an intrinsic part of the moviemaking process" (149). For on the day that *Snow*

White opened, Kamen had in place a complete merchandising campaign that involved agreements with over seventy companies, thereby marking the start of an elaborate nexus of entertainment and advertisement that would eventually become a model for the American film marketplace.

More than simply establishing another possible source for capital funding, though, this new emphasis on combining entertainment and merchandising also helped propel the worldwide popularity of Disney's films and had a major impact on the company's entire production process. Certainly, this emphasis marked the beginning of a fruitful and enduring pattern of integration that would increasingly come to identify the company, to mark its unique place in American culture as the most successful example of the entertainment-marketing conglomerate, and eventually, I would suggest, to script the terms for the company's entry into the field of television and then other mass media. For Disney's first efforts in using the new technology of television show the influence of this internal company model. In 1950, responding to overtures from television, Disney created a one-hour Christmas special for NBC entitled "One Hour in Wonderland," featuring film and radio star Edgar Bergen and his dummy Charlie McCarthy as its hosts. The show took the form of a children's Christmas party at the Disney studio, providing the "guests" and television audience glimpses of the lot and soundstages, a sneak preview of Disney's upcoming theatrical release *Alice in Wonderland* (1951), and live-action scenes involving the voice- and image-model for Alice, the young English actress Kathryn Beaumont, and Bobby Driscoll, the child star of the studio's just-released live-action feature *Treasure Island*, as well as earlier efforts like *Song of the South* (1946) and *So Dear to My Heart* (1948). The show proved so successful at attracting a television audience that in the following year CBS approached Disney about doing a similar special. More important to Disney, though, was the fact that the first show had measurably contributed to the success of *Treasure Island* and helped to build a large audience for *Alice*; one commentator estimated that the telecast was "worth $1,000,000 at the box office. . . . I think Disney has found the answer to using television both to entertain and to sell his product" (quoted in Cotter 4). Consequently, Disney prepared "The Walt Disney Christmas Show," a special with the then-record television budget of $250,000. Designed as a Christmas party for children of different nationalities, Walt himself served as host, introducing several cartoons and animated segments drawn from the Disney archives, and once more providing lengthy previews of the studio's upcoming releases, this time *Snow White and the Seven Dwarfs* (entering rerelease) and *Peter Pan*.[1] Again, the result was a favorable critical and commercial reaction, confirming the possibilities that Disney had foreseen for integrating television with the company's other entertainment projects.

As the studio continued to study how it might move into television on a more elaborate scale, then, it was already anticipating that the new medium would function as part of a much larger media construct, one that would eventually extend far beyond both traditional film exhibition and the then-current model of television broadcasting, and that would open up various new synergistic possibilities.[2] In fact, this vision of television as part of an integrated media environment was one reason why the two leading networks initially balked at buying into Disney's ideas for a television series. While the networks viewed a deal with the studio largely in terms of the existing program paradigm, with Disney creating the product that they would sell to advertisers and then exhibit by broadcasting over network stations, Disney had another view of the new technology's potential, one in which the network distribution and exhibition would promote and help finance the studio's larger entertainment agenda. For Walt linked the creation of a television series to his idea for a Disneyland theme park. He wanted to leverage the negotiations for the former to provide funds for building the latter, while conceiving of each as advertising and drawing an audience for the other, as well as supporting the ongoing work of the film studio. Thus Walt and Roy Disney "made it clear that the Park was an integral part of the package they were peddling—no support for Disneyland, no show" (Cotter 58). Under such unconventional and potentially risky terms, CBS withdrew from negotiations, and while NBC continued discussions for several months, it too finally balked at making a commitment to the dual project. After Roy personally called new ABC head Leonard Goldenson, though, a deal was quickly struck, and on April 2, 1954, the new partners officially announced plans for the television series, as well as their financing deal for the theme park. Under this agreement the network would pay Disney $2,000,000 for twenty shows (rather than the typical run of twenty-six), provide $500,000 for a 35 percent ownership in the proposed Disney theme park, and guarantee up to $4,500,000 in loans for the park's construction (Thomas, *Walt* 249). While the studio had not yet even determined the precise format for its *Disneyland* show, those negotiations officially set in place a key component of the new sort of vision machine that would eventually become a fundamental part of the American cultural landscape.

Premiering in 1954, the *Disneyland* show took the shape of an anthology series, a flexible format that would allow the studio to draw on the great variety of material in its archives, while also maximizing opportunities for further synergistic exploitation.[3] The show that resulted, hosted by Walt, pointedly sold both old and new Disney: by packaging its large archive of short cartoons into thematic programs; by condensing or serializing its animated and live-action features; by creating sneak-preview episodes that promoted both new releases and films that, with its unique releasing plan, the studio regularly rereleased to ever-increasing profits; by pioneering "behind-the-scenes" or "making-of" documentaries that publicized the latest films; and by regularly reporting on the building and subsequent development of the Disneyland park. Thus, in its initial season the *Disneyland* show offered a condensed version of *Alice in Wonderland* and a two-episode presentation of *Treasure Island.* The "Operation Undersea" episode described the making of the new Disney feature *20,000 Leagues Under the Sea,* particularly emphasizing the technological challenge of shooting its many underwater scenes. And several shows during that first season, including the initial episode, chronicled the various stages in the park's preparation, while also stressing the links between the theme park and the television show. As Walt himself explained to viewers at the start of the first episode, he believed that "Disneyland the place and *Disneyland* the TV show are all part of the same," and since the format of the show—weekly offering episodes from Fantasyland, Adventureland, Tomorrowland, or Frontierland—paralleled the planned structure of the park, that connection was consistently underscored. And conversely, since the park itself was, as Michael Real notes, "consciously designed as a total environment made of dramatic productions complete with plot, scenery, and characters," each visitor would, by design, pass "through a Disney experience just as a viewer is carried through scenes in a film by a camera" (47). Thus the genre contexts—of park, film, and television—gained a natural continuity, even a kind of *narrative similarity,* as they played off of the studio's origins in the world of film.

The success of this format was immediate, as the show provided ABC with its highest-ever rated program—a number six Nielsen ranking for the year—and garnered a series of awards that quickly raised network prestige. For the initial 1954–55 season, *Disneyland* received Emmy Awards for Best Variety Series, as well as for Best Individual Program of the Year and Best Editing (both for the "Operation Undersea" episode); it gained nominations for both Walt Disney and Fess Parker in the category of Outstanding New Personality; and it won a Peabody Award for Outstanding Youth and Children's Program. Although in 1955 86 percent of the profitable television stations in the country were affiliated with the CBS or NBC networks, it was also the first year in which ABC became profitable—a result due in large part to the Disney agreement, since *Disneyland* generated nearly half of ABC's advertising revenue that year (Boddy 117). Moreover, the partnership with a successful film studio helped vault ABC to the status of a major competitor to the other networks. Meanwhile, the show became a key component in a kind of internal negotiation, particularly in Walt's plans to, as Christopher Anderson explains, "transform the Disney studio from an independent producer of feature films and cartoon short subjects into a diversified leisure and entertainment corporation" (137). Yet what may be even more important is that the development of this show heralded the start of a larger transformation of the entire entertainment industry in the United States, since it demonstrated that television and the film industry could no longer simply ignore each other or act as antagonistic competitors. Rather, they began to recognize the mutual benefits of working together, of following Disney's own guiding synergistic principle that began from the assumption "that entertainment was the same in any medium" (Thomas, *Walt* 242).

While many of these benefits could be traced directly to the economic agreements involved in the move to television, there remained other areas to be negotiated. For although the agreement between Disney and ABC allowed the studio to advertise its base product, obtain working capital, construct and promote a completely new product (Disneyland the park), capitalize on its older films, and even foster future cooperation between the film and television industries, the very success of the *Disneyland* series produced new and unexpected challenges both to Disney's synergistic structure and to its approach to popular narrative. Certainly, the studio could calculate that the "Operation Undersea" episode would positively impact the release of *20,000 Leagues Under the Sea,* and the immediate success of that film, as the previous chapter noted, quickly bore out that prediction. Yet Disney was obviously taken aback by the public response to several other episodes during that initial season, most notably the three Davy Crockett shows that aired on December 15, 1954, January 26, 1955, and February 23, 1955, sparking a national craze for which Disney, even with its successful merchandising history, was rather unprepared. As has often been chronicled,[4] the studio's three-part mini series gave birth to what Margaret King terms "one of the great popular culture events" of modern America (143), one that would bring both an unexpected demand for Crockett merchandise and a new level of critical response to the television medium.

Certainly, the success of the Crockett series was due largely to its being the right sort of story at the right time. Deep in the Cold War and in the immediate wake of the very bloody Korean conflict, contemporary America readily responded to the sort of traditional hero it depicted, and especially to the distinct sense of identity and purpose embodied in Crockett's persona. One immediate measure of its impact was the success of the show's theme song, "The Ballad of Davy Crockett," which was the number one pop song in the nation for five straight weeks, was covered by singers of every sort, including Fess Parker (who played Davy), and sold approximately seven million copies in six months. While initially surprised by the way the series resonated with the American public and, perhaps more to the point, that any television show would have more immediate and measurable impact than its films, the studio rushed to capitalize on the popularity of both the figure and the actor who portrayed him. As Paul Andrew Hutton notes, in the effort to catch up to public enthusiasm, "every conceivable kind of item" was quickly branded with the Davy Crockett label (31), not only the naturally linked products, such as buckskin jackets, moccasins, jeans, toy guns, action figures, and especially coonskin caps, but also such items as bathing suits, bedspreads, bicycles, guitars, lunch boxes, mugs, pajamas, pillows, purses, puzzles, soap, thermos bottles, underwear, and wallets.[5] With the success of "The Ballad of Davy Crockett," Disney quickly formed a subsidiary for releasing records, and costars Parker and Buddy Ebsen wrote and recorded a song for it, "Davy Crockett's Motto—Be Sure You're Right (Then Go Ahead)." Fess Parker was signed to a long-term contract, while the studio quickly looked for other properties that might exploit his sudden popularity. And in an unprecedented move, in fact, one that went against the prevailing wisdom of the time that said that audiences would not pay to see what television offered for free, the studio edited together a film version of the series, *Davy Crockett, King of the Wild Frontier*, which was rushed into theaters in June of 1955 and earned $2 million (Anderson 149). Meanwhile, executives began to consider how the studio might develop additional material on its new franchise figure, even though Crockett had died at the end of the third episode. As Walt Disney candidly admitted, "We had no idea what was going to happen on Crockett. Why, by the time the first show finally got on the air, we were already shooting the third one and calmly killing Davy off at the Alamo. It became one of the biggest over-night hits in TV history, and there we were with just three films and a dead hero!" (quoted in Cotter 63).[6]

Yet even as the studio rushed to create a follow-up miniseries for the next season, one depicting an earlier Davy Crockett, Disney found itself facing questions about its approach to popular narrative. Certainly the three Crockett episodes had proven wildly popular and profitable, but critical voices had also appeared. The most noteworthy was that of John Fischer, who, in a controversial *Harper's* essay, denounced the Crockett phenomenon as the product of what he termed "a simonized, Disneyfied version of history," one that was "as phony as the Russian legend about kind Papa Stalin" (16). Other critics and historians quickly followed Fischer's lead, weighing in not only on the Crockett material, but, what was far more important, also on the impact of both Disney and television in shaping our sense of history and our broad cultural perceptions. In retrospect it seems that the Disney portrayal was not so far off the mark as some of these accounts initially suggested. In fact, historian William Jamborsky claims that "for the most part Disney played reasonably straight with history," producing what he terms "a mature production . . . not expected by many critics of Disney" (105–6). Even Richard Schickel, often critical of the Disney films' social dimension, retrospectively found the Crockett material to be "a pleasantly exuberant adventure story," mainly because he felt that it "stood . . . outside the Disney mainstream" (256).

Perhaps a more significant reaction, though, might be seen in the way the studio approached the new Crockett episodes it had rushed into production ("Davy Crockett's Keelboat Race" of Nov. 16, 1955, and "Davy Crockett and the River Pirates" of Dec. 14, 1955). For these shows pointedly pull back from any illusion of a historical account and instead emphasize the Crockett of legend, as if trying to assure audiences that Disney's Crockett was from the start an amalgam of, as the Frontierland introduction announces, "tall tales and true." What had quickly become clear was the power of the new television technology to reach a broad audience, to affect popular opinion, and also to engender serious criticism—criticism that could eventually influence company sales. The response to the Crockett shows, both positive and negative, suggested that Disney would have to give more attention to the narrative power of the new technology, and that its television series would necessitate a new range of negotiations.

II

It is . . . our common destiny to become film.
—Paul Virilio, "The Last Vehicle"

When the studio began work on the *Disneyland* series in 1954, it quickly found that, despite its flexibility, the anthology format posed something of a programming problem, one manifest in the show's very rhetoric. For as every episode began, a voice-over announced that the show would offer episodes drawn from four categories—Adventureland, Fantasyland, Frontierland, and Tomorrowland. While Disney had in its archives ample material to produce shows on the first two topics and had already explored frontier themes and characters in some of its cartoons, the staff had no previous experience and few ready ideas to fill the promise of what it termed Tomorrowland. As we have previously noted, science fiction was not part of the studio's prior fantasy vision, and the genre's typical themes did not easily lend themselves to the sort of family-oriented narratives that were Disney's strength. Moreover, Walt initially insisted that any Tomorrowland episodes be "science-factual" (quoted in Watts 311), a term that staked out a different and certainly more realistic path than that followed by traditional science fiction and that might involve the studio in a larger public discourse about science and technology. For these reasons and because, as Bill Cotter notes, "no one was quite sure exactly how to portray the future," the studio at first almost ignored this section of the show (64). Yet when a few episodes were produced in this vein, they were well received and some were released theatrically as shorts. Behind that accomplishment was the studio's response to a problem it had begun to recognize and that we have observed in *20,000 Leagues Under the Sea:* the difficulty of talking about a subject that had, in the mid-1950s, largely been drawn into the orbit of a sensationalized science fiction film genre, that "imagination of disaster," as Susan Sontag famously termed it, a description that obviously put the subject at some odds with the usual Disney family agenda.

In this chapter I examine the problem these early Tomorrowland television shows faced as they tried to develop a rhetoric that would allow for a balance between sensationalistic science fiction and that more realistic "science-factual" aim. This effort to negotiate a suitable way of talking about both science fiction and the "science-factual" would result in a narrative pattern that draws heavily on established Disney efforts in other areas, yet also shows a clear sense of that popular cinematic mode against the background of which these episodes would be seen and measured by the television audience. That pattern, however, would prove to be unstable, as the *Disneyland* episodes collectively known as the *Man in Space* series—"Man in Space" (Mar. 9, 1955), "Man and the Moon" (Dec. 28, 1955), and "Mars and Beyond" (Dec. 4, 1957)—gradually lose that balance. Despite Walt Disney's directive, a rather conventional rhetoric of science and technology would increasingly become colored by the practices of a cinematic fiction, with science and technology becoming essentially the backdrop for a project imagined in filmic terms. While these episodes represent some of the best of early *Disneyland* programming, garnering international attention and establishing a *potential* for speaking about scientific and technological issues in a thoroughly entertaining manner, they also evidence some of the problems of narrative negotiation at which the Davy Crockett shows hinted. For they suggest a level on which Disney's efforts, like the larger cultural move in this direction, were already being influenced by a kind of postmodern "destiny," as Paul Virilio puts it, one that would continue to shape the rhetoric of the studio's later feature efforts in science fiction.

In this instance, too, Virilio's critique of modern technological society, and especially his notion of how we are increasingly being "cinematized," can help us link the trajectory of these early Disney shows to later Disney science fiction, and even to other media efforts at talking about science and technology, at addressing what we today often term "technoscience."[7] Simply put, Virilio's sense of our "destiny to become film" is reflected in the "destiny" of the Disney *Man in Space* shows.[8] Virilio uses the cinema as a trope for a key effect of our technological society, the manner in which it distances us from the real by blurring the boundaries between the factual and the fictional (or, as he offers, "the relative fusion/confusion of the factual . . . and the virtual"), by replacing our normal experience of the world with what he terms a "reality effect" (*Vision* 60), and by troubling the very manner in which we describe the factual and the fictional—which was, of course, a criticism leveled at Disney's most successful television effort, the Davy Crockett shows. In the early Disney television episodes about technology, we see further signs of that effect, as if shows originally fashioned with a new format in mind and approached with a different, even scientific, sort of rhetoric gradually succumb to the "reality effect" Virilio identifies, effectively finding their destiny to become, quite simply, "cinema." We might say that while the Disney staff was puzzling over how to speak about or "portray" tomorrow, tomorrow was already finding its own voice—one largely derived from science fiction—and in the process already framing our postmodern fate.

The *Man in Space* shows derive from a series of articles on the possibilities of space travel, published in *Collier's* magazine between 1952 and 1954. Among the contributors were such luminaries of this new field as Dr. Fred Whipple, chair of Harvard's Astronomy Department; Dr. Joseph Kaplan, professor of Physics at the University of California; space illustrators Chesley Bonestell and Fred Freeman; the writer Cornelius Ryan; and a group of German rocket and space experts, including

Willy Ley, Heinz Haber, and most notably Wernher von Braun.[9] Several pieces coauthored by Ryan and von Braun detailed proposals for launching an Earth-orbiting satellite, traveling to the moon via multi-stage rockets, and eventually journeying to Mars using nuclear propulsion, and all were done in a heavily illustrated, color format aimed at appealing to a lay audience. As the first issue's cover trumpeted, "top scientists" would tell how "man will conquer space soon . . . in 15 startling pages." The rhetoric of this "come-on" certainly struck a sensational note of its own, and in what was more a show-business than journalistic spirit, *Collier's* even organized a large-scale publicity campaign to promote the series, providing radio and press kits, releasing photographs to the large news syndicates, and arranging television interviews for von Braun on a number of nationally broadcast programs. While the point may have been to try to claim a share of the public's attention from the currently fashionable films of alien invasion and atomic apocalypse—films like *The Thing* (1951), *Invaders from Mars* (1953), and *War of the Worlds* (1953) that had already done their share to sensationalize science—one effect of this media campaign was to take on some of the aura of popular science fiction.

Both the quasi-scientific articles and the exaggerated publicity surrounding them caught the attention of artist and senior Disney producer Ward Kimball, who had been tasked with finding suitable subjects for the proposed Tomorrowland segments of the new Disney television program, and he suggested adapting part of the *Collier's* series. Serving as producer and director for the three shows that eventually aired over the course of *Disneyland*'s first four seasons, Kimball certainly faced a difficult task in bringing the essays' popularized science to a television audience more familiar with the likes of *Captain Video; Tom Corbett: Space Cadet;* and *Rocky Jones, Space Ranger.* He had to find a way of marrying the various approaches typically used in Disney films to the hard science of the magazine articles—a task made more difficult by Walt's *new* suggestion that the programs combine "comedy interest and factual interest. Both of them are vital to keep the show from becoming dry. You need a good balance to keep it from becoming too dry or corny" (quoted in Watts 310). At the same time, he still emphasized that they "be based on scientific fact, not science fiction," and that "fantasy" be kept primarily to the Fantasyland segments (Piszkiewicz 84). Acquiring the services of Ley, Haber, and von Braun as technical consultants and even on-air commentators assured a strong emphasis on factual detail, scientific probability, and a sense of authority—all, of course, reinforced by their pronounced German accents. However, the initial packaging of these elements, along with the rocket scientist commentators, into a "science-factual" show would remain a difficult proposition that later episodes would have to renegotiate.

In introducing the first *Man in Space* show, Walt explained to viewers what he hoped to accomplish: that the program might effectively combine "the tools of our trade with the knowledge of the scientists to give a factual picture of the latest plans for man's newest adventure." Within that commentary is a suggestion of the larger rhetorical strategy on which Kimball and his group had settled. The tools, of course, were largely animation, with which the studio was practically identified and which was one of the key resources it brought to the *Disneyland* television series. However, Disney had also developed a facility with documentary techniques, thanks to both the studio's wartime work doing military training films and its more recent success with its "True-Life Adventure" films.[10] Through these efforts the studio had worked out the techniques for deploying a seemingly objective, detached camera, for structuring the images so captured in a "natural" manner, and for using voice-over narration to reinforce the apparent "truth" of those images without undercutting their impact. And implicit in those practices were the two goals the studio hoped to present as complementary: entertainment and education.

In fact, the difficult balancing of these goals points to the major problem Disney would have as it developed the Tomorrowland segments. All three of the *Man in Space* programs, as well as several subsequent Tomorrowland episodes, extensively employed new animated footage, particularly for their early sequences. The first episode combined animated images and archival footage, including scenes from Méliès' *A Trip to the Moon* (1902) and Fritz Lang's *Die Frau im Mond* (1929), to explain the history and basic scientific principles of rocketry, and it offered an animated comic figure, labeled "homo sapiens extra terrestrialis," to demonstrate the physical problems of life in the conditions of space. In the second episode, "Man and the Moon," a lengthy sequence of animated images humorously explains mankind's historical fascination with the moon and illustrates various silly legends and superstitions that have grown up about it. "Mars and Beyond" provides a collection of animated speculations on the physical and mental nature of possible Martian inhabitants and culminates with a comic cartoon version of a typical "pulp" story about Martian invaders. The narrative pattern is quite similar. While each episode appropriately places science within a cultural context, suggesting how scientific knowledge arises from everyday experience and is constantly being constructed by that experience, each also places the audience at a comfortable distance—both historically and aesthetically—from this construction, treating those prior assumptions lightly, making fun of their misconceptions, literally *drawing* a historical technoscience so broadly as to make it the subject of ridicule. The broad implication is that these historical constructions were not quite science, and that the contemporary audience has effectively—and thankfully—emerged from this dark period, as if in the modern world science and technology were finally free from all such cultural influences.

As a balance, and ultimately in contrast, the *Man in Space* shows underscore recent scientific efforts to better understand the problems of space flight, of travel to the moon, and of exploring Mars and the other planets in our solar system. In doing so, they treat scientific knowledge not as something culturally constructed, but rather as something solidly objective, to be articulated by those figures Kimball had marshaled to provide the shows with a sense of authority. Thus each episode offers its authorities: Ley to discuss rocketry; Haber to talk about the stresses the body faces in space flight; von Braun to lay out the scientific principles behind rocket flight and the practical problems of building a space station and reaching the moon; and astronomer E. C. Slipher to explain how scientists use the telescope, spectrograph, and other instruments to predict conditions on other planets. The general effect of these experts—typically dressed in business attire or lab coats, bearing slide rules, and wielding models, charts, and graphs to press their points home—is to shift the tone and to serve as a documentary-style counter to the earlier, predominantly animated scenes. These commentators present science in a very different light, as a set of hard and fast rules discovered and ready to be employed in the conquest of space by a sober modern America.

Yet each episode concludes with a sequence that ultimately seems nearer science fiction than fact. For extrapolating into a future created by the scientists' speculations, each show dramatizes the predicted events, and in a way that increasingly troubles the sort of balance at which they seemed to aim. For example, after von Braun's description of his "design for a four-stage orbital rocket ship" in "Man in Space," an animated sequence details the efforts involved in preparing and launching just such a ship. The style here is starkly dramatic, with a massive rocket poised against a dark sky on "a small atoll of coral islands in the Pacific," while "square-jawed technicians study their consoles," as the narrator ponderously describes the scene, and mankind begins to "bet his life against the unknown dangers of space travel." Its animated images are dramatically backlit and composed with a sense of the monumental, and its voice-over commentary lends an awe-filled tone. The result is, very simply, a stilted and suspense-filled sequence that melodramatically constructs our attitude towards this scientific undertaking almost as much as did the initial humorous scenes.

"Man and the Moon" similarly concludes with a dramatization of von Braun's two-stage plan to reach the moon, starting with the construction of a space station and continuing with the launching of a rocket from there to the moon. After the animated depiction of the space station's construction, though, the following sequence uses live actors to portray astronauts who are journeying to and around the moon. That trip is not presented with the sort of clear calculation of the earlier scenes, but is narratized as a suspenseful adventure involving a meteor collision, which precipitates another animated sequence to dramatize how the moon rocket might be repaired in space. Because so little was known about the moon's surface and about its "dark side," though, the combination of animation and live-action never produces the expected climax of a moon landing, simply a trip around the moon, and thus a promise of more to come from future voyages—or cinematic sequels.[11] Moreover, that ending, by its very inconclusiveness, holds the technology depicted at a kind of distance from the audience, framing it not in terms of any perceptible social impact, but as adventuring on a grand scale, somewhat akin to the action of the television space operas, like *Rocky Jones*, that Disney had originally disavowed.

For "Mars and Beyond" the studio again produced an animated depiction of a proposed flight to Mars, designed, as a narrator tells us, by von Braun and Ernst Stuhlinger, another German rocket expert. In this instance, the technology is all speculative—or as the narrator offers, "still a dream for the future"—no longer involving the rockets with which audiences were by now becoming quite familiar through newsreels and television reports, but an atomic-powered spacecraft theorized by these scientists and oddly saucer-shaped, rather like the sort of craft associated with popular visions of alien invaders. In fact, we might note that this episode begins with animated images of three archetypal flying saucers heading into dark space, dissolves into a robot that introduces Walt Disney as the show's host, and, after an animated vision of a trip to Mars aboard a fleet of Stuhlinger's atomic spacecraft, concludes with another image of three flying saucers taking off from Mars, entering into the belly of a giant saucer that then speeds off into the darkness of space, bearing, as the narrator says, "our space pioneers of the future." The rhetoric of these framing images establishes a rather different atmosphere for this episode, one that draws on a certain limited factual base—although as the expert Slipher allows in his segment, "astronomers cannot draw too many definite conclusions about Mars"—in order to fashion another sort of story, a primarily animated meditation, somewhat akin to Disney's classic *Fantasia* (1940), on the possibilities of life beyond Earth, life "with infinite variation," as the narrator offers, "on other planets throughout the universe."

Of course, this episode is intent on making precisely this point: the increasing coincidence between what many conceived of simply as science fiction and what was coming to be seen as "science-factual." But the various images of flying saucers, robots, atomic spacecraft, and alien creatures were very much the language of those exaggerated science fiction narratives with which audiences of the period had been bombarded; they all too easily evoked a kinship with films like *Earth vs. the Flying Saucers* (1956), *This Island Earth* (1955), and even *Invaders from Mars.* They hinted, in effect, that our destiny was, as Virilio offers, "to become film," or at least to embark on a future that was *like* that seen in those popular films, one that seemed adventurous, if also a bit cold and foreboding, full of unknowns that were, on the one hand, less than comforting to the traditional Disney audience, and on the other, rather problematic for those expecting the sort of authoritative scientific grounding at which the *Collier's* articles and the series' first two episodes largely seemed to aim.

Those images also did something more. They pointed to an increasing difficulty that the studio seemed to have in talking about the world of science and technology, or at least in balancing the different rhetorical elements it used to depict this world. While animation, the studio's stock-in-trade, was crucial to visualizing both ancient ideas and the projected possibilities of space flight, it occupies increased screen time in each episode and dominates the third, and this at a time when audiences were finding footage of real rocket tests and flights increasingly common in the newsreels and on television. That animation emphasis also created some problems of tone and perception, for the early animated sequences in each episode are pointedly encoded as humorous, as "comedy interest," thanks to their exaggerated styling, visual puns, and frenetic pacing. And that effect naturally has some fallout for the later, documentary-style animation that closes each show. The authorities are the linchpin, occupying the central sequences of each narrative and helping to adjust the tone for the concluding sequences. And while this strategy works effectively in the first two episodes, "Mars and Beyond" retreats from that authoritative commentary. In fact, in what was probably stock footage from the earlier episodes, von Braun and Stuhlinger are simply shown— but not heard—discussing their model for a spacecraft, while a narrator notes that this is "still a dream for the future." Effectively, the scientists serve as little more than visual icons of authority here, touchstones for those who had seen the previous episodes.

The future at Disney, however, would see little development of the dream they represent—at least apart from the latest theme park attractions, such as the Rocket to the Moon ride that had opened in the Disneyland theme park, or its later descendants, such as Epcot's much-ballyhooed Mission: SPACE. In fact, Disney would offer only two more shows that followed this pattern before eventually dropping such episodes altogether. The first, "Magic Highway U.S.A." (May 5, 1958), aired in the same season as "Mars and Beyond," and further traces the sort of narrative pattern we have described. In illustrating what Walt Disney in his narration terms "our magic carpet to new hopes, new dreams, and a better way of life for the future," that is, the modern American system of automotive transportation and superhighways, the episode offers an animated history of roads and automobiles, humorously done as in the *Man in Space* shows, and it follows those images with live-action film, or to be more precise, a hybrid film that mixed restored footage of travel along the first cross-country highway in 1913 with new scenes shot in the style of early silent comedies, parodying the problems facing those early motorists and speeded up to give the film a Keystone-like tone.[12] Subsequent live-action scenes of present-day highway construction techniques are mundane, offer little sense of new technology, and so eventually they too are speeded up and scored to humorous music to lend them the same comic tone as the earlier scenes. And absent here are the kinds of authorities marshaled for the *Space* shows, figures like von Braun and Haber; in their place the episode employs an *actor* who, dressed in the requisite lab coat, *portrays* a "modern highway engineer," offering a monologue about America's future requirements for modern superhighways. The show's final vision of future travel, another animated sequence, is done in an abstract rather than realistic style and follows from a series of cartoon caricatures of the various types of American citizens who have specific demands for future roads: the farmer, salesman, businessman, housewife, and so on. While obviously not quite science fiction, the show hardly seems driven by the sort of "balance" Disney had outlined for the first *Space* episodes.

The problem is not that the episode does not offer enough of the "science-factual"; in fact, by 1958 this vision of superhighways criss-crossing a continent was an all-too-familiar part of daily American life. Rather, it was the nature of the show's rhetoric, for in straining to avoid a mundane reality or trying to draw out the construction of our scientific and technological knowledge in this area, Disney literally transformed the real into the cinematic: blending archival footage with re-creations to fashion a comic hybrid, "undercranking" scenes for humorous effect, "casting" his expert, and situating the audience as a set of comic caricatures, of "types" that were the staple of the era's domestic comedies. Virilio has suggested that "a mobile people" might well become "entirely victims of the set," seduced by the cinematic reality they seemingly inhabit (*Art and Fear* 79), and this episode points to just such an effect. For in describing the very mobility of the modern American audience and the promise of ever-increasing mobility, "Magic Highway" has clearly exploited the trappings of the set, the conventions of a cinematic world, conceiving its viewers as simple types who already inhabit a cinematized reality.

The last show in this vein, "Spy in the Sky" (Apr. 1, 1962), again credits Ward Kimball as co-director and co-writer, and similarly combines live-action and animation, the fictive and the factual, while pushing the pattern of "Magic Highway" to what we might term its destined extreme. The first half of the show, all live action, is essentially a half-hour trailer for the forthcoming Disney feature *Moon Pilot* (1962). That film is a broad comedy about the space race of the 1960s that takes the very authority figures who had served so successfully in the first two *Man in Space* shows—scientists, government representatives, the military—and makes them the subjects of its satiric thrust, as blocking characters who bumblingly interfere in an intergalactic romance. Several comic scenes from the film lead into what is supposed to be backstage at the Disney studio, as the actors rehearse and prepare to shoot additional footage— which is, of course, all carefully rehearsed and staged for the show's cameras, with the "real" interaction between the show's two leads, Tom Tryon and Dany Saval, scripted to parallel their comic-romantic relationship in the film, to suggest that their real life is *like* the film's story. The result is a dissolving of distinctions, as the backstage events prove every bit as contrived as the movie they promote, as the actors effectively "become film," and in the process point the way for the audience's future as well.

Awkwardly linked to this promotional piece through Walt Disney's narration, a theatrical short, originally released in 1959, concludes the episode. It mixes animation with a few brief live-action scenes, focusing on recent efforts to place satellites in orbit around the earth and linking those efforts with practical uses of such satellites. As in the *Man in Space* shows, this segment opens with animated footage, done in a comic vein, describing mankind's "questionable weather forecasting devices" of the past, and follows with a combination of animated footage and drama-tized live action—like the trip to the moon sequence of "Man and the Moon"—showing how satellite and rocket technology might someday be used not just to predict but to control the weather, thereby helping, as the narrator suggests, to transform the earth itself. The abrupt shift from the lengthy comic trailer to the dramatized scenes of rocket and satellite use suggests the larger trajectory that these shows have followed, as the ex-perts disappear and narrative takes over—the broadly comic one of *Moon Pilot* and the dramatic, mainly animated one speculating on our control of the elements. Seen in retrospect, Walt Disney's introduction to this episode, wherein he notes how "every achievement in outer space opens the way to more distant goals," rings hollow as the episode becomes an extended ad for the studio's latest film and a literal demonstration of a level on which the real "destiny," the most important of those "distant goals," was that of the cinema itself, or more precisely, the synergistic one of producing and promoting popular films, drawing on the studio's expertise in comedy and animation—and by now, science as well.

We might note as well that this now-familiar mix of comic scenes of the past, factual footage of the present day, and dramatized images of tomorrow operates within a new context, for this episode, we learn at the start of the show, comes to us "from the wonderful world of ad-venture." When Disney moved its anthology show from ABC to NBC in 1961, retitling it *The Wonderful World of Color*, the earlier thematic divisions that had given us Frontierland and Tomorrowland, and partly inspired the *Man in Space* series on the *Disneyland* show, had disap-peared. And the change in format allowed little room for the hard science and factual emphasis that had initially energized the space trilogy, nor for the sort of distinctions Disney had originally emphasized between fantasy and science. Contrived "adventure," what we might think of as a *cinematic* reality, was simply edging out "the real thing." While the following season would see one last entry that recalls the Tomorrowland shows, "Inside Outer Space" (Feb. 10, 1963), it was just a compilation of the animation produced for the *Man in Space* series, linked by narration from a new "authority," the Disney cartoon character Ludwig Von Drake, clearly evoking the many German authorities who were so prominent in postwar American science, but sanitized of their real-world Nazi as-sociations. The shift from von Braun's authoritative voice to Von Drake's comically befuddled one, and from science presented in an entertain-ing way to what became an extended cartoon on various space themes, seems telling. Scientific speculation and the educational dimension of that speculation were being swallowed up by entertainment media; the lines between the different elements of the formula Disney had tried to articulate were blurring precisely as the "space race" itself became a big show, a kind of popular entertainment done before cameras for the masses—a great cinematic and cultural spectacle that was already available, almost daily, on every television channel.

In this context, Neil Postman's somewhat jaundiced warning about television and the nature of its public discourse is worth considering. He argues that, "Television is at its most trivial and, therefore, most dangerous when its aspirations are high, when it presents itself as a carrier of important cultural conversations" (*Amusing* 16). During the Cold War and in one of its key theaters of operation—that of scientific and technological development—the conquest of space was certainly among the most significant of those ongoing "cultural conversations." In fact, it was part of our national agenda, as a result of a series of momentous decisions by presidents Eisenhower and Kennedy,[13] and the rhetoric surrounding it—talk of thrust, escape velocity, capsules, reentry, recovery—had quickly entered into the popular discourse as Americans began to "talk science." In attempting to participate in that conversation, the *Disneyland* series demonstrated the sort of "aspirations" that would win it a number of awards,[14] make it one of the most watched and longest-lived shows on television, and indeed, demonstrate once more the power of this new technology to intervene in a national dialogue. Yet at the same time, the series displays some symptoms of that trivializing effect Postman charges television with, as it increasingly framed the larger human aspiration for transcendence and knowledge within a decidedly cinematic context, as a series of what Disney in other circumstances might well have simply described as "True-Life Adventures."

Further fallout of this effect shows up in the technoscientific trajectory developed and depicted in subsequent Disney film productions. While, as we have noted, original programming on scientific and technological concerns nearly disappears from the television series following the "Spy in the Sky" episode, those concerns did quite literally become cinematized by mutating into a staple cinematic product of the studio, a move that we can trace in a series of increasingly trivial yet also consistently profitable efforts over the following decade. For films like *The Absent-Minded Professor* (1961), *Moon Pilot* (1962), *Son of Flubber* (1963), *The Misadventures of Merlin Jones* (1964), and *The Monkey's Uncle* (1965), among others, would become typical of Disney live-action features in the late Walt Disney era, and they would provide an archive of such material that, in turn, would later be programmed on the very Disney television show from which they had taken inspiration—in effect, completing the cycle of cinematization.

In all of these films, science and technology, along with their befuddled Von Drake-type scientists, typified by Fred McMurray's characterizations, simply become cartoon-like elements and point toward the even broader comic context in which they would continue to operate in later Disney films like *The Cat from Outer Space* (1977), *Honey, I Shrunk the Kids* (1989), *Flubber* (1997), or *Rocketman* (1997). In these works the science and technology that were essential to the ongoing space race and at the core of Disney's educational thrust of the mid-1950s seem increasingly detached from real-world conditions, or in a film like *The Rocketeer* (1991) with its 1930s context, rendered as nostalgia, much as had been the case with *20,000 Leagues Under the Sea*. Despite Walt Disney's idea for using television to develop a new way of addressing and popularizing the concerns of science and technology, one that even acknowledged an element of the cultural construction of science and technology, that rhetoric would be altered by the studio's recognition of what would best "sell," as well as by the general trajectory of our media culture—a culture that all too readily renders everything as part of the "set." In fact, that effect might help explain the persistence of the popular myth that the moon landings never really occurred but were simply "staged" by the U.S. government.

Under this same pressure, as well as a desire for an easily consumed product, science and technology would prove difficult components for negotiating into Disney narratives. Rather, they consistently become circumstances of comedy, regularly function as conventions of a cinematic world that all too neatly matches up with the cinematized reality we were coming to inhabit, or what would come to *pass for* reality, especially amid today's preoccupation with what we, without a proper sense of irony, all too readily term "reality programming." These early Disney television efforts provide us with a kind of early warning, and most vivid illustration, of this effect. In the way they try to speak to, and market science and technology to, a popular audience, they demonstrate not just a rather predictable trajectory, that is, the transformation of the "science-factual" into the science fictional, but also a mechanism—Virilio's cinematization and its production of a "reality effect"—that in the light of contemporary television programming increasingly seems almost a defining characteristic of our media landscape.

6   The "Inhabitable Text" of the Parks

Disney shrewdly perceived television's ability to link diverse
cultural practices that intersected in the domestic sphere
of the home. In effect, Walt identified the program with the
park in order to create an inhabitable text, one that would
never be complete for a television-viewing family until they
had taken full advantage of the postwar boom in automobile
travel and tourism and made a pilgrimage to the park itself.
—Christopher Anderson, *Hollywood TV*

We have seen how Disneyland, the Disney Company's original
theme park, was quite literally produced by negotiations over another
new technology, that of television. In light of Walt's long-standing interest in developing another sort of family-oriented type of entertainment, a park where parents and children might go to "play" together,
and Roy's insistence on a sound plan for financing any such project, the
studio agreed to produce *Disneyland* for ABC largely in exchange for the
network's backing of the proposed park. And on the first episode of the
series Walt himself emphasized the connection, suggesting a new concept,
that audiences think of the park and television show as elements in an
integrated entertainment system. Christopher Anderson sees this linkage
as part of a crucial economic strategy for the burgeoning Disney empire
and a sign of the growing complexity of the synergy that had long been

a guiding company principle. But Anderson's explanation can also help us see a key attraction of the parks: the way in which they technologically extend the film experience in a manner that anticipates present-day discussions of virtual reality entertainment. In the Disney theme parks, fully supported by their complex "production" technology, guests are "cast" into a new kind of text, gaining the chance "to perform in the Disneyland narrative" (153). But more importantly, we should note that this narrative is hardly an empty one. It celebrates its own technological base, lets audiences play in what Scott Bukatman has described as the "technological spectacle" of "popular American culture" (2), and in the process underscores our inevitable relationship to the complex technologies of modern life. One of the key attractions of the Disney parks, consequently, is the way they help us negotiate our own place in the postmodern scene; for a price we "inhabit" a new and promising space, engaging in an almost physical version of what Bukatman terms "the narrative process of technological accommodation" (28).

But to create that sort of "inhabitable text" and allow for that process of "technological accommodation," Disney would ultimately have to negotiate more than just the financing deal with ABC. For while amusement parks were already an established component of modern American culture, thanks partly to the success of Coney Island early in the century, to the midways that had appeared in a variety of major American cities slightly later, and to the widely publicized entertainment zone featured at the 1939–40 New York World's Fair,[1] Walt Disney clearly had in mind something rather different, something that would involve the studio in the development of a number of new technologies. To transform the older *idea* of an amusement park into the reality of the contemporary theme park with a wide appeal, into what Stephen Fjellman, speaking of the elaborate offspring of Disneyland, Walt Disney World, has described as "the most important entertainment center in the world" (10), would necessitate both significant reconceptualization and additional technological innovation. While Walt admired and acknowledged being inspired by Copenhagen's Tivoli Gardens, with its order, cleanliness, and sedate atmosphere, he also recognized that what Bob Thomas terms the "battered and tawdry" nature of the latter-day Coney Island and its cheap imitators had come to represent the amusement park experience for most Americans (*Walt* 241). To change that cultural perception would require rethinking how the amusement park might best work in the contemporary environment, how it might attract a new audience. Part of the solution would be to approach it as a kind of entertainment technology, much like the movies that were the studio's stock-in-trade and a comfortable model of popular entertainment. Another part would be discovered more slowly. It was the creation of specific technologies that would fundamentally transform the experience, enabling the amusement park to become a true *themed* park, that is, a three-dimensional, immersive entertainment experience that would foster the sort of "accommodation" Bukatman describes. And both developments would involve Disney in negotiating between two conflicting cultural attitudes towards technology itself—attitudes born out of an increasing awareness of technology's ideological implications.

The first step in developing Disneyland—and its subsequent offspring—involved creating a kind of entertainment hybrid, an amalgam of the amusement park and movie experience. Of course, since in the early 1950s Disney was still primarily a film studio, much of the initial thinking about a theme park inevitably grew out of this background. The artistic roots of Disney were, after all, firmly planted in the movies themselves, and as Fjellman notes, the various stories Disney has told, whatever their original source, were typically "transformed in the interest of cinematic presentation" (257). As our earlier discussion of the cartoon *Babes in the Woods* suggests (see chap. 2), European fairy tales were not simply given a new ideological flavor—or what some would term "Disneyfied"—but were also usually reconceived very much in filmic terms. Moreover, Walt's first musings on the theme park concept in various ways centered precisely on the work of his film studio. As early as 1940, he had begun talking to colleagues about ways to showcase "Disney characters in their fantasy surroundings," and in 1952 he sought permission to create a facility adjacent to the studio—one that would combine studio tours with various fantasy attractions (Watts 384–85).

An additional emphasis on this cinematic dimension naturally followed from several key staff additions Walt brought in to assist him in thinking about the park project. Art directors Richard Irvine and Marvin Davis were both hired from Twentieth Century-Fox to help suggest and design the attractions that would fit into the general park design initially drawn up by Walt and Harper Goff, a Disney animator. Other studio artists were soon added to the design staff—John Hench, Ken Anderson, and Marc Davis—forming a design group that approached the park project in a familiar way, as if it were a kind of film, as they not only looked for links to specific movies that might lend themselves to translation into an experiential medium, but also drew storyboards for all the proposed attractions, just as they did for their cartoons, and paid careful attention to point of view, as if they were conceiving of the rides and their details precisely in terms of camera placement. And as Bob Thomas notes, Walt himself reinforced this cinematic inflection. For just as he had with the studio's films, Walt contributed his own vision of the rides' narrative dimensions, for example, describing "the entire Snow White ride as if it were a movie cartoon, visualizing all the park's attractions for the designers just as he had brought cartoons to life for his animators" (*Walt* 243).

The finished products were, additionally, laid out according to a pointedly cinematic organizational principle. In his analysis of Walt Disney World, Fjellman has shown how "attractions, lands, and worlds are put together in acts and scenes," and how the various elements of each attraction are presented as "cinematically short" scenes, with the overall entertainment effect depending on careful "editorial decisions" that point the audience's attention to one element and away from another (257). Lighting, point of view, and movement through space, all linked to a simple narrative trajectory, are the key elements in this kind of live cinema, although Fjellman adds that we might also view them as components within a much larger filmic scheme. For he reads all of the Disney parks as "cinematic metastories," with each attraction functioning like "a scene in a large production" that is the park experience itself (258). This universalizing view sees all of the attractions as "edited" parts of a film-like whole, and even the frequent interruption of audience movement by the various souvenir shops becomes simply another version of the typical movie concession stand. While Fjellman's comprehensive interpretation may seem to force the point a bit, its emphasis on a cinematic principle that has largely guided the various Disney parks seems inescapable. It is a point often made by commentators, and one given an added dimension by Jean Baudrillard, who has described the Disney park experience as an "immense reality show" in which visitors become not simply spectators but "interactive extras" (*Screened* 153).

Yet even as the park's design team drew on their background to construct a new kind of filmic experience, Walt also insisted on a key element of difference from the movies. He wanted both the park and its individual attractions to be open to constant change. As Walt would explain, he conceived of Disneyland as "something that will never be finished, something I can keep developing, keep 'plussing' and adding to. . . . It will get better as I find out what the public likes. I can't do that with a picture; it's finished and unchangeable before I find out whether the public likes it or not" (quoted in Thomas, *Walt* 244). It is an approach that reflects two rather different concerns that Disney was apparently intent on balancing: first, the lure of the technology itself, and of what each new development might make possible; and second, a desire to speak to the public's interests and concerns, and thus to adjust the park's attractions to constantly address those concerns. If the first of these issues suggests Walt's natural enthusiasm for what might be done, for tapping the excitement bound up in new technological development and using it to consistently enhance the entertainment experience, the second hints of a kind of simple ideological consciousness, a desire to speak to and reaffirm "what the public likes," as Walt increasingly came to see the company's products, as Steven Watts offers, "in terms of a stewardship of Middle American values" (401)—values that could be woven into narratives, weighed via ticket sales, and adjusted to meet changing attitudes. Negotiating between these elements has resulted in a constant dynamic that is crucial to the continuing success of the various Disney parks, but also perhaps responsible for some of their continuing criticism, as the company pushes these values, these manifestations of a constantly shifting pop culture, as universal or multicultural.

A second key element was the development of a specific technology that would help translate the two-dimensional conceptions of the various attractions into an effective, three-dimensional form—one that would practically demonstrate the "inhabitable" nature of these texts. This technology is what Disney would come to term Audio-Animatronics, a kind of primitive robotics involving, as the title implies, a combination of sound, physical animation, and electronic controls that would push the studio's earlier "illusion-of-life" aesthetic into another dimension. The seed for this new development was apparently planted with Walt's purchase of a bird automaton while on a trip to New Orleans in 1949 (Imagineers 118). Fascinated by its workings, he enlisted the help of Roger Broggie of the studio machine shop and art director Ken Anderson, having them translate the principles of the bird's movements to human models: initially, that of a nine-inch dancing man, based on the filmed movements of actor Buddy Ebsen,[2] and later, a miniature barbershop quartet, which could "sing" to prerecorded music. Both of these early efforts were relatively simple mechanical devices, driven by cams attached to levers that, in turn, moved wires that controlled the figures, enabling them to imitate basic human movements.[3] Later, the system would incorporate magnetic audio tape to send signals regulating the cam-generated movements, and eventually it would develop into what Disney terms DACS or the Digital Animation Control System, "a sophisticated computerized signal controller" that "sends the programmed digital signals—twenty four electronic frames per second—out to the various mechanisms," servos that could produce ever more complex figure movements (Imagineers 120). The ultimate goal was life-like motion, initially realized in animals or other simple figures, and later in human models, all of which could be worked into the park's operation, allowing for the sort of constant, repetitive movements needed for ride displays and producing consistently convincing illusions to help support the larger cinematic fantasy of the parks.

While these first Audio-Animatronic figures could only execute simple, repetitive motions, they were, as Walt would put it, "sort of another door that's opened for us" in the use of technology (Jackson 96), a possibility for developing "another dimension in the animation we have been doing all our life" (Jackson 99). These initial developments proved suitably promising and effective enough to warrant being worked into the design of several of Disneyland's first attractions. Guests traveling along the Rivers of America, for example, were greeted by a rather primitive version of this technology, an Indian Chief waving to them, and in the African section of the "Jungle Cruise" ride they could see natives dancing on the riverbank. Of course, there were also simpler mechanical figures in these same rides, such as the elephants and hippos of the "Jungle Cruise," which sprayed water, surfaced and submerged, or charged at the passing river boats on cue. A more elaborate development of this technology soon resulted in one of Disney's longest-lived attractions, the "Enchanted Tiki Room," which grew out of another sort of synergistic plan, for creating a park restaurant that would also offer Audio-Animatronic entertainment. The technology reached new levels of realism, though, with the studio's efforts to create a series of exhibits for the 1964–65 New York World's Fair, all of which would make extensive use of Audio-Animatronics. Some of these exhibits, such as the Pepsi/UNICEF "It's a Small World" show, deployed the technology in a highly stylized manner, while others, particularly the state of Illinois' "Great Moments with Mr. Lincoln" exhibit, aimed for a new level of lifelike presentation. In this latter case, Walt had urged his engineers (or "Imagineers," as they would eventually be termed) to push for verisimilitude: "I want him to breathe. I want him to be alive!" (Imagineers 118). And to further that illusion, Disney modeled its figure on a life mask of the president that had been created in 1860. This effort produced a mechanical Lincoln who could rise from his seat, gesture with either hand, and move head, mouth, and eyes as he addressed the audience on the meaning of liberty.[4] After the fair ended, Lincoln was moved to Disneyland, where he eventually became the centerpiece of the "Hall of Presidents," an attraction that showcases Audio-Animatronics by replicating the original idea, producing mechanical versions of every American president. Over the years this attraction would be constantly updated with the figure of each new president and improved with the latest developments in Audio-Animatronic technology. And joining Lincoln were all of Disney's other Audio-Animatronic-featuring exhibits created for the fair, including the General Electric "Carousel of Progress" and Ford's "Magic Skyway." Together, these creations—several still in operation today—established the model for most of the subsequent Disney park attractions. Already "peopled" with Audio-Animatronic characters, the various rides and shows quite literally demonstrated for guests the parks' "inhabitable" nature, while also encouraging them to "cast" themselves as extras in these ur-virtual, technologically driven worlds.

Yet the real advantage that the Audio-Animatronic creations offered was not simply their mechanical efficiency or even the uncanny appeal that inevitably attached to such robotic figures. Rather, it was the implication of their rather ghostly habitation. For through their operations those figures helped to negotiate our own place in this "reality show"—or rather, the larger reality show outside of the parks. The "Carousel of Progress" is a particularly telling example. Moved to Disneyland after the World's Fair and later, in a slightly altered version, installed in Walt Disney World's Magic Kingdom, this attraction is a modern version of a rather old-fashioned entertainment idea—the cyclorama. However, in this updating the circular central exhibits remain in place while the theater, and thus the audience, revolves around its series of vignettes: of an American family at the coming of the twentieth century, of a family in the 1920s, of the same figures in the post–World War II era, and of those family members in contemporary times. In keeping with its original sponsorship by General Electric, the "Carousel" details the progress of electronic technology during approximately a century of American life. It balances the constant march of technological development during these eras with, in each case, comic instances of the mishaps and frustrations that often attend the adoption of new technologies—blowing fuses, misusing appliances, burning the family dinner—to produce a humorous illustration of that constant process of "technological accommodation." Of course, by catching us up in its unusual revolving format, in effect, by rather slyly engaging us in a "ride" throughout the presentation, the "Carousel of Progress" from the start assumes a kind of physical power over its audience, one that also hints of the authority of its narrative. But the family depicted here is also key, since it obviously stands-in for the audience, suggesting our place in this ever-changing technological world—and technology's permanent place in the domestic realm. That family's easy embrace of the latest developments, albeit self-consciously, as the father's address to the audience suggests, establishes their function here as tutors. For they effectively model the technological attitude, one largely unburdened by cultural concerns, that the audience was expected to adopt.

Of course, the "Carousel of Progress" is a unique attraction in both structure and format. While it points up the rethinking of the theme park that Disney had begun, particularly with its emphasis on realistic and quickly shifting visual scenes and controlled point of view, and it demonstrates how the Audio-Animatronic technology could be effectively deployed to model audience attitudes, its rather didactic approach to issues of "progress" and technology's cultural role would need to be reconsidered. While it had constructed a kind of "inhabitable" space, the text played out in that space would require further development for an increasingly sophisticated audience, one that already inhabited a highly technologized realm. By examining several of the more recent inheritors of the model offered by the "Carousel," the rest of this chapter will illustrate how many of the Disney attractions have developed a more complex and pointedly self-conscious approach to technological concerns. In fact, in another example of that "blatantness" that Byrne and McQuillan have described, many later Disney attractions, as we shall see, even foreground some of the cultural issues that were largely erased from the "Carousel of Progress" but are inevitably involved in our ongoing negotiations with an increasingly technologized world.

II

"Profit is simply a by-product we have learned to live with."
—Chairman, X-S Tech

As visitors queued up for the now-closed "Alien Encounter" ride at Walt Disney World's Magic Kingdom, they would go through a series of chambers that gradually immersed them in the context for that experience. In one they were greeted on monitors by representatives of the X-S Tech Corporation, an alien, but humanoid company that markets technological gadgetry throughout the galaxy. In a broadcast interview, the X-S chairman asserts his company's belief in its "important obligation" to market its high technology to "help less fortunate planets," while he allows that the great profit resulting from these sales "is simply a by-product we have learned to live with." In the next room visitors would see a live (Audio-Animatronic) presentation of the latest X-S discovery, a matter transporter, which a robot representative of the company then demonstrated on a typical Disney animal—shifting the cuddly creature from one side of the room to the next, but also leaving it singed, in some pain, and clearly reluctant to repeat the process. That demonstration, while good for a quick laugh, also quickly undercut the enthusiastic spirit of the first presentation and would leave visitors wondering not only what awaited them in the next chamber, but also precisely what sort of bargain was being struck here with the latest technology, particularly when they saw the technology itself—in the form of the robot—conducting its experiments on an organic creature that is ultimately not so different from ourselves.

That question obviously carries a kind of self-conscious weight for the world of Disney—one that is, by reputation, and particularly under the former leadership of Michael Eisner, more than a bit much like the X-S Corporation. Disney is, of course, a vast conglomerate, made up of various "worlds" that stretch across this human one—Paris, Tokyo, Hong Kong, Orlando, Anaheim. And it does offer for our entertainment and, in many cases, education, the latest technological innovations. One of the pavilions in Epcot, entitled "Innoventions," provides hands-on introductions to recent electronic developments—in computers, gaming, virtual reality experience, and so on. The location of "Alien Encounter," at least until its transformation in 2003 into a more kid-friendly format as "Stitch's Great Escape," was the Magic Kingdom's "Tomorrowland," which offers not only the usual amusement park thrills but also technology like the WEDway People Mover, originally conceived by Walt as a technological solution to the problems of urban mass transit and also exhibited at the New York World's Fair. Even a number of the rides and exhibits in the most nature-oriented of the Disney parks, Walt Disney World's Animal Kingdom, rely on Disney's signature Audio-Animatronic figures of the sort found in the "Alien Encounter" introduction and indeed in nearly every Disney attraction. Moreover, with its own technological developments the Disney Corporation consistently promises to transport us, if not across the galaxy at least to wholly different "worlds" or "lands," to teleport us all to tomorrow. Finally, we all implicitly understand, at least from having paid for entry to a Disney park, that these technological wonders all come at a price, and that through the business of such introductions and applications this company, too, manages to make enormous profits that, after early years of struggle, it has now "learned to live with."

In sum, the "Alien Encounter" ride presents us—as it did Disney's guests—with an intriguing but also troubling proposition that foregrounds two major yet closely linked concerns: Disney's relationship to the technological and our own relationship to the technological wonders that are those parks that have become the company's premier revenue source and America's top leisure attraction. In a rather unusual moment of ideological commentary, this encounter practically defines technology as both a fascinating lure *and* a tool of exploitation, even as it rather curiously seems to signal its own metonymic link to the larger Disney enterprise, which has become fundamentally reliant on such cutting-edge technology as a way of selling itself to us. In fact, while many successful rides typically present themselves as immersive experiences, ones in which we not only monetarily but also psychologically "buy into" their stories, and while they try to make that buying a relatively easy proposition—usually by employing a series of chambers and increasingly detailed introductions to gradually contextualize the guests, to produce a certain calculated perspective, as if the guests themselves were products of an assembly line or technological process—this attraction and an increasing number of others seem to trouble that deal a bit by rendering the whole process so transparent and suspect. Seen in retrospect, all of this has to make us wonder how we are supposed to put aside the overall Disney-*ness* of this "encounter" in order to better participate in and thus derive the full fun from such a ride, when the attraction so clearly underscores notions of corporate manipulation, amoral profiteering, and pious posturing—all of which have at times, fairly or not, been associated with the Disney project. Put more simply, these estranging effects make for what should strike us as a rather strange "attraction." Yet they are also effects that help foreground another manner of technological negotiation that has become crucial to the success of the Disney enterprise, as it has come to redefine itself from film studio to a comprehensive entertainment and leisure corporation.

That troubling impression is hardly unique to the "Alien Encounter" ride, though; in fact, it is one that, with just a bit of attention, we can begin to note all around us in the various Disney parks. The renowned "Pirates of the Caribbean" ride, for instance, a staple of both Disneyland and the Magic Kingdom, and the last ride that Walt Disney himself helped design, puts us in the world of "fun-loving" Audio-Animatronic plunderers—also a context some would see as metaphoric of the Disney project, and an effect that is only redoubled when one exits from the ride, as typically happens in the Disney parks, through a series of high-priced souvenir shops designed to plunder guests' pockets. The "Kali River Rapids" ride in Animal Kingdom puts guests on a raft, floating through tropical lands that, as the ride's backstory tells us, have been clear-cut for development by an international corporation—a situation that eerily suggests the original Florida development project for Disney World. And

"The Great Movie Ride" of the Disney-MGM Studios park celebrates the illusory power of both the movie industry and the theme park, with its guide who is chased off by a character who steps out of one of the movie sets, but eventually reemerges from another film set later in the ride to displace that movie figure, as if guide and character were equally illusory—and equally manipulative and controlling figures. These and many other park and film offerings might simply be seen as instances of that rather curious Disney "blatantness" we earlier noted, that is, its seeming self-consciousness about its corporate strategies and supposed ideological aims. However, I would suggest that these and many other rides and attractions, in the way they project a kind of self-awareness about both their technological underpinnings and their entertainment purpose, are acting out another approach to that negotiation with the technological that operates both within and through the Disney theme parks. It is a kind of self-reflexive strategy that provides another—and subtly effective—sort of accommodation to the technological.

The rest of this chapter will focus on this strategy of obviousness as it operates in a variety of the technologically themed attractions found throughout the parks. To more precisely focus this part of the analysis, I want to draw on the work of Constance Penley and Andrew Ross to emphasize several rather different, even conflicting attitudes that have come to dominate contemporary discussions of technological culture and seem pointedly implicated in these rides. A widely held attitude that Penley and Ross describe sees technology as a largely neutral, but potentially liberating force that promises to open up "utopian" possibilities for all. This view, which they suggest is rather naïve, has often been ascribed to Walt Disney by his biographers, is implicit in the Richard Schickel epigraph with which this book opened, and can easily be observed throughout the commentary offered in the "Carousel of Progress" attraction. In contrast, Penley and Ross argue that in recent times technology has most often served a culturally repressive function, that it has largely become a force manipulated by "the all-powerful sponsors of control technology" (xii–xiii). Yet between those "liberating fantasies," as they term them, and the "technology-as-social-control school of thought" that seems to characterize much academic discussion, there seems to be a possibility for dialogue, perhaps another version of what I have broadly termed negotiation; for while the technological may well serve as a tool of "social agency" or control, it also most often develops, as Penley and Ross allow, out of "real popular needs and desires" (xiii), embodying those desires in ways that can never fully be disguised or denied. Disney, as most people would recognize, has been singularly successful at recognizing and catering to many of those "needs and desires," and indeed, as we see in other areas such as the computer industry, Disney tends to follow rather than to create those desires, to maximize its appeal by reflecting popular attitudes, even those that might seem critical of the company itself. It is in that space of negotiation, in Disney's ability, seen throughout the theme parks, to both acknowledge and balance off these rather different attitudes towards the technological, that the company comes to seem so "blatant," but it is also the point at which it becomes something more valuable—perhaps even culturally vital—than many of its critics would allow.

As this book has repeatedly emphasized, technology is at the heart of much of the Disney experience, and certainly its presence is palpable everywhere in the theme parks. We have noted how the trademark Audio-Animatronic system of endowing three-dimensional figures with technological life now supports most of the rides and attractions in the theme parks, making them seem *inhabited* and, more importantly, the world they describe as *inhabitable*—that is, acceptable to the audience. The rides themselves are marvelous technologically controlled experiences, with each one carefully timed and designed to provide a predetermined, even cinematic, vantage for maximum entertainment. And all of the parks function much like giant machines, with their support mechanisms largely hidden from public view and their driving values implicitly those of a technologically oriented culture, mainly those Cecelia Tichi sees as fundamental to modern America—speed, efficiency, and stability.[5] Indeed, with their efforts to process guests as quickly as possible (a goal enhanced by the new "Fast-Pass" ticket system), to move them through queues, onto the rides, and off of them as quickly and efficiently as possible, and to make the total experience as safe and predictable as possible, the parks not only depend on technology, but are themselves great technological marvels, massive machines ruled by a combination of machine values and revenue considerations arising from the intersection of amusement and profit that similarly marks the film industry. And that conflation of entertainment and technology is hardly accidental or even unexpected, given Disney's origins in that preeminent technological art form of the twentieth century. In his pioneering study of Disney, Richard Schickel notes how both Walt and the people around him always saw "a certain implicit fitness about this meeting and mingling of the great forces of the age, Disneyism and electronic scientism" (284), or more simply put, fantasy and technology. We can better understand this "mingling" and its implications for the technological by examining a number of the attractions in the various Disney parks, which, like "Alien Encounter," share a certain level of postmodern self-consciousness that foregrounds how Disney has sought to negotiate between those conflicting technological attitudes that Penley and Ross identify.

As those machinic "values" cited above indicate and as Penley and Ross would emphasize, technology is never simply neutral, nor without its own attendant effects that require some careful bargaining. Efficiency, for example, always comes at some cost. We can especially see the terms of this bargaining in one of the newer and more popular Disney rides,[6] the Animal Kingdom's "Dinosaur: Countdown to Extinction." In some ways a rather traditional ride and typical of those found throughout the many Disney worlds, "Dinosaur" takes guests through a scenario drawn from and using the imagery of one of the company's successful films, the animated *Dinosaur* (2000). Centering on popular contemporary theories about dinosaur extinction, the film depicts the effects of a massive meteor shower on the dinosaur population during the Cretaceous period. In a narrative development of this view, the ride places guests on "time rovers" that take them back to the very end of the dinosaur era, there to rescue a young Iguanodon—like the central character of *Dinosaur*—before a meteor storm can wipe out his kind, and perhaps the time rover as well. Once rescued, as the ride's backstory explains, the creature is to be returned for study to "The Disney Institute"—both the building that houses the ride and a supposed foundation for paleontological study that is supported, as a sign informs us, by "a generous grant" from the Mc-Donald's Corporation. This link between the corporate realm and world of science and technology obviously echoes the situation we initially noted in "Alien Encounter" and confirms a familiar fact of contemporary life, while the actual ride, with its close calls from a carnotaurus, a pterodactyl, a meteor shower, and other dangers, metaphorically hints at some of the dangers that might attend that scientific-corporate connection.

"Dinosaur" adds an intriguing dimension to this formula with its emphasis on the ride's starting and end points, the putative Disney Institute. In fact, this framing device is both an effective model of how the best Disney attractions work—through elaborate planning and attention to detail that produce both atmosphere and efficiency—and a key to its particular manner of technological self-consciousness. For the queue to the ride's technological centerpiece, the time transporter vehicles, begins in an elaborately detailed, classically designed building that indeed resembles what it purports to be, a museum. Guests walk past various display cases of dinosaur-related artifacts, see fossils of different Cretaceous Period creatures, view a large mural depicting the era, and read about the creatures on display, as well as the theories surrounding their extinction. In fact, we should admit that this *is* actually a museum of sorts, since its displays of real artifacts and plaster casts of skeletons and other remains, along with the appropriate informative and educational placards and paintings, represent precisely the sort of mix we would find in any "real" museum. The setting thus reminds us of one of the great appeals of all the Disney lands, that once in them, as Umberto Eco explains, "the public is meant to admire the perfection of the fake" (44). However, we should qualify Eco's remark, since in this case the "fake" makes just as legitimate a demand on our belief—or admiration—as does the content of any "real" museum of natural history or paleontology, and even carries much the same educational force. The extensive research that went into the ride's creation ensures that the science here is quite genuine, is in keeping with current theories about the end of the dinosaur era, and offers a solid grounding for the ensuing technological experience, a supposed ride into the past.

Yet Eco does sound an important cautionary note, as he reads a technological valuation even in such playing about with the real, or what he terms the "hyperreal." He suggests that this kind of carefully constructed imitation also carries a troubling message by implying "that technology can give us more reality than nature can" (44). It is a point that resonates when we enter the "Orientation Room" of the "Dinosaur" ride, where Dr. Marsh, supposed director of the Disney Institute—and it is worth noting, in this context, how often Disney gives a female face to authority in its more recent attractions—addresses us from a video monitor, explaining the "perfect blending of science and technology" that we are about to experience. As she offers, the institute's time machines will make traditional historical study obsolete; or as she ironically puts it, "the future of history is the past." Indeed, insofar as this time trip is supposed to let us experience a simulacrum of a crucial moment in Earth's history, we might well feel that this experience is more "than nature can" offer. Yet there is also another sort of payoff attached to this technology, something beyond this hyperreal experience and similar to the crude capitalist calculations foregrounded in "Alien Encounter." For the backstory or deep content to this ride involves a kind of profiteering by breaking the rules, as our next host, a video tour guide who is introduced in an inner, industrial-styled section of the institute (as if he were the industrial/business voice of the institute), speaks to us conspiratorially about the prospects of bringing back a souvenir from our time travel, a specimen from the past that might be displayed—or sold, perhaps even turned into a movie—in the present. If the introduction to this ride, with its scientific/historical frame and educational connotations, suggests the sort of context we might conventionally associate with Disney, thanks in part to the "True-Life Adventures" nature films that were once a staple product of the studio, this deeper, "revealed" circumstance lets us glimpse the profiteering dimension that has also attached to the company's educational efforts, and thus begin to gauge other possible payoffs or consequences to the technological here.

In fact, the ensuing ride allows little opportunity to explore the "reality" of the past at all, since once we are strapped into our time rovers and hurtled into the past, we find ourselves racing to accomplish that profit-oriented goal: to locate the dinosaur our guide wants to bring back—a willing, docile type, much like the guests who have been recruited for this venture—before a meteor shower can destroy us as well. In a kind of high-tech variation on older haunted house-type rides, then, that search quickly moves us from one hazard to another—meat-eating dinosaurs, falling meteors, crashing rocks and trees—as our car dodges and accelerates, all while our guide, who remains safe back at the institute, encourages us via radio transmissions to ignore the hazards and keep trying to find the Iguanodon he has selected, and while an automated voice in our car builds tension by counting down the seconds to catastrophe. Being snatched back to the present at the very last moment, we are left at ride's end to balance several things: the exhilarating sense that we have raced with our own "extinction," the notion that we have indeed seen the past and even saved a part of it, and a realization of how that past, in keeping with McDonald's sponsorship of the ride, might be reprocessed for profit (perhaps as Dinoburgers to be sold at the McDonald's franchise restaurant just across from the ride's entrance). In any case, what we have saved this creature for remains unclear, as the monitors now show a computer-generated image of the dinosaur wandering through the corporate halls of the institute, bringing chaos. It is a final reminder of both what nature can offer and what the modern, technological world might do—or fail to do—with that offering, and thus an effective caution about the uses to which we might put our science and technology, much after the fashion of the film *Jurassic Park* (1993).

"Dinosaur" initially presents the technological as serving the cause of science, as ideally extending the traditional museum experience by allowing us to travel physically to the scene of those fossils and artifacts we are only able to glimpse on entry, and even then, we see them only as *virtual* artifacts—plaster casts and plastic models of the fossil record. Yet the ride gradually shifts how we read the work of science, presenting us with just the sort of "unstable" cultural codes Byrne and McQuillan discern in other Disney texts (5). While the institute director outlines the realistic and educational potential of such historical travel, she gives way to the self-serving young technician, our assigned guide, who has his own plan for our travel, who literally wants to bring the real home—and profit from it. As technology takes hold, the slow and relaxed pace of the museum experience shifts into a breakneck ride into the past, along with its unexpected dangers. And the "authentic" nature tour becomes a frenetic grab for a souvenir of our trip—that is, another model of a common Disney tourist experience, here replicated at the ride's exit shop. Of course, these shifts all contribute to the ride's excitement, its fast movement and suspenseful plot, but they are hardly *essential* (a simple time-travel scenario, again to the dinosaur era, structures the older "Ellen's Energy Adventure" attraction in Epcot). What they point to, what they self-consciously acknowledge, is the way in which the technological, and even the amusement park itself, can easily shift value, becoming by turns a tool of knowledge and a suspicious device for profiteering, an opportunity for *experiencing* the real or simply for *playing* with it as a version of Eco's "hyperreal."

For a second example of how the parks address our accommodation to the technological, I want to look a bit more closely at the "Alien Encounter" ride initially described and pursue its technological commentary beyond those introductory rooms that similarly serve to gradually immerse guests in its science fictional context. While less a traditional ride than "Dinosaur," it is also connected to film, in this case through the influence of a major figure of cinematic science fiction, George Lucas, who helped design it, along with an earlier Disney attraction, the Michael Jackson 3D film, *Captain Eo.* As we might expect from Lucas's films, particularly the *Star Wars* series, his participation lends an interesting edge to this ride's backstory and its alien experience. Lucas's first feature, *THX 1138* (1970), is a dystopian view of a future in which people are kept drugged and impassive by a corporate state apparatus. And the original *Star Wars* (1977), we might recall, while depicting a broad array of alien beings, ranging from the friendly "walking carpet" Chewbacca to the repulsive, slug-like Jabba the Hutt, ends on a rather troubling compromise. It juxtaposes the voice-over reminder to Luke Skywalker that "the Force will be with you always" with the image of his nemesis (and father) Darth Vader escaping from the destroyed Death Star—a reminder that evil too will be with us "always."

That vision of a compromised future and of a persistent, menacing evil found its way into "Alien Encounter" and helps account for what many would see as its rather harsh tone. In fact, Bob Sehlinger's *Unoffi-*

cial Guide to Walt Disney World, 2001 warns visitors, particularly those with very young children, that "there is no uplifting message and no happy ending. There is death in this attraction, and its tone is dark and foreboding . . . we consider it mean and twisted" (422–23). At its core is a future in which the Earth has become a new market for the latest technology from more advanced civilizations in the galaxy—a kind of "third world" world, or as the chairman of X-S, L. C. Clench puts it, one of the "less fortunate" civilizations. And thanks to that status, Earth is also open to beta-testing, to being involved in X-S Tech's manifestly still experimental teleportation technology. As another of those unstable codes we have noted, that experimental character allows for both the humor in the ride's introduction—the cute, Disney-esque creature's reluctance to be teleported—and the foreboding, especially as the animal arrives "singed," that forecasts the darker tone of the eventual "encounter" and compels the audience to wonder what might go wrong in the next test. The eventual malfunction brings a creature that more nearly resembles the devil of *Fantasia* (1940) than it does any *Star Wars*–type alien. In effect, it visits us with an image of pure evil, a flesh-eating creature that reacts hungrily to every sound, every scream that the audience makes, and a creature that effectively stands in for the menace that is bound up in X-S itself, or simply in the *excess*-ive uses of technology. And in the face of this double menace—of both the predatory alien and the predatory technology company—we seem almost helpless, thanks to the machinery that has accidentally transported this creature across the galaxy while we sit strapped in place.

The sense of helplessness this ride created, then, also owes much to its construction, for in order to witness the latest advance of X-S Tech, this intergalactic transporter, audiences entered a round chamber, were seated around a central transporter tube, and were then effectively "locked" in their seats by shoulder and head harnesses that automatically lowered. Ominously suggesting that *we* might be going on some sort of trip, one that would require substantial safety restraints, this harness device was a key to the resulting "encounter." For when the transporter demonstration goes wrong, the lights go out, and the carnivorous alien, instead of the head of X-S,[7] is deposited in our midst, the harnesses kept each person in place and, with the aid of the darkness, technologically constructed the alien's presence for the individuals in the audience: blowing hot air that represents its breath, spewing spray that suggests its saliva or the blood of its victims, offering mysterious clicking sounds that hint of its biting, and in other ways indicating its menacing movements. In a most effective paradox, then, the unmoving individual seat here became the essence of a new sort of ride that suggests the double nature of the technological. The apparatus immobilized the "riders" and then, with the aid of darkness and a variety of individually aimed nozzles and speakers, proceeded to transport them into their own darkest imaginings.

Yet even given this effect and that "dark" assessment Sehlinger offers, the ride was rated as a "headliner," and it is one that was, as Sehlinger notes, at its opening "heralded as the showpiece of the 'new' Tomorrowland" (Guide, 2001 422). It could be so rated because, like many of the other rides in the various Disney worlds, it not only took us into the dark and threatening situation described above, but also snatched us safely back from that threat when the creature is recaptured and transported back to its world. And it accomplished these effects in a highly technological way that speaks to the larger and complex Disney attitude towards the technological that we have been tracing. For it reminds us that technology has its boons and its flaws; that it can serve and also victimize us; that it can be a source of both wonder and fear (or transport and restraint). In fact, the ride implicitly suggested that buying into the former potential typically means that we accept the potential of the latter as well. The bargain here is thus our own, as is the responsibility for that bargain, as corporations, aliens, and humans all simply do what they do. The ride, like the technology, came with its warnings, and in ignoring those warnings, in accepting the ride, we accepted the technology along with its problematic character.

Perhaps more significantly, "Alien Encounter" reminds us with this disturbing caveat emptor context that technology is not simply an autonomous thing, not just a system to be neutrally deployed, but rather that it is shaped by various social and cultural forces that are often practically invisible in our everyday lives. Here the technological is "the latest innovative wonder" that is being "sold" to us by the self-proclaimed "galaxy's number one authority in technological innovation." Perhaps more surprising for the context of Disney entertainment, it was also something that binds us, that restrains us for the purposes of that selling. It was part and parcel of a larger system in which corporations identify people as users, those users as markets, and the markets as profit sources. It was also a system in which—since humans are by definition alien to the technology and its creators, since they are the true "alien encounter" here—human considerations play only a secondary role; as we overhear one of the engineers in the background commenting, X-S is "putting sales before science *again.*" When audiences were released from those technological bonds, when at ride's end the head and shoulder restraints lifted off, they emerged from this encounter with a certain wariness about the land of tomorrow (surely an ironic effect in Tomorrowland) and an almost visceral appreciation that technology is not just things but a certain set of practices involving our relationship to those things—a relationship that can help define us as human or alien and one that necessitates our active participation.

That rather sober appreciation may well have come at too great a cost for Disney. As we have noted, "Alien Encounter," while highly rated, was also criticized for its dark and potentially frightening vision, and especially for its rather overdone element of an alien feasting on human victims. It should hardly be surprising, then, that in 2003 Disney reworked this attraction in hopes of making it a tamer, less challenging experience, and consequently, one whose point is muted. Retitled "Stitch's Great Escape," it now substitutes the comic alien of Disney's animated film *Lilo & Stitch* (2002) for its previous flesh-eating "star," and eliminates much of the corporate commentary, including the profit-driven Chairman Clench. While retaining the same intergalactic transportation scheme and the movement-restricting seats and harnesses, and even warning of great risk in the process because of the extremely dangerous creature that is to be sent, the ride shifts menace into mirth as an Audio-Animatronic version of Stitch appears and goes on a playful rampage: breathing on the helpless humans, pinching them, sneezing on them, licking them. Instead of embodying the rapacious potential of corporate technology, "Stitch's Great Escape" simply gives technology an impish embodiment, suggesting its unpredictable and often uncontrollable potential, while backing off of much of the self-criticism found in the attraction's earlier version. Of course, a sense of our own helplessness in the face of this trickster remains, and thus some subversive suggestion of what Penley and Ross term "control technology." But it is a helplessness without real danger, producing an atmosphere that, instead of horrifying, simply elicits laughter or mock recoil. The result is a negotiation that seems all too easy, a comic experience that precisely reaches the attraction's new target audience—the young children who had made the animated film a success.

As a final example of the parks' efforts at technological accommodation, I want to consider an attraction that is even further removed from the traditional style of ride but is also based on a film, in fact, one that critics have fittingly described as a kind of thrill ride itself. This attraction also initially seems little concerned with a conventional technology, but it effects the same sort of value shift noted in "Dinosaur." The "Indiana Jones Epic Stunt Spectacular" of the Disney-MGM theme park, a show typically staged for audiences of two thousand, draws its structure from the movie *Raiders of the Lost Ark* (1981), but it is essentially about the larger experience of the movies, and particularly the special effects technologies that make their illusions both possible and convincing. It is, in fact, one of the most technology-intensive attractions at any of the Disney parks, and it very self-consciously puts that technology on display. Thus, with one of the largest moving sets ever designed, it begins by replicating Indiana Jones's famous escape from a falling, ball-shaped rock in *Raiders*, follows with a series of stunt fights and a truck wreck that recall other events from the film, and culminates in a gunfight and the explosive destruction of an airplane that, as in the movie, is intended to transport the Ark of the Covenant to Nazi Germany.[8] These actions all correspond to specific scenes from the movie with which the audience is presumably quite familiar, and they are presented in a way that also assumes some familiarity with how films are made. Yet, while the show isolates these few key plot elements from the film and restages them for viewers, its real concern is with how such scenes "work," that is, the technology behind film's illusions: the machinery involved in the set designs, the technology required to move massive sets, the pivoting poles, air bags, and hidden trampolines that enable its stunt work, the techniques of staging car chases and mechanically flipping or rolling the cars, and the controlled creation of fires and explosions. Its particular pleasures largely derive from letting us see behind the scenes, inside the machinery, through film's "trickery," and thus in emphasizing the illusion-making technology on which not only the movies but, as we cannot help but recognize, the theme parks themselves fundamentally depend. The very machinery of the hyperreal, implicit in the other rides we have discussed, is here simply laid out for our inspection, amusement, and even a sense of mastery.

With its emphasis on this movie technology, found as well in such near kin as "The Great Movie Ride," the "Backlot Tour," and the recent import from Disneyland-Paris, the "Lights, Motors, Action! Extreme Stunt Show," the "Indiana Jones" presentation engages us in a particular sort of "blatantness" that is obviously fundamental to the attraction of the whole Disney-MGM park. For visitors to this park, even more obviously than in the other Disney worlds, are invited to celebrate the movies—or more accurately, to celebrate the illusory power of movies, television, and indeed the entire entertainment industry, including the theme park itself. Working in this vein, other rides here show how sound effects manipulate our perceptions (Drew Carey's "Sounds Dangerous"), how drawings take on the illusion of life ("The Magic of Disney Animation"), and how models and miniatures are mixed with actors and full-sized props to create seamless action scenes ("Backlot Tour"). Moreover, they emphasize the pleasures bound up in such technological wizardry—experiencing the interrelations of our senses, seeing the "magic" of animated figures being brought to life, vicariously enjoying the most improbable situations. Throughout this park, as Stephen Fjellman simply sums up, we are in a great variety of ways "shown how Disney constructs its cinematic effects—how it produces its real fakes, its fake reals, and its fake fakes. We are let in on some of the secrets—secrets carefully kept from us" elsewhere (283). The implication, of course, is that others, insiders, have fully mastered the technology of the movies, and that, with our newfound experience and knowledge, we too have gained at least some small measure of that mastery; we understand how the mechanism works on—and for—us.

Yet, in several ways the "Indiana Jones" show pushes these effects and the process of revelation a bit further than most of the other attractions. While stunt shows are hardly novel and even figure as attractions in other amusement parks,[9] "Indiana Jones" offers a special context that emphasizes its technological links and makes it a fitting cap for this discussion. For it is hardly just a display of stunt skills, but rather a show about tricks done for and with the camera eye. Hovering around every scene are constantly shifting cameras and sound equipment arranged on dollies and booms; one of the central figures is introduced to the audience as a "second unit director," who in turn introduces his assistants and various technicians—cinematographer, sound person, pyrotechnics expert, stunt coordinator, and so on; and each scene begins with initial dialogue about camera angles and lighting arrangements, with sound checks, and with the traditional clapper board. In effect, this show constantly foregrounds and establishes as its context the techniques and technology of the movies—the unstated context for all the Disney parks— and even plays with our ability to distinguish between actual filming and the *representation* of filming.[10] So even as it offers a discourse about constructing realistic effects, about the secrets of fashioning a convincing reality illusion, it also advances another discourse about the role of cinematic technology—not as a recording device but as an elaborate and even necessary apparatus of deception, and one that relies for its success in part on our own contrived participation.

Another of those effects derives from the way "Indiana Jones" amplifies this notion of participation. For rather than just playing to its large audience, it begins with a "casting call," drawing volunteers from the audience and placing them in the show, having them work like actors in this "movie" experience, letting them experience its magic from the inside, inhabiting this text. Fitted with appropriate costumes, they are brought down to the "set" to serve as extras, fight with the stunt performers, and become involved in the crashes and pyrotechnics of the scenes. It is the sort of immersion that underscores several key thrusts shared by the movies and the theme park, even as it also suggests that being in a movie is an experience very much like being in an amusement park—and vice versa. More particularly, it emphasizes the deceptive power that both wield, how they are equally able to sell us their illusions, while it also, as a key term in this negotiation, practically celebrates our participation in that deception, our complicity in the bargain being offered for our consumption, ultimately calling into question just who actually wields the "control technology" here. In fact, as our selected fellow guests engage in staged fistfights and gun battles, and even as we recognize the carefully choreographed and technologically enabled nature of these events, we cannot help but enjoy the prospect of such participation, even of being applauded for it by our fellow guests. Much of the appeal here is that strange sense of being both bound up in and yet fully aware of the illusion being fashioned, of becoming, as it were, *hyperreal ourselves.*

Through this process the technology of illusion undergoes its own shift in valence. It does become a ride instead of a display of tricks, as well as a rather different sort of reality, thanks to Disney bartering some of its secrets—secrets of how sets carefully control viewer perception, how hidden mechanisms propel both people and vehicles, how explosions and fires produce dazzling effects but no real damage—for another level of audience satisfaction or pleasure. If this show works, on one level, to demystify film technology, then on another (as another sort of unstable code), it draws a level of power from that same revealed technology. In this context we might recall Eco's similar observation about the buildings encountered throughout the Disney parks, particularly those of the ubiquitous Main Street, USA. While not built to normal scale past their first story, the Main Street buildings still *seem* habitable and indeed function as shops, restaurants, displays, offices. Their purpose, he offers, is not "to make us believe that what we are seeing reproduces reality absolutely," but rather to emphasize "that within its magic enclosure it is fantasy that is absolutely reproduced" (43) for us and, in part, by us. What the "Indiana Jones" show manages—and it is ultimately a move central to all of the Disney parks—is to draw out of the technological the power of fantasy, to suggest, as Penley and Ross might put it, that film's technology, while highly manipulative, also provides us with "liberating fantasies" that are, particularly in experiences like this one, both satisfying and accessible to us all.

The highly reflexive dimension of this and the other "encounters" here, I would suggest, is important to managing that negotiation between the manipulative and the liberating, just as it is for that between the real and the fake or hyperreal. As we have noted, the Disney-ness of these rides and experiences never quite disappears, despite their authentic detailing and even as we proceed in a carefully calculated way through their often immersive architectures. While audiences waited to be greeted by Chairman Clench of X-S Tech, for example, they also saw on the surrounding video monitors an advertisement for "Lunar Disneyland, the Happiest Place Off the Earth." And if the Disney Institute of "Dinosaur" blurs any distinction from a traditional museum, its name and the posted corporate linkage to McDonald's—which reminds us too of the product tie-ins between the movie *Dinosaur* and the restaurant chain's "Happy Meals"—inevitably draw us up short. We simply do not get away from Disney or its particular uses of technology. And yet the rides and shows give a high level of pleasure, bringing guests back time and again; their particular reality, or hyperreality, apparently offers much satisfaction. If their effect translates as a kind of "blatantness," it is one that opens onto those negotiations previously described. For this effect reminds us that in its parks Disney finally negotiates *through the hyperreal.* Its attractions offer not just an illusion or pleasant fantasy but a different measure of awareness. They *do not* simply fool us; rather, they wink at us and induce us to acknowledge our own complicity with the technological world—which is Disney's complicity as well—and all that it so attractively promises to deliver.

Part of the payoff is that, for all of their capacity to deliver technological illusions, the Disney parks also thereby help us manage our own difficulties with the real and the technology of the everyday. For in them we do not just escape from a dreary technoculture or become part of what Mark Dery in his discussion of amusement parks derisively terms a "flight from public space and social responsibility" (172). Such explanations do little to account for the curious ways in which Disney repeatedly calls attention to issues of technology and its often exploitative, dangerous, and manipulative uses by capitalist enterprises—like itself. In the contemporary world, we often feel, as Jean Baudrillard has effectively described our condition, like we are living within "a hypothetical machine, isolated in a position of perfect sovereignty, at an infinite distance from [our] original universe; that is to say, in the same position as the astronaut in his bubble, existing in a state of weightlessness which compels the individual to remain in perpetual orbital flight" (*Ecstasy* 15). In various ways, all of the rides described here evoke an element of this all-too-familiar detached sensibility; in a peculiarly postmodern manner they attest to the reality we ultimately inhabit—along with our Audio-Animatronic stand-ins—as strange and even Disney-like as it might be. And we naturally take some, if perhaps unwitting, comfort both in that acknowledgement and in the possibility for reconnection they also seem to hold out.

We might do well to see the Disney parks, and indeed much of the larger Disney enterprise that moves throughout the dimensions of the media and entertainment landscape of our technoculture, as specifically attuned to a central characteristic of modern life. Dery argues that, throughout contemporary Western culture, we can find "a technodeterministic tendency . . . to map the mechanical metaphor of the moment onto human affairs and the natural world" (241). Thus the computer and its various digital dimensions have come to provide us with what seem to be increasingly pertinent metaphors for much of contemporary life. But that tendency speaks of more than just a kind of metaphoric fashion; it reminds us of how consequential, even inescapable, the technological is for human experience—including human amusement—and how we are constantly trying to interpolate it into our everyday world, conduct our own negotiations with it, even on a linguistic level, and even when we are supposedly *vacationing from* that world.[11] Part of the problem we face, of course, is technology's very character, its own unstable nature, as it offers different potentials that we, much like Disney, have to negotiate. In the Disney parks, technology simply is everywhere, and its signature, as we have seen, is not, as we might expect, erased to aid the fantasy, but writ surprisingly large. In that presence the parks effect a significant version of this mapping, writing out Disney's relations to the technological in stark characters that can be, as we might only expect, both pleasant and a bit disturbing, or as I earlier offered, an *estranging attraction*. In the process, they also assist in our own bargaining with the technological conditions of modern life, suggesting that here is one of those places where people might go to work out, even if only momentarily and within the parks' precincts, what can seem an acceptable, even pleasurable balance between what Paul Virilio has rather starkly termed the "totalitarianism . . . latent in technology" (Oliveira 2) and what many with equal assurance see as its great liberating potential.

7 Course Correction: Of Black Holes and Computer Games

> "You know, we shouldn't be needing a
> [course] correction at this time."
> —*The Black Hole*

In the opening scene of *The Black Hole* (1979), Disney's first serious science fiction film in twenty-five years, one of the characters notes a strange force acting on the exploratory spaceship *Palomino*, a force requiring the crew to adjust their course unexpectedly. It is an effectively suspenseful way of introducing the central focus of the film, their encounter with a massive black hole that is pulling everything towards it and requiring, even before they have detected it, an unscheduled course correction. It is also a comment that speaks unwittingly to the creation of this film, as well as to another Disney science fiction effort that would follow in just a few years, *Tron* (1982). For both films spring from a sudden effort at what might be termed course correction within the Disney Company, at pulling the studio out of a kind of creative "black hole" that was beginning to threaten its future, by engaging in what had become a popular discourse about technology. Executives, particularly those in the feature film division that, as Jon Lewis has chronicled, was quickly becoming "a significant liability," rather than the core of the company's activity (98), sought for ways of reaching an audience that seemed to be changing and looking elsewhere for entertainment. The "correction" that resulted involved an intriguing combination—of films *about* technology and films that *involved* major technological development and investment. It was a correction, however, that did little more than stake out important territory, pointing in a new technological direction that Disney and, indeed, the rest of the American film industry would not fully pursue for another decade.

In the period following Walt Disney's death in 1966, the company increasingly struggled to maintain its traditional audience. In both the 1967–68 and 1968–69 seasons, the company's flagship television series, now renamed *The Wonderful World of Color,* suffered serious drops in its ratings, while its feature films in the same period produced only a few hits, with *The Love Bug* and its sequels (1969, 1974, 1977) the major exception. While Disney had in the 1960s finally risen to the ranks of a major studio, thanks to its leadership in television and a string of both live-action and animated hits, including *Swiss Family Robinson* (1960), *101 Dalmatians* (1961), *The Parent Trap* (1961), *Mary Poppins* (1964), and *The Jungle Book* (1967), the late 1960s began what many saw as a long period of decline—in both the quality of film productions and their overall profitability. Admittedly, in the decade following Walt's loss, the company as a whole progressed from $12.4 million in profits in 1966 to $74.4 million in 1976, ranking it second only to Universal in profitability during that period. However, those figures do not tell the whole story. Highly profitable rereleases of the company's earlier animation hits, the growing contributions of its theme parks, and an increased effort at marketing its trademarked products—all elements of the company's deeply engrained synergistic strategy—partially disguised the problem besetting Disney's core filmmaking unit. In just a few years, between 1976 and 1981, Disney's share of the American box office would drop from 7 percent to just 4 percent (Mills 52), the lowest of all the major film studios.[1]

And yet, the live-action feature program had hardly been neglected. Under the guidance of Walt's son-in-law Ron Miller, it had not only stayed active after Walt's death, but had actually increased production. But while Disney turned out a large number of films, most were hardly innovative efforts, and the decision makers, as Bart Mills has noted, too often seemed to be "making their decisions while looking over their shoulders at what was done before" (56). There were attempts to recapture the spirit of *Mary Poppins* (1964) with similarly hybrid efforts such as *Bedknobs and Broomsticks* (1971) and *Pete's Dragon* (1978), sequels to a number of earlier successes, such as *Herbie Rides Again* (1974) and *The Shaggy D.A.* (1976), and animal-focused comedies and adventures, like *$1,000,000 Duck* (1971) and *The Bears and I* (1974), recalling the sort of programming that had proven most successful on the Disney television show.[2] As Leonard Maltin has characterized the studio's feature films during the post-Walt era, "It was difficult to dispel the feeling that they were being turned out with a cookie-cutter" (268). And the animation program, the foundation upon which the company's reputation had been built, was faring no better. In the fifteen years following Walt's death, few original animation projects were begun, mainly weak efforts such as *The Aristocats* (1970) and *Robin Hood* (1973). And a further blow was struck in 1979 when top animator Don Bluth left the studio to form Don Bluth Productions, a competing animation company, taking with him sixteen talented young animators, the core of the next generation of trained Disney artists. As Charles Solomon has suggested, at this point it seemed like the very "spirit of advancement and experimentation faltered" at the studio (50).

In analyzing the problem facing Disney at this time, Mills put the blame primarily on the appeal of the film product. As he observed, while "the studio kept churning out sweet, gentle family films . . . the families stopped coming" (52). Certainly, the declining birth rate that left Disney with fewer young fans might have contributed to the problem, but a bigger issue was simply changing attitudes and tastes. As Mills notes, it was becoming apparent that "youngsters seemed to be growing up faster" (52), looking for cinematic subjects that appealed to the more complex tastes of the moment, and not finding them in Disney's formulaic fare. At this point in film history, the big, special-effects laden science fiction film had begun to establish itself as among the most popular of film genres, thanks to the phenomenal success of a cluster of remarkable movies: *Star Wars* (1977), *Close Encounters of the Third Kind* (1977), *Superman* (1978), and *Alien* (1979). So moving in this technologically focused and technologically dependent direction must have seemed like an appropriate "correction," even if the genre in its latest manifestations had also become, thanks to the very technology involved, an increasingly sophisticated and unusually expensive proposition.

Of course, Disney did, as we have already seen, have some limited background in the science fiction genre, having produced the highly successful *20,000 Leagues Under the Sea* in 1954 and the *Man in Space* series, created for the *Disneyland* show but also released theatrically to much acclaim. Yet as we have also noted, in the wake of these rather ambitious, costly, and certainly serious efforts to focus on science, technology, and their attendant themes, the studio had eventually shifted in a less ambitious—and less costly—direction, as it developed a formula of comic science fiction that quickly became a staple. This narrative recipe commonly involved bumbling scientists, technology gone wrong (generally harmlessly so), or encounters with friendly aliens. And thanks to its typically comic atmosphere, it usually suggested that the world of science and technology had little significant impact on everyday life. In fact, the formula typically treated science in the fashion of what we today term technoscience, that is, as a kind of cultural construct, reflecting the attitudes and ideologies of the moment. Doing so was itself a kind of negotiation with a subject matter that, during the Cold War and against the backdrop of the race to the moon, was seen as culturally significant. With this approach the studio could treat science and technology with less seriousness, situating them as comic mirrors of both our individual and cultural foibles, as a long line of films in this vein demonstrate, works like *The Shaggy Dog* (1959), *The Absent-Minded Professor* (1961), *The Misadventures of Merlin Jones* (1964), *The Computer Wore Tennis Shoes* (1969), and *The Cat from Outer Space* (1978). Looking at these and a number of other titles in the post-Walt era, Brian Attebery has suggested that, "What is most interesting about Disney SF is not that it advances the genre in any significant way . . . but that there is so much of it and that it is so much alike" (150). Formulaic, generally cheaply done, and aimed at a young audience, these films occupied a place largely outside of the mainstream of science fiction cinema of the 1960s and 1970s, and they generally demonstrate little in common with those major science fiction productions that had so caught the public's attention in this era. No longer quick to take chances, Disney had struck a rather simple economic and narrative deal with the genre and was reluctant to alter the terms of that bargain.

One major effort at correcting this course was *The Black Hole*, at $18.5 million Disney's most expensive production to that time, as well as its most elaborate special effects effort. Five years in development, the film began as a story entitled "Space Station One" under the guidance of longtime Disney writer and producer Winston Hibler. And as originally envisioned, the story would have stayed very close to traditional Disney narratives. As producer Ron Miller admits, "We tried to force a kid and animals into it to make it a sort of Disney science-fiction situation" ("Producer" 41). But after Hibler's death in 1975, the project was refocused to emphasize an encounter with a black hole, a phenomenon that had only recently become a topic of scientific discussion. In shifting this encounter "from a minor part of the story to its heart," the studio was essentially committing itself not only to a new *kind* of story, but also to the sort of complex and costly special effects work that had become the hallmark of major science fiction films—in fact, work that would involve a major investment in new technologies (Culhane 20). But the hope was that in so doing, *The Black Hole* would stand a better chance of attracting an audience increasingly interested in the big-budget, special effects-driven films. Ultimately, the special effects work did prove impressive, earning the film Academy Award nominations in both Best Cinematography and Best Visual Effects categories. However, the film itself proved disappointing and the box office equally so. The film earned just $25.4 million on domestic release, a weak showing for a film offered as the studio's prestigious Christmas season release, and particularly disappointing when compared to the $79 million domestically earned earlier in the year by another science fiction production, Twentieth Century-Fox's *Alien*.

Still, the production marked a significant shift in direction, not simply because of its budget or subject, but for the new sense of commitment it represented to move beyond the sort of "cookie-cutter" efforts we have noted and to once more push the development of new film technologies. Disney began to participate in co-productions with other studios, resulting in such un-Disneylike releases as *Popeye* (1980) and *Dragonslayer* (1981), and, in one of the few successes for Ron Miller's leadership, eventually created its Touchstone label for developing and releasing more adult fare. In the area of film technology, it made a first halting move in the direction of computer-assisted production, developing several new programs that would, in fact, allow for the effective combination of this new area of effects with the company's more traditional investment in matte painting. *The Black Hole* represented, in short, Disney's recognition of the need for a commitment to new approaches to the production and distribution process, as well as to reevaluating the very nature of filmmaking.

As a sign of this new commitment, we might note that, while *The Black Hole* had a prestigious cast, more than half of the film's budget was eventually devoted to its special effects work. With a nod to the past, Disney lured out of retirement veteran artist and production designer Peter Ellenshaw to lend experience to the project.[3] Ellenshaw had previously provided matte paintings and special visual effects for a long line of popular and successful Disney adventure films, including *Treasure Island* (1950), *20,000 Leagues Under the Sea*, *Third Man on the Mountain* (1959), and *Swiss Family Robinson*, and he had won an Academy Award for his visual effects in *Mary Poppins*. Put in complete charge of *The Black Hole*'s visual design, Ellenshaw painted or supervised the creation of more than 150 mattes and designed a total of 550 visual effects shots—both Hollywood records at the time and far more than had been used in *Star Wars*, the matte work for which had been done by his son Harrison (Culhane 19–20).

But along with this link to the past and to traditional ways of doing visual effects, the film also pointed in a more contemporary and challenging technological direction by exploiting some of the new possibilities for integrating the computer into film production, particularly for linking the computer to the camera. Probably the most significant of these applications was ACES, the Automated Camera Effects System, which employed a computer to plan and control camera movement. As described in *American Cinematographer*, this Disney-developed system involved "a servo controlled camera, carriage and dolly, model stand, process projector and other ancillary devices which can be moved through a complex continuous or stop-motion shot with exact repeatability" ("Automatic" 60). Simply put, it used a computer to map out and control camera movements so that models or animation could be shot and then combined with live-action or matte images shot with precisely the same camera motion. Also developed was a program called Mattescan, which allowed the camera to move in relation to Ellenshaw's matte paintings, producing elaborate tracking shots such as that which introduces the spaceship *Cygnus* and helps lend it an impressive three dimensionality. And to visualize its central effect, the black hole, the film employed the longest computer graphics sequence in film to that date. In combination with Ellenshaw's more traditional effects techniques, these state-of-the-art developments helped earn *The Black Hole* Academy Award nominations for both cinematography and visual effects, and suggested a new commitment at Disney to negotiating with the latest technological and narrative fashions.

The key to *The Black Hole*'s promise, though, was probably also one of the keys to its disappointments, for it was clearly a film that in some ways seemed to look more backwards than forwards, particularly in terms of the narrative and its themes. For even as Disney's live-action feature unit was at this time trying to push in a new direction, or at least one that the current vogue for effects-oriented science fiction had staked out, the film owed much to a cultural and studio past—a link that also helped to argue for its production. The film's plot particularly seemed to rehash that of the studio's most successful science fiction effort, *20,000 Leagues Under the Sea*, which was itself a nostalgic story, based on the Jules Verne novel and set in the previous century. Certainly its central figure, the megalomaniac scientist Dr. Hans Reinhardt, seems drawn directly from the earlier film's Captain Nemo, his fantastic space ship, the *Cygnus*, recalls Nemo's famous submarine, the *Nautilus*, and even specific scenes, such as a burial in space or the gathering of the central characters around Reinhardt's dinner table, seem modeled on similar episodes in the earlier film. In addition, the film's basic visual design also owes much to that sense of the past, as the set for most of the film, Reinhardt's ship, has a distinctly nostalgic look. Trying to create, as he says, "a different version of a spaceship than any other we've seen" (Culhane 24), Ellenshaw fashioned a massive image of steel tracery and glass that evokes the Crystal Palace of 1851, and seems an anomalously fragile structure poised next to the powerful black hole on which the film focuses. While that unusual, rather baroque look, which markedly contrasts with the stark white spacecraft audiences were accustomed to, thanks to films like *2001: A Space Odyssey* and *Star Wars*, served an effective narrative function, helping to project the bizarre and imperious nature of its designer, Dr. Reinhardt,[4] it also seemed unsuited to the world of the narrative.

The attempt to give a thematic resonance to the narrative also pulls viewers into a distant cultural past, as the film almost from the start establishes Dante's *Inferno* as its other master text. The black hole, of course, readily lends itself to such a comparison, its swirling, descending circularity visually suggesting the multiple circles of Dante's hell, but to underscore the point the reporter Harry Booth exclaims, on first sighting the phenomenon, "My god, right out of Dante's *Inferno*," and his later embellishment, "I expect to spot some guy with horns and a pitchfork," not only reinforces his initial comparison but also points toward the film's narrative expansion of the image. For Reinhardt's master creation and ultimately his alter ego, the robot Maximillian, is deep red in color and equipped with various appendages that readily suggest the archetypal "horns and a pitchfork." The final image of the black hole's interior, populated by the damned figures from Reinhardt's crew, fantastically landscaped in fire and rock, and supervised by an inexplicable amalgam of Maximillian and Reinhardt, leaves no doubt that the desire to take his crew and ship, at all costs, into the black hole has quite literally brought the scientist into a most traditional version of hell. While this reincarnation of Nemo similarly seems driven by his "genius," as one character observes, and has great knowledge to share with mankind, including his gravity neutralizer, he is presented from the start as practically inhuman; as Harry matter-of-factly observes, he "sure loves to play God." As a result of this exaggerated vision, the narrative is never able to offer a compelling vision of the scientist or his work, one in keeping with contemporary cultural attitudes or even commensurate with that of 20,000 *Leagues Under the Sea*. Instead, it simply plays out, almost like a medieval allegory, an uncomplicated and starkly drawn conflict between good and evil, set in the far reaches of space.

Still, *The Black Hole* did involve a host of elements that acknowledge the film's kinship to the recent spate of successful science fiction films, supporting the general impression that, in this instance, the studio appeared to be jumping on a pop culture bandwagon. It offers a vision of deep space exploration; includes elements of mysticism with its Dantean conclusion and its attributing of telepathic skills to Dr. Kate McCrae; and it gives central roles to several of its robot characters, particularly to V.I.N.C.E.N.T. and Bob, who seem clearly modeled on *Star Wars*'s comic/heroic robots, R2D2 and C3Po. At the same time, the narrative's concern with space exploration lacks any clear point. The *Palomino* and its crew have simply been charged with the by-this-time trite—not to mention illogically phrased—directive articulated by one of the crew, "to discover habitable life in outer space." With Dr. McCrae's telepathy we see the powers of "the Force" replaced with pseudoscience. And, with the notable exception of Maximillian, the robots here are weakly, even rather cheaply realized: their eyes painted circles, their flying enabled by wires that are visible in several shots, and their ability with laser weapons a plot contrivance. While provided with many of the trappings of other recent efforts in the science fiction genre, then, *The Black Hole* never seems quite at home with those elements, only ineffectually working them into its narrative, which seems essentially a stage for its special effects work.

Yet in one other respect *The Black Hole* does seem to be charting new territory, to be correcting course in a way that Disney would later exploit more successfully. For the film seems as if it could well have been inspired not only by a classic work like 20,000 *Leagues Under the Sea*, but also by another area of Disney success, the theme park ride. Its five chief protagonists are, after all, largely undeveloped characters, simply riders in a spacecraft broadly directed "to discover . . . life." They encounter a series of escalating thrills: damage to their ship, attacks by Reinhardt's robots, an encounter with a meteor storm, and the black hole itself, which eventually sucks them into its maelstrom-like center. Reinhardt's ship is populated, like every Disney ride, with the equivalent of Audio-Animatronic figures, engaged in typically routine, repetitious activities—his roboticized crew. And the movement through the black hole, the climax of this space "ride," leaves the surviving protagonists safe and sound, apparently headed back to their home planet. Nothing much has been achieved, apart from the series of *frissons* and narrow escapes provided by the narrative, and the film simply concludes, as do so many theme park rides, with a sense of relief. By this point, of course, the company had already begun mining its films for new ride "plots," a process it would eventually reverse—most spectacularly with a work like *Pirates of the Caribbean* (2003, 2006, 2007)—by turning some of its best rides into films. *The Black Hole* simply seems like a work already conceived in these terms, a film that would make full use of ride technology and techniques, and indeed provide audiences with a new sort of experience, not so much that of the classical film narrative as that of the "film ride."

With a second big-budget science fiction effort, *Tron*, Disney would advance that course correction even further, exploring important new avenues in project participation, subject matter, and film technology. Tom Wilhite, appointed new head of film production at Disney in late 1980, emphasized this shift in direction in an interview linking *Tron* with what he described as Disney's "new direction": "Perhaps change hasn't occurred as often as it should here, but we feel we're moving in the right direction with the kinds of pictures we have in production now. . . . We're discovering the essence of what made this studio what it is: change, chance, risk-taking, escapes, innovation, upbeat films" (Solomon 51). That policy statement promised much—"change," "innovation"— but it also sought to link those promises with Disney's successful and profitable past, as Wilhite clearly tried to negotiate his own place in the company, distancing his regime from recent failed leadership while also establishing his respect for the studio's traditions.

While it could certainly be classed as a "risk-taking" project, *Tron*, like *The Black Hole*, still maintained a number of readily identifiable links to the past and to Disney practice. The film was originally born as an animation project, brought to Disney by Steven Lisberger, head of a small animation company. And the finished product involved much old-fashioned, labor intensive work; as co-supervisor Richard W. Taylor offers, the back-lit animation technique employed for much of the film involved "handpainting of hundreds of thousands of cels and as many as forty hand-flopped passes under the animation cameras per scene." Moreover, Harrison Ellenshaw, Peter's son, co-produced the film, created the matte paintings used in the production, and co-supervised the visual effects. The intent of the project, however, was to integrate these traditional elements into a totally new approach to filmmaking, thereby taking both animation and science fiction into the future, an impulse that Taylor described with a paradoxical promise, that *Tron* "will remind you of something you have never seen before" (Sorensen 5).

Yet in order to move in this new direction, Disney would ultimately need to break with a number of long-established studio traditions. Foremost among them was its approach to production, one that originated all projects within the studio and did not strike partnership deals. That approach was quickly becoming unrealistic—and undermining profitability—in the post-studio era of Hollywood, where projects were shopped from one studio to another, talent was "packaged" to accompany a specific project, and profit participation was a common part of the larger "deal." As a result of the poor showing of its feature film unit, though, in the early 1980s Disney began making exceptions to these long-standing policies, particularly by negotiating production and distribution deals with various independent filmmakers. Thus, in a flurry of such deals it invited independent producer Tim Zinnemann to make his film *Tex* (1982) at the studio, accepted the rather large talent package put together by Jack Clayton for *Something Wicked This Way Comes* (1983), and gave profit "points" to director Carroll Ballard for his project *Never Cry Wolf* (1983).[5] All part of that general "course correction" we have already described, such moves signaled Disney's efforts to move beyond its old production formula and to become competitive in the new industry environment.

That old way of doing business was more than just an economic barrier, though, for it had effectively cut the studio off from new ideas and projects that could help it maintain its audience share or attract a new audience. With the production of *Tron*, Disney seemed to be pointedly addressing such conceptual concerns as well, for in this instance the studio was accepting a project already visualized by the team of Steven Lisberger and Don Kushner, previously responsible for a two-part animated film for television, *Animalympics*. And as part of the deal—one necessitated by the very nature of the project—Disney agreed to work with a team of production specialists that Lisberger and Kushner were already assembling. These were people who were skilled at two elements they saw as crucial to their film concept, back-lit animation and computer graphics. Among them were set designer Syd Mead, architectural consultant Peter Lloyd, and especially Richard Taylor, an animation expert who had recently become the art director for the fledgling computer effects firm Information International, Inc., or Triple-I. Overall, the group that set to work on the project had the sort of experience that was simply not available within Disney's traditional animation-oriented family, and they came with impressive industry credentials, having already earned a total of six Clio awards for commercial work.[6] Dubbed "the new kids on the block," by Disney veteran Harrison Ellenshaw, the *Tron* group, according

to Richard Taylor, saw their task partly as one of reinvigoration, as helping to "wipe out a few of the cobwebs" at the studio, "trying to create a
new energy level" (Mills 54).

Certainly, the very subject matter of the film was partly responsible
for that "energy," since it was something far removed from the usual run
of Disney subjects and even unlike any other science fiction films of the
era. The project would, very simply, allow the studio to once again assume
a position of industry leadership, both technologically and thematically.
Tom Wilhite quickly acknowledged this lure, admitting one of the things
that made the project most attractive to the studio was that its subject
seemed "very much on kids' wavelengths," since *Tron* was "the first
Hollywood film dealing with electronic games" (Mills 53). In a period
when a company like Warner Communications had begun to earn more
money from its computer games than from its feature film output, this
subject must have seemed especially promising. Moreover, the subject
opened onto a whole new thematic territory, namely the relationship
between the real world and an electronic simulacrum; as Lisberger offers, "I was really intrigued with the duality of the two worlds in the
film. There's the real world where the 'users' live, and . . . the theatre
of the electronic world" (Sorensen 6). And that concern with "duality"
would increasingly become a major focus of the science fiction genre,
in fact, arguably its most dominant concern over the next two decades,
as films like *Virtuosity* (1995), *The 13th Floor* (1999), *Dark City* (1999),
and *The Matrix* (1999) and its sequels testify. No longer just jumping on
a bandwagon, as seemed to be the case with *The Black Hole*, Disney was
in this instance clearly anticipating a major trend of the genre.

But in order to explore that new terrain convincingly, Lisberger and
Kushner felt that *Tron* would need to involve the computer world at a
most fundamental level, drawing digital technology into all elements of
the film's creation, and in the process laying the foundation for one of
the most important course corrections in both Disney and Hollywood
history, the embrace of digital animation and effects. As the concept for
Tron developed, they recognized that the narrative would grow out of
three distinct dimensions: the back-lit animation that was their original
focus, traditional live-action scenes, and computer-generated imagery
(CGI). In order to make these elements fit seamlessly together, though,
additional contributions from computer technology, including specially
created software, would be needed. Peter Blinn, who had previously
done special effects work for another pioneering film in this vein, *Star
Trek—The Motion Picture* (1980)—developed a computer program that
controlled light intensity for the various back-lit effects that were prov-

ing particularly time consuming and labor intensive. As on *The Black Hole*, a computer-controlled camera stand and motor proved essential for blending live action with the animation. And even the logistics of the film became computer-dependent; as Peter Sorensen explains, due to its complexity *Tron* became the first Disney film to employ "a computerized frame-by-frame bookkeeping system of scenes" (16)—now a commonplace production approach.

The computer effects created for the film, though, were certainly its most complex element and that on which most reviewers and commentators would eventually focus. Because it was such a groundbreaking work, involving diverse areas of expertise in an industry that was still in its infancy,[7] *Tron* would ultimately pull in four of the pioneering CGI companies, all of which were already involved in creating the new marriage between the film industry and digital media. Since Taylor, one of the top experts in back-lit animation, was already working for one of the main computer graphics companies, Triple-I, and had previously worked for another such firm, Robert Abel and Associates, those two companies were quickly approached to aid in the production, with Triple-I doing much of the striking imagery found in the second half of the film, particularly the CGI animation of the MCP, of Sark's Carrier, and of the Solar Sailer, with Abel handling many of the transitions and creating the opening title animation. Digital Effects, Inc., working from a design by Taylor and animator John Norton, created the Bit, a floating digital figure inside the computer world where much of the film's action occurs, while Mathematical Applications Group, Inc., or MAGI, oldest of the CGI companies, handled much of the first half of the film. MAGI's in-house system, known as Synthavision, was a "solids modeling" system, which worked in a very different way from those of the other companies involved. As a result, the film manages to achieve a distinctly different look as the narrative moves further into the world of the computer, shifting from MAGI-produced (and styled) CGI to that primarily created by Triple-I.[8]

The overall result of these various complementary efforts is a look that takes advantage of the very limitations of the then state-of-the-art CGI effects, their clearly nonrealistic appearance. Fully three quarters of the film occurs within the world of the computer, a kind of electronic alternate reality, as computer genius and game designer Flynn is sucked into the mainframe of computer corporation ENCOM in order to stop him from investigating the theft of various game programs he had created. What he encounters there is a world that, while obviously modeled on the real world, ultimately does not quite correspond to anything that actually exists, and indeed seems cobbled together from the various programs the ENCOM mainframe has appropriated for its own uses. As Charles Solomon has recognized, the key images we encounter in this stylized computer world—the light cycles, tanks, rooms, and furnishings—are easily recognizable and yet "their computer-generated shapes and textures don't correspond exactly to anything that really exists. . . . [They] look something like drawings and something like photographs, but not entirely like either" (52). And even those recognized correspondences are placed in a constantly shifting context that furthers this sense of a hybrid world. Lead special effects animator Lee Dyer explains that scenes were designed to be dominated at times by a pointedly "geometrical" look, while at other times they were to have "more of an organic feeling," such as when we see Tron in Yori's "apartment" within the computer world (Sorensen 31). The sort of compromise aesthetic that results helps build that sense of an alternate reality without completely estranging audiences from this pointedly constructed, unnatural world.

And yet that alterity remains one of the central attractions of this film, indeed, an essential element of its story. For *Tron* is very much about the lure of the digital, about the great attraction of the new world of video games and electronic appurtenances of every sort that were starting to suck everyone into their environment, much as the computer whiz Flynn is suddenly digitized and drawn into the ENCOM mainframe. Of course, this principle applies to most science fiction films, which almost invariably have to cope with a curse of their own inevitability. That is, one of their central attractions—perhaps even their raison d'être—lies in their ability to imagine and visualize other times, other places, other worlds. Fritz Lang clearly recognized this connection when he created that landmark of the genre, *Metropolis* (1926). For despite the dystopian horrors he envisioned in his futuristic city, that city still proved to be his film's central fascination—that on which critical commentary would inevitably settle and that would then provide the model for many subsequent futuristic cities, both utopian and dystopian, to be found in films ranging from *Just Imagine* (1930) to *The Fifth Element* (1997). As a balance to that lure, *Metropolis* includes a discourse about seduction, as it uses the figure of the robot Maria to metaphorize the ease with which the city's inhabitants are taken in by its gleaming promise, by all that the technological world offers. That problem certainly lingers in *Tron*, and in some ways provided its makers with a more daunting challenge, since in visualizing that alternate reality within the computer, they faced a world with no models, or as Lisberger puts it, "a totally alien environment, where whatever ideas one wanted to generate one had to think up from scratch" (Sorensen 6).

Of course, despite Lisberger's comment, the look of this world was not completely without a model. Solomon reminds us that *Tron*'s interior world was from the start "designed to resemble a video game" (51) with its emphasis on straight lines, simple geometric shapes, and the pulsing lights that its back-lit animation particularly highlights. The starkly stylized realm that followed from this model would, it was hoped, resonate with younger viewers, while also providing an important context for the larger struggle that the film describes. For the video game was already being seen in many quarters as a kind of mixed development, offering a new and engaging form of entertainment, while also exercising its own seductive pull on children and teenagers, drawing them away from other culturally valued activities, such as reading, sports, and simple human interaction. So the film's look, as in the case of so many other science fiction films, provided the attraction while also suggesting the central problem that the narrative explores—the fascination or lure that this new electronic world, this potential other reality, holds for us, together with the dangers bound up in that alluring yet also insubstantial world.

To manage this dual potential, the film, by turns, valorizes the world of the computer and the video game, and recognizes its threatening potential. It accomplishes the former by presenting what has come to be known as gaming culture in a positive light, primarily through the character of Flynn. He is a top game designer, operator of a popular video game parlor, and a champion game player himself, who seems to be practically worshipped by the teens and young adults who frequent his place. That we see some of them invited into his living quarters, his home, further establishes his link to these kids and even the general wholesomeness of the gaming activity. Not a part of the corporate world—he was forced out of ENCOM after creating its top-selling games—he is a hacker and an important part of this electronic culture, a new kind of rebel who also helps to bridge generations by demonstrating that the computer game is not simply child's play. And yet the film also points up the dangers here, with its easy localizing of a dark intent in the corporate world that has created and marketed the most popular games, while eliminating employees like Flynn who care about the games and those who play them. It is one more instance of a Disney film striking a populist note and apparently aligning itself against the large corporate entity—one that is in some ways like Disney itself—just as we have seen in a number of the theme park attractions.

In order to effect this strategy, the film focuses the problem primarily within the technology itself, or rather, on a technology gone bad and abetted by a weak individual. Of course, the ENCOM facility, as it is visualized, is a world that closely resembles the computer environment we later see, with its emphasis on order, security, controls, and even the rectilinear styling of the building; and its chief officer, Ed Dillinger, is responsible for maneuvering Flynn out of the company and depriving him of any royalties for his game designs, largely out of jealousy of Flynn's skills. Yet ultimately it is less the corporate world than the MCP itself (the Master Control Program) that the film identifies as the culprit and the real threat here. Like a number of other movies in this period, such as *Futureworld* (1976), *Demon Seed* (1977), and *War Games* (1983), *Tron* postulates a computer intelligence that becomes self-conscious and begins reaching for more and more power, including power over its human creators. Thus, through the information the MCP contains, it can blackmail and wield control over Dillinger, and then attempt to broaden its power, as if an ever-increasing power and control—as its very name implies—were the ultimate and indeed natural goals of the MCP. Its surprising ability to take control of an experimental atomizing device, enabling it to digitize and suck Flynn into its strange environment, simply plays out our fears of the computer itself, anticipating the vision of a much later film like *The Matrix*, while also neatly metaphorizing the subtler power of the new computer culture seemingly to draw everything into its orbit. With the computer here no longer controlled by men but rather threatening to take control, as it has with ENCOM, the narrative literalizes our deep-seated fears of the computer's power in and over contemporary culture without clearly casting any human blame, beyond the simple jealousy and greed of Dillinger, who had initially empowered the MCP. Of course, this view is a common one for the era, reflecting the general cultural mystification that was forming a kind of aura around the computer. But by localizing the problem within the technology itself rather than implicating the corporate or cultural contexts that abetted these developments, the film could achieve a simple narrative resolution, and certainly one more in keeping with Disney's treatments of technology in its comic science fiction films of the previous decades.

With Flynn's triumph over the MCP—fittingly aided by the personification of his game creation Tron—the film emphasizes the power of the individual, along with our human ability to contain the power of the computer and to use it effectively. And like those theme park rides that critique corporate uses of technology, it is also able to humanize the corporate environment. For once Flynn liberates the information about his game designs from the MCP, he almost magically appears as ENCOM's head, the hacker rebel and counter-culture figure now its corporate leader and new identity. As he flies off in a helicopter from the roof of the ENCOM building at film's end, Flynn seems the perfect model of the new type of entrepreneur—Bill Gates, Steven Jobs—born from the new technology industries and armed with a new approach to both industry and technology. He has demonstrated that gaming—both designing and playing—is a legitimate path to wealth and success in the corporate world, that, as most young people seem to take on faith, the computer is not to be feared, and even that high-tech industry (or perhaps a high-tech business like Disney) can have a human face.

Of course, that very neat ending represents a rather difficult nego-tiation, and one that is not without some fallout for the technology that is the narrative's centerpiece. For while *Tron* ultimately supports that computer world and affirms the popular attraction to it, the film also manages, like *Metropolis*, to warn against some of the abiding charac-teristics of its technology, particularly the potential for the technology itself to determine our actions—to become "Master." And while it pro-vides a dazzling visual design for its inside-the-computer scenes, that inner world invariably seems cold and uninviting, as devoid of any real complexity or life as the simple games the film visualizes. As a result, the narrative ultimately seems less a satisfactory compromise, less an imaginative response to the broader cultural anxieties about the com-puter and the culture it was creating, than a rather stylish sidestepping of what were quickly becoming important cultural concerns. And that unsatisfying vision was mirrored at the box office. While costing slightly less than *The Black Hole, Tron* did only marginally better in receipts, hardly encouraging further efforts in this vein or heralding a successful "course correction," despite its interesting mixture of important new film technology with a narrative about our culture's latest technological concerns.[9]

As a film like *20,000 Leagues Under the Sea* demonstrated, Disney had in the past often tried to hedge its bets when dealing with narratives in the science fiction genre, trying to maintain a hold on the past even as it told stories that invariably pointed towards the future. When we add into consideration films like *The Black Hole* and *Tron,* we see how that linkage—and the negotiation to which it attests—consistently re-lied upon a number of key elements: nostalgic settings; familiar plots; established techniques, such as matte painting; and veteran technicians like Peter and Harrison Ellenshaw, who well understood the traditional Disney "look." The resulting element of compromise between past and future seems to suggest, on the one hand, an ongoing corporate desire to "play it safe," to approach the new and challenging carefully, by anchoring narratives—and thus audiences—in a comfortable and at times nostalgic context. Yet on the other hand, it also points to the underlying Disney desire to integrate into its generally familiar offerings contemporary concerns and cutting-edge technology, and to develop a strategy for successfully achieving that aim. The goal, of course, was to maximize viewers, to reach both traditional and new audiences by speaking in both conventional and quite new ways. But with *Tron*, the conventional anchor simply does not hold; there is no easy compromise with its vision of a computer-driven, computer-fascinated world. While honest and described as "brilliant," Flynn remains a rather "edgy" protagonist. And this narrative provides us with no family—even of the broken sort that so often shows up in traditional Disney narratives—to lend a sense of comfort and normalcy to the story. In this sense, it does seem a major course correction, yet one that simply did not play well either with traditional Disney audiences or with those who controlled the company's finances. John Taylor notes that a financial analyst for Montgomery Securities, "after screening the movie . . . advised his clients to sell Disney. Other analysts followed suit, and Disney's stock fell 2.5 points in one day" (24). Rather than opening up new directions for the studio, as practically every technological innovation seemed to have done during Walt's tenure, *Tron* and its heavy investment in the digital world ultimately left the company's executives wondering, much like the crew in *The Black Hole,* if indeed Disney needed this sort of correction. The retirement the next year of company CEO Card Walker and the resignation the following year of Ron Miller, partly orchestrated by Roy E. Disney as part of an ongoing power struggle, only seemed to confirm that doubt.

Still, the technical developments pioneered by these films did eventually open important doors for the studio. The development of computer-controlled camera systems and of groundbreaking—if still a bit primitive—digital effects, as the next chapter will discuss, did prove crucial for future film production, both at Disney and throughout the film industry. After finishing work on *The Black Hole,* Eustace Lycett, head of Disney's Special Photographic Effects Department, observed that the future of optical effects "will be electronic" and that the entire effects process would "be a whole new ball of wax" ("Screen Magic" 85). Of course, Disney would prove reluctant, even under the new management team of Michael Eisner and Frank Wells installed by the new majority owners, the Bass Brothers, to undertake similarly elaborate science fiction efforts for some time—*Armageddon* (1998) is probably the closest match in terms of budget, effects technology, and technologically focused narrative. However, both *The Black Hole* and *Tron* were important points of negotiation as Disney struggled with once again developing new technologies for filmmaking, with undertaking new story types that would help it reach a wide audience, and with creating the sort of production partnerships that would let it operate more effectively in a rapidly changing film industry.

8 *"Better Than Real":*
Digital Disney, Pixar,
and Beyond

I

It was taking elements from reality and making them into a
heightened reality, because I didn't want to make it photo-
realistic. I think it looks better than real.
—Ralph Eggleston (in Lawrence French, "Toy Story")

And what if reality dissolved before our very eyes? Not into
nothingness, but into the more real than real?
—Jean Baudrillard, *The Ecstasy of Communication*

In describing his approach to the "look" of *Toy Story* (1995),
art director Ralph Eggleston points to an interesting bargain that was at
work as Disney and its new partner, Pixar, set about creating the first all-
digital feature film. Traditional Disney animation had long been lauded
for its efforts at realism, for what had come to be known as the "illusion-of-life" approach, so the partnership with Pixar may have seemed
a curious move. After all, as we noted in our discussion of *Tron*, early
film efforts with CGI had some difficulty with that reality illusion since
they depended on what director John Lasseter terms "geometric primi-
tives (basic geometric shapes)" to construct their subjects, which usually

resulted in images that looked either too angular for reality or just "unnaturally clean" and plastic (French 24, 35). The resulting visual style
had been adequate and even quite appropriate for some of the first feature
film CGI efforts, which were meant to look stylized, such as the inside-
the-computer environment of *Tron* (1982) or the fantastic angular figure
of the stained-glass knight that was featured in *Young Sherlock Holmes*
(1985). But this stylized imagery hardly measured up to the polished if
rather conventional realism of late Disney animation. Progress on CGI
effects proved so rapid, though, that, as Pixar founder Ed Catmull notes,
by the time the company signed its exclusive co-production deal with
Disney in 1991, realism was beginning to pose a rather different sort of
difficulty: "The problem is, the closer you get to reality, that's when the
brain starts to kick in with its auto-recognizers, and thinks something
is a little weird" (French 20). The problem he identifies is both technological and psychological in nature, and it would necessitate developing
a complex aesthetic to address this response. First worked out in the
initial Disney/Pixar feature effort, *Toy Story* (1995), the aesthetic that
was negotiated has proven essential to the success of the new type of
animated films the now united companies have produced, and it reveals
much about the sort of bargaining with the real that the larger world of
digital filmmaking seems inevitably to implicate.

As Lasseter explains, the animation team at Pixar, thanks to the
software the company had been developing since its formation, rapidly
began to find that it "could produce settings that looked absolutely real"
(French 32), and that CGI films need not settle for the pointedly stylized
look that characterized such pioneering efforts as *Tron* and the non-
Disney film *Lawnmower Man* (1992). But simply exploiting the software's photo-realistic capabilities posed another problem, the creation
of what Andy Darley describes as an image track that is almost "too
pristine" (20), too clean and perfect for audiences to accept. Instead, and
in contrast to other digital animators, Pixar began to pull back, aiming
not to project a perfect realism but rather to create a kind of "caricature
of reality" (French 32), to, in a sense, strike a bargain with the real. Of
course, this sort of approach is hardly new, and it represents one of the
key links between traditional film history and the development of digital film. We find another version of it at the very beginnings of modern
cinematic history, as Georges Méliès made his definitive break with the
cinema of *actualities* of the Lumière brothers. Given a new ability to hold
a mirror up to the everyday world, to go the naturalistic impulse of the
late nineteenth century one better, Méliès instead moved in a different
direction. With his magic-inspired approach he developed not a cinema

that functioned as abstract art, but rather a cinema that was a vehicle for fantastic reality, something he might well have described as "better than real."

In reassessing Méliès' impact on the trajectory of the cinema, Paul Virilio argues that, in the course of his "wresting cinema *from the realism* of 'outdoor subjects' that would quickly have bored audiences, Méliès had actually made it possible for film to remain realistic" (*Aesthetics* 15). For Méliès' cinema, with its highly fantastic look, depended not on simply recording things, on observing surfaces, but on the power of the unseen—the tricks of substitution, of shifted perspective, of superimposed shots: "What he shows of reality is what reacts continually to the absences of the reality which has passed" (*Aesthetics* 17). For all of their often startling images and sudden transformations, his films ultimately relied upon the real as a measure of their magic, using it as a point of reference, gauging it through its very absence. In the process they underscored how much the real always bears traces of what is not simply surface, not even captured on film, something a bit wondrous. As Walter Benjamin, in his now classic treatment on the subject offered, one of the camera's key accomplishments, subtly appraised in Méliès' work, is the way it "introduces us to unconscious optics as does psychoanalysis to unconscious impulses" (237). Méliès' very technique thus opened onto an important thematic territory for film, something completely omitted from the cinema of trains approaching stations, workers leaving factories, and walls being demolished.[1]

Toy Story, like the subsequent Disney/Pixar films, in deploying the new digital animation technology that was already raising questions about the very nature of cinema, builds very much on this sort of bargain with the real and on its thematic implications. Armed with a rapidly developing digital technology for realistic reproduction, yet consciously trying to avoid a purely photo-realistic aesthetic—partly because of lingering limitations, such as the difficulty in reproducing skin and hair textures, but also partly because of that uncanny effect Catmull describes or what Darley broadly terms "uncertainty" (18)—they have generally demonstrated a visual compromise that has also prompted, or worked most effectively with, certain thematic emphases, as was also the case with Méliès' efforts. More specifically, these films have been marked by an emphasis on various reflexive elements that underscore the rather porous boundaries that separate the real world from the fantastic. As Eggleston further explains, he and the others involved in developing the first full-length digital film determined that, as they designed the look of *Toy Story* and its successors, they would "tread a fine line between making the settings too realistic and too cartoony" (French 33). Yet in treading that line, in fashioning a CGI world that is a caricatured yet near-realistic environment, they also managed, like Méliès, to suggest the depths of the reality we inhabit: not the sort of estranging hyperreality, the "more real than real" that Jean Baudrillard has described as part of the contemporary human condition, but a real of which we have simply lost sight, in part because seeing itself has become so constrained, so conditioned by the various vision machines that are everywhere around us and that mediate our experience of the modern world.

Even beyond those stylistic and technical considerations behind *Toy Story*'s sort of realism, though, Disney was, in committing itself to co-produce such a film, already opening the door to a variety of other necessary compromises that could easily have proved troublesome if not calamitous. The very partnership with Pixar was the most obvious difficulty in this mixture, since it involved branding with the Disney name, which was generally identified with traditional, craftsman-like animation, the work of a new cutting-edge studio working in fully computerized animation—what some might have claimed was a betrayal of the artistic legacy of Walt Disney.[2] Actually, as the previous chapter indicated, Disney had been one of the first traditional studios to recognize the benefits of the computer, as evidence the CGI work that was employed in films like *The Black Hole* (1979), *Tron*, and even the animated *The Great Mouse Detective* (1986), as well as the company's adoption in 1990 of the CAPS program, jointly developed with Pixar, to computer paint the feature *The Rescuers Down Under* and all of the studio's subsequent traditionally animated films.[3] Yet while Disney had even begun to hire animators who had been schooled in computer-aided animation, its animated product still looked quite conventional—deliberately so—and it continued to be marketed as consistent with the long and popular tradition of Disney cartooning.

Of course, thanks to the involvement of director John Lasseter, Disney was able to maintain something of a link to its past, both stylistically and thematically. For Lasseter had been trained at the Disney-founded California Institute of the Arts, had worked at Disneyland and interned at the Disney studio while still in school, and after graduation had worked for five years in the studio's feature animation department, assisting in the creation of films such as *Tron* and *Mickey's Christmas Carol* (1984). In 1984 he moved to George Lucas's special effects company, Industrial Light and Magic, to work in its computer graphics division, and when Steve Jobs purchased that division, Lasseter was offered a major creative role in the company that came to be known as Pixar Animation Studios. Lasseter was, in sum, familiar with Disney technique, thoroughly engrained in and appreciative of its story values, and very much aware of the studio's place in the whole tradition of animated cinema. At the same time, he brought to the task a reputation as one of the leading figures in the new field of computer animation, having already received an Academy Award for *Tin Toy* (1988), the short that would become the basis for *Toy Story*, and a nomination for his earlier effort, *Luxo Jr.* (1986). As a further measure of this link between past and present, we might note that when in 1997 *Wired* magazine, one of the major forums for the new digital culture, offered a run-down of the major "players" in the "new Hollywood," it singled out Lasseter. Surveying the various "people who are reinventing entertainment" through digital technology, it counted him as one of the key figures in the emerging digital cinema and, tellingly, described him as "the next Walt Disney" (Daly 212)—an appellation that seems only too apt given his new appointment as Chief Creative Officer of Disney.

Another way in which *Toy Story* would bring the past and present together was in its style. Lasseter has claimed that reading the book *Disney Animation: The Illusion of Life* by old-time Disney animators Ollie Johnston and Frank Thomas effectively set him on his career path as an animator. That book gives an inside account of Disney's traditional illusion-of-life aesthetic, the driving impulse to create not so much an animated imitation of reality, but a world that was recognizably human and that clearly worked according to the familiar laws of nature. Certainly, *Toy Story* in every instance demonstrates the influence of that aesthetic, not only with its naturalistic shadows and shading, its highly realistic outdoor imagery, and the great attention to detail throughout its mise-en-scène, but more particularly with its figures that have a consistent and demonstrable heft, that conform to and deform with perceived external pressures, that move naturally in accord with their physiologies and the laws of nature, and that both demonstrate and evoke human feeling. While the world and characters of *Toy Story* remain recognizably artificial, then, they also clearly stake out the potential for computer animation to bring traditional cartooning to a new order of realism, and in this bargain to elicit from viewers what Michele Pierson has termed a new level of "wonder."[4]

In fact, Pierson's study of contemporary special effects work provides a useful lead in helping us further measure the dimensions of the "better-than-real" aesthetic that informs *Toy Story* and its digital brethren. She describes how in Hollywood two rather different emphases have, almost from the start, informed the development of digital imagery, particularly as it has been applied to the field of special effects. The first is the industry-driven emphasis on "the creation of photorealistic imagery," a fascination with seeing how closely—and quickly—digital technology would allow filmmakers to come in creating convincing replications of the real world and its inhabitants. This emphasis has been driven by a host of Hollywood imperatives, among them, economies of scale,[5] substitution for expensive location shooting, and simply more convincing and complex special effects work. In the context of this emphasis, we might note that the RenderMan software, developed by Pixar and now an industry standard, was originally developed under the name "REYES," an acronym that denotes the sort of totalizing realism that was the ultimate aim of this tool: "*Render Everything You Ever Saw.*" As its developers explain, the program was designed to produce images "virtually indistinguishable from live action motion picture photography" and "as visually rich as real scenes" (Cook 95). Seen purely in this context, a digital cinema driven by such software simply represents the latest development in an established cinematic tradition. As Thomas Elsaesser theorizes, we should think of it as "not new in itself, but a possibly more efficient and maybe in the long run cheaper way of continuing the longstanding practice of illusionism in the cinema" (204).

The second emphasis Pierson notes, though, complicates this focus on "illusionism." It is a concern with "audiences' perception of this imagery," a phrase that suggests more than simple observation or viewer immersion, and that partly speaks to the uncanny effect Ed Catmull and others have recognized, and also to how that imagery functions within the narrative context. This concern with perception reflects a long-standing fascination with and even "desire for a cinema of astonishment" (48–49), one that, on a fundamental level, still mines the sort of appeal found in Méliès' early films. Too perfect an imitation of the real, Pierson believes, tends to make that "astonishment" disappear, as we see dramatized in the plot of a film like *Simone* (2002). Examining the fallout from a perfect CGI illusionism, it describes how movie audiences and critics alike simply and readily accept the computer-generated title character as a real person and accomplished actress. With such digital possibilities in sight, Pierson argues that any discussion of the film industry's rhetoric about an aesthetic of realism, with its seeming fixation on what can be done through CGI technology, needs to be balanced against a certain level of practice, against what *should* be done. Particularly, she emphasizes an appreciation of the importance of "reception"—a reception that is conditioned by a tradition within special effects and fantasy cinema of an "experience of wonder" that audiences of such films not only expect but actually find enjoyment in (52), as the loyal following for the stop-motion effects films of Ray Harryhausen suggests. In fact, Pierson argues that this sense of "wonder" has been essential to the appeal of the big-budget, effects-driven films of recent years, works such as *The Matrix*, *Pearl Harbor, The Day After Tomorrow*, and especially the *Lord of the Rings* trilogy.

One of the many reasons the Disney/Pixar films have been so successful is because they have managed to balance off the real and the wondrous, primarily through an approach implicit in that rhetoric of the "better than real." It is a method that, as the comments above suggest, is most immediately apparent in the films' visual style, which the comments of the animators and filmmakers seem almost invariably to address. For example, it is obvious that *Toy Story's* creators approached their subject in a rather conventional way; in giving life to their toy subjects, they were guided by a traditional realistic imperative. That is, the toys' bodies and actions always function plausibly, are consistent with what is physically possible; thus a character like Buzz Lightyear, despite his own belief to the contrary, cannot fly, although he is certainly capable, as the film's conclusion demonstrates, of "falling with style." The *Toy Story* characters, consequently, never suggest the sort of plastic/elastic figures and hyperkinetic motions that characterize the animation in a film like *Who Framed Roger Rabbit* (1988) or that are an essential element and certainly a major part of the appeal of the Warner Bros. Tex Avery and Chuck Jones cartoon tradition.

In addition, the film's imagery seems to insist, in keeping with the Disney tradition of naturalism and illusionism, that we see its world as an extension of our own. Thus, its visual look readily suggests a familiar human environment, with its colors, in most scenes, muted rather than oversaturated, lighting and shading consistent with natural light sources, and all of its images insisting on their three dimensionality instead of the two of traditional animation. In fact, built into the RenderMan software are various effects designed to reinforce this reality illusion, such as "motion blur," which produces smooth character movements, a "dirt" program to make things look appropriately used or worn, and a capacity to simulate lens flare whenever the virtually created "camera" turns towards the sun or other depicted light source. As layout artist Craig Good notes, even the virtual camera's "movement" in *Toy Story* was designed to imitate "what you would see in a live-action film," and to avoid the sort of "fantastic gyrations" that are always a temptation for those who simulate camera movement in the computer—movement that certainly *could* work in ways that would be impossible on any live-action set (Street 84) and that we find used to good and ill effect in such digitally dependent films as *Spiderman* (2002), *The League of Extraordinary Gentlemen* (2003), *Van Helsing* (2004), and *The Fantastic Four* (2005). As a result of these effects, *Toy Story* (and even more so, its sequel, *Toy Story 2* [1999]) does at times bring us up short in its resemblance to live action and as it repeatedly nods in the direction of a photo-realist aesthetic; but even its bringing us up short functions to good effect.

And yet, we can also recognize instances when the film's creators sought to check that naturalistic impression by exaggerating or "pushing" elements of *Toy Story*'s world beyond the parameters of the real. As Eggleston points out, even as they worked within those broadly realistic guidelines, the filmmakers also carefully designed "the doorknobs bigger, the baseboards higher, and the doorways narrower" than normal, "taking elements from reality and making them into a heightened reality" (French 33), much as a traditional filmmaker might use forced perspectives or special lenses to create particular atmospheric or thematic effects. Certainly, the characters—both humans and toys—all have eyes that are much larger than normal. In certain instances the size and scale of objects clearly become fluid, such as when on Sid's porch the light fixture can by turns fit through a hole or sit securely atop the same hole, as if it were resting on its edges. Sound effects were designed by following a principle of making them "bigger" than ordinary sounds. To create the barking of Sid's dog, for example, the filmmakers combined "dog sounds with tiger sounds to make it bigger and more impressive," effectively "caricaturing" a dog (Street 83). And for scenes in Sid's room the animators created a pointedly stylized look by employing a wide-angle lens effect that warped straight lines in order to help build, as Eggleston says, "a creepy feeling" (French 33). While staged within what we might generally describe as a believable digital environment, these effects also repeatedly qualify how we perceive that environment, presenting us with a world that, by virtue of being both like and unlike our own, helps produce just the sort of "wonder" that Pierson describes.

That experience of wonder, as well as the negotiation with the real that is behind its production, however, extends beyond the purely stylistic realm to the level of narrative development in *Toy Story*. Andy Darley has observed in other digital animation a similar strategy, what he describes as a pattern of "self-referentiality and surface play" that also characterizes much of "visual postmodernism" (16). While the Pixar films might not initially suggest the postmodern, they do, as in Méliès' case, demonstrate a level on which story design and thematics seem to draw out the implications of that stylistic bargain that is at the base of the films, particularly the potential for revealing the rather fluid boundaries between the real world and the fantastic, and in the process suggesting a world that is, after a fashion, "better than real," at least as the real is commonly conceived. It is an effect that another Disney/Pixar film like *Monsters Inc.* (2002) deftly inserts at the heart of its narrative with its central imagery of doors that, like wormholes in reality, connect to all parts of the human world, or that we find in *The Incredibles* (2004) with its vision of a world of hidden, even domesticated superheroes, of "incredible" potential secreted away in the heart of suburbia. To develop a similar potential, *Toy Story* opens its own sort of "holes" by consistently foregrounding narrative, especially cinematic narrative, as a practice that constructs a world from—and affirms a link between—real and fantastic elements, and with that combination effectively influences our lives. The result of this connection between the film's special stylistics and thematic self-consciousness is one of the peculiar pleasures of *Toy Story*—and of many of the best CGI films to date—as we find ourselves able to be caught up in a sense of its constructed wonder, in fact, to see its wonder as possibly shading over into our own world, opening onto it and revealing its "wondrous" nature as well.

The most obvious way in which *Toy Story* evokes this reflexive potential is by reminding us, at practically every narrative turn, of the world of the movies, and more specifically of the world of fantasy films. The books in Andy's room, for example, bear the titles of several Pixar films, and the "star" figure of the first Pixar movie to gain major recognition, the lamp from *Luxo Jr.*, sits prominently on Andy's desk. Rex the Dinosaur speaks several lines taken from the character George McFly in *Back to the Future* (1985). When Buzz is knocked out of Andy's window and falls into a seeming jungle of grass outside, the theme from *Raiders of the Lost Ark* plays on the soundtrack. Sid's lines as he begins to torture Woody evoke several films in this same adventure vein, although most specifically *Star Wars*. When Woody comes to life in Sid's hands, he uses the famous 180–degree turn of the head from *The Exorcist* (1973) in order to scare Sid. And as Woody and Buzz try to catch up to Andy's family in the final scene, we hear "Hakuna Matata" from Disney's *The Lion King* (1994) playing on the car radio. These and various other reflexive notes struck throughout the film remind us that we do inhabit a world that, as Virilio argues, has become "cinematized," and that we are constantly moving through and participating in what seems like "an entirely cinematic vision of the world" (*War* 66)—a vision that, the film implies, has the potential of opening up a wondrous dimension in our lives.

Even beyond these many instances of what Darley would term "surface play," though, *Toy Story* demonstrates a remarkable and telling pattern of narrative self-consciousness. The opening quickly establishes this trajectory, as it confronts us with the construction of an imaginary world, a kind of analogue for the creation of the film's digital world. Filling the frame are obviously stylized and systematically arrayed clouds set against a bright blue background—too blue to be real, too evenly spaced, and certainly not the sort of "natural" imagery we might expect in a film that was demonstrating state-of-the-art CGI. The images, in fact, call attention to the *artificial* nature of this world, an artifice further underscored by the exaggerated voice-over that we hear, as the boy Andy adopts different voices in acting out a melodramatic encounter between a variety of mismatched toys with which, we soon realize, he is playing. As the virtual camera tracks back, we recognize, especially as we see a contrasting view through an open window of "real" clouds and a truly blue sky, that the initial skyscape was just the wallpaper in Andy's room, a fake setting for his naïvely constructed play narrative, and only marginally more real seeming than the cardboard "buildings" that he has constructed and even labeled for his toy characters.

In beginning on this reflexive note, this almost literal "surface play," the film immediately foregrounds its nature as narrative and addresses us with a rhetoric of artifice. Of course, while we quickly recognize the nature of this construct, take some pleasure in watching the boy's private imagination at work, and acknowledge the pleasure involved in the play itself, these elements also lead us in, direct us to read the "real"—the world of Andy's room—in contrast, as a level beyond that which the narrative has encoded as constructed and a product of the imagination. And while clearly not a photo-realistic representation, as we have noted above, the world *of* Andy's room and that *in which* it is situated hardly resembles the exaggerated, cartoonish realm (with its crudely lettered signs, unscaled characters, and childish wallpaper backdrop) of his play. In the course of juxtaposing these different realms, the film has managed to catch us up in its own narrative reality, in a kind of in-between world, a world of wonder, yet one that also lays some claim on our everyday reality experience. It is a place where narratives easily develop, where the imagination can happily play, in fact, where it can play out a useful moral story about the rescue of the innocent, of Bo Peep and her sheep, and the triumph of good over evil—a story that forecasts the larger trajectory of the film wherein rather similar events occur. And yet it is a place that, we have been assured, exists within *our* walls, our own humanly constructed world.

If Andy's abandoning of his play narrative and rushing off at his mother's call seems to simplify things—returning to a level of normalcy wherein toys are simply toys, distractions from the real, and the realm of the imagination is easily distinguished from the normal world—the unexpected reactions of the toys quickly recoup that sense of wonder by molding another compromise between real and fantastic worlds. For while Andy's toys come to life as soon as the boy leaves the room, when "the coast is clear," as the cowboy figure Woody calls out, their surprising "lives," the film quickly establishes, follow a carefully worked out and mundane scenario, another level of narrative in which they assume an unexpected level of control and function not as if they are simply toys, but normal beings with specific jobs and functions, governed by strict laws, and from which they emerge, on cue, to play their assigned roles as toys. As John Lasseter explains, "We decided that the toys approach their relationships with their child as a job" (Street 83), one in which their very purpose is to serve as the raw material for the fantasy worlds he creates. Thus, while Woody calls a "staff meeting" of all the other toys, we see a number of them "rehearsing" their basic functions: Mr. Potato Head is trying out new facial configurations, including one that he terms "Picasso"; Rex the Dinosaur is practicing his scare tactics; and Etch-a-Sketch, as Woody observes, has been "working on that draw." At the subsequent meeting, Woody has a clear working agenda, one in which he goes over the toys' timetable for the upcoming move of Andy and his family, recalls the recent seminar they held on "Plastic Corrosion Awareness," and announces a change in the schedule for Andy's birthday party. For those worried about being replaced by any new toys received at the party, he reminds them about the nature of their "job": "We're here for Andy when he needs us." Precisely because they are so fantastically *alive*, the toys are, we see, very much like us, their lives like ours, even as they practice for their roles in the construction of a child's fantasies. In fact, their link to reality, their job, is precisely to assist in the creation of wonder by playing their appropriate or assigned parts.

Of course, with this emphasis on the toys acting and reacting just as humans would, while also playing roles in humanly created scenarios, *Toy Story* is simply further developing a long tradition in Disney animation. We need only recall such works as *Midnight in a Toy Shop* (Silly Symphonies, 1930), *Broken Toys* (Silly Symphonies, 1935), and to some extent *Pinocchio* (1940). In the first two of these, toys, once humans are not around, reveal their secret lives—lives that do not simply mimic human actions, but, wondrously, demonstrate an inner life as well, as they seem driven by the same complex psychic causality that moves people; and when people are present, they willingly return to their roles as props for the human imagination. In *Toy Story* that human-seeming depth is mated to a visual three dimensionality unlike that found in any traditional animation, and that combination all the more impels us to match this world against our own, and to interrogate our own normal sense of—and sensitivity to—reality, in fact, to consider how our own narratives help us deal with the reality of *our* experience.

With the introduction of Buzz Lightyear that interrogation takes on another dimension, as he represents a toy that, while similarly alive, has apparently not yet reached the same level of self-consciousness as the others. He is, in effect, a figure stuck within the sort of fantastic realm depicted in the film's opening, his "life" completely scripted for him—literally written out on his box, as Woody notes—much like the naïve narrative in which Andy has awkwardly placed all of his toys at the film's opening. Admittedly, that lack of perspective, that inability to see his place within the real, is one key to Buzz's appeal; he is naïvely comfortable within his scripted narrative in a way that we would all like to feel comfortable in our life roles. And yet this also becomes one of the central problems that the film has to work out. He has to become aware of and learn to accept his place in the world, the bargain between the real and the fantastic that his life represents: as the other toys have had to do, as Woody must in the face of new challenges, and even as we too must do as life's realities become ever clearer to us.

These problems are most pointedly addressed in the sequence introducing Andy's neighbor Sid's house, the first scene of which pointedly parallels the film's opening. For it too illustrates how a child constructs a narrative for his toys, as we see Sid bring Buzz and Woody to his room and begin to cast them within his own sort of stories. Set up as a parallel to Andy's room—similarly on the second floor of his house, its window exactly opposite Andy's, its floor littered with his toys—Sid's room is, as we have noted, visually stylized to create a darker, more ominous atmosphere. As Lasseter explains, the filmmakers sought to treat it "in terms of contrasts. . . . In Andy's room, it's fairly clean, the lighting is warm and cozy, and the toys are well taken care of. In Sid's room it's dirty, dark and cluttered, and . . . the mutant toys look horrific" (French 27). That atmosphere, though, also casts into relief Sid's own type of "play," the kinds of narratives he fashions (and, we might suppose, given the posters on his walls, the kinds of narratives that have helped fashion him): a violent and even cruel activity that does not manage any sort of productive compromise between the real and the fantastic, and certainly does not imbue his toys with imaginative life, but rather treats them as elements within a cruel joke, fit only for mutilation or destruction, as if reality itself were just a nightmare.

In fact, as the film further develops its reflexive dimension, it also presents Sid as a darker version of Andy, as we see him creating his own narratives for his toys. However, they are narratives that, unlike Andy's, have very stark consequences for those involved. Seizing his sister Hannah's doll, he puts on a deeper, menacing voice, that of a "doctor," as he announces that she's "sick" and in need of "an operation," "a double-bypass brain transplant." After donning a mask as if he were a surgeon, Sid then places the doll, described as his "patient," in a vise, forcibly removes its head, inserts the head of a toy pterodactyl, and returns the mutilated, now horrific toy with the satisfied assertion that it is "all better now." Buzz's observation, "I don't believe that man's ever been to medical school," comically understates the situation, while also dissipating some of the disturbing fallout of his actions, including Sid's own obvious impression that what he has done is in some way quite funny. However, it also points up the power of narrative to assert its own reality—a power reinforced by the images that, rather naturalistically, decorate the room, among them: a roadside "DANGER" sign with bullet holes in it, a poster for a film entitled *Web of Terror*, a skull and crossbones, another toy's head suspended in a lava lamp, and the remains of a toy melted into a waffle iron.

Sid's horrific scenarios also have an easily measured effect, as we watch Woody and Buzz's subsequent reaction to the room and its toy denizens. For Woody and Buzz immediately view the other toys as reflections of this world and extensions of Sid's persona, as mutant monsters created by this "mad doctor" and equally intent on doing them harm. Surrounded by the various mutant toys of Sid's creation—among them a baby's head on a spidery, erector-set base, a jack-in-the-box with a disembodied hand, and a jet pilot's torso grafted onto a skateboard—Woody hides behind Buzz, urges him to use his laser and karate-chop action, and announces that "We're gonna die!" Caught up in this fake reality, of course, he forgets that these are all toys, like him, forced into horrifying roles, fully scripted by their owner, not "cannibals," as he fears. Yet it is an understandable response, springing from a confusion that recalls our own ambiguous view of Andy's room at the start of the film, for here there is no clear demarcation between the real and the fake, no cardboard "buildings" or crudely lettered signs to remind them that this is a world of play. And indeed, with Sid's brand of play, there is ultimately little distinction, as we see when, after slipping into another narrative wherein he casts Woody as a spy, Sid announces that "we have ways of making you talk" and begins torturing the toy, using a magnifying glass to burn a hole in the doll's forehead. Instead of a world that is "better than real," Sid (his name perhaps hinting of his sadistic nature) has deployed his imagination to create a nightmarish realm, one in which there are ter-rifying consequences for his toys, as is clearly demonstrated by his new narrative, one in which he plans to have Buzz "blast off" into "orbit" while strapped to a skyrocket that will eventually explode and destroy him.

Appropriately, the counter and solution to these sadistic narratives that victimize the toys proves to be another narrative, this one gener-ated by the toys themselves. For to escape from Sid and return to their proper place as Andy's toys, Woody and Buzz must concoct their own story—one that drives home the consequences of Sid's horrific tastes. Returning to their "professional" attitude, Woody and Buzz recruit Sid's monstrous creations, assign each a specific task (their jobs, after the fashion of Andy's toys), and even script them into a most fitting narra-tive, a cinematic one recalling the horror film poster seen on Sid's wall. Their inspiration is a subgenre of the horror film especially popular in this era, wherein "playthings" suddenly come to life and become vio-lent, as we see in films like *Child's Play* (1988) and its sequels, *Puppet Master* (1989) and its sequels, *Demonic Toys* (1991), and even *Pinocchio's Revenge* (1996). These films provide Woody with his plot; the resulting narrative draws on the genre's various conventions—figures arising as if from their graves (in a child's sandbox), reaction shots underscoring Sid's terror, low-angle shots to make the toys look larger and more powerful, quick cutting to each mutant toy's sudden appearance; and specific im-ages evoking the world of horror cinema, such as Woody's imitating the head-turning scene from *The Exorcist,* as he warns Sid that "We toys can see everything . . . so *play nice!*" Of course, creating this rather effective cinematic context, this most obviously reflexive moment, pointedly blurs the borders between the real and the fantastic, the world of humans and that of toys. As Woody explains to the other toys, though, "We're going to have to break a few rules, but if it works, it'll help everybody." And that *helping* effect is precisely the point, here and in the film as a whole. It is the payoff bound up in that otherwise disconcerting blurring of boundaries, and ultimately the return for that sense of wonder this film evokes through both its stylistic and reflexive negotiations.

The film concludes, we might note, at a more traditional point of wonder, as Andy's family celebrates Christmas in their new home. Pres-ents are being opened, new possibilities appearing, and the toys have settled back into their routines—carrying on with their own concerns (Bo Peep conspiring with her sheep to get a kiss from Woody), scouting out the new toys Andy and his sister are receiving, and once more worrying about whether or not they will be replaced. Narratively, it brings us back to the start of the film, to a new potential for play and for wonder, and to a new round of negotiations with the real world, the world of humans, that is the lot of the toys. It thereby reminds us that such negotiations are a kind of constant. Of course, they are child's play, but also toys' work, and, as we might add in the context of this discussion, even the occupation of digital animators whose task is to try to draw a sense of wonder out of the "more real than real."

II

Disney's move into digital technology has clearly had an impact far beyond the realm of its traditional animation projects and has increasingly affected the studio's efforts in live-action fantasy. As background on this impact, we might consider Thomas Elsaesser's comments on how the new digital cinema has inspired an ongoing debate about the "status of the moving image," largely because of its potential for undermining "deeply-held beliefs about representation and visualization." More specifically, he notes how it challenges our traditional investment in the representational nature of photographic and cinematic images by calling into question their seemingly natural or indexical character. Elsaesser suggests that, as a result, the digital has come to function partly "as a 'cultural metaphor' of crisis and transition" (202), and partly as a site of our ongoing "mourning for the real," a testament to that supposed disappearance of the real that Baudrillard has trumpeted, as the "more real than real" displaces our ordinary experience of reality (*Simulations* 46). In fact, Lev Manovich's observation in 1991 that "film itself" is increasingly "being undermined by three-dimensional computer animation" (13) no longer seems a cry of alarm, but more a description of an ongoing event, of the passing of film, and perhaps of our cultural investment in the cinematic as it has been conventionally conceived.

While notions of "crisis and transition" might seem a bit out of place in a discussion of digital Disney, we have already noted a marked change in the Disney animation enterprise—one we can only expect to become more profound with the full acquisition of Pixar and the placement of its key figures, such as Lasseter and Catmull, in prominent and powerful positions in the company. Moreover, we have described how a work like *Toy Story*, as well as the many other successful films produced by the Disney/Pixar partnership, does raise questions about the real and even about the nature of film, thus helping us to see some of the shadows cast by the new digital regime. However, the Pixar films so easily and comfortingly remind us of the essential pleasures of the cinematic experience, of the wonder that, from their inception, the movies have evoked, that mourning hardly seems an appropriate attitude. For even as the digital images of films like *Toy Story* participate in this inevitable interrogation of the real, their aesthetic negotiates a comfortable position for us, particularly by finding some common ground with the past and especially with Disney's "illusion-of-life" tradition. And *Toy Story*'s thematics, especially its consistent pattern of "self-referentiality and surface play," only further that effect by, on the one hand, foregrounding the film's constructed world and, on the other, by reminding us of how firmly that construct is rooted in our own world, thereby opening doors into a wondrous spirit they share. In this respect, we might describe *Toy Story* as intent on what philosopher Owen Barfield once termed "saving the appearances,"[6] letting us hold on to that visual faith a bit longer by working its compromise between photo-realism and fantastic effects. Yet it is a "saving" that also relies on an ability to let us see beyond those "appearances," reassuring audiences by offering them something that might seem a bit better than the real, at least as the postmodern world, with its emphasis on surfaces and its promise of fashioning the "more real than real," usually construes the real.

These concerns about the construction of the real and the effect of that construction on viewers are implicit, then, even in what many would see as a simple children's film about children's toys, a plaything about playthings, for the very technology of *Toy Story* tends to raise big and even necessary questions for film and for the whole trajectory of visual media. And we can see how those questions surface even more obviously in several non-Disney films that seem almost like experiments with the collapsing boundaries between animated and live-action cinema, films like *Final Fantasy* (2001) and *Sky Captain and the World of Tomorrow* (2004). The former film, based on a series of video games, is, like its source material, completely the product of digital animation, but also an ambitious effort at rendering both the digital world and its characters in photo-realistic fashion, and asking viewers to accept them, to buy into their reality, in just the way we might with the actors and narrative of a conventional live-action film. In the latter film, virtually everything that we see *apart from* the central characters—sets, props, backgrounds—has been digitally created, so that the film can offer us an intriguing combination of the real and the fantastic—a combination that, while not quite compelling, does suggest an impulse to negotiate the audience's relationship to this hybrid world. For better or for worse, the effect in both films is a decidedly different, even challenging experience, one nicely described by Roger Ebert in his review of *Sky Captain*, wherein he discusses how the digital vision of such films "removes the layers of impossibility between the inspiration and the artist" (Ebert).

Against this background I want to briefly consider one of Disney's most successful recent efforts, in this case a live-action film that also makes great capital from CGI effects, *Pirates of the Caribbean: The Curse of the Black Pearl* (2003). It is a film that faced a difficult conceptual task, as it tried to strike a balance between the historical period in which its action is set and the vaguely historical theme park ride of the same title, a central attraction at all of the Disney parks that provided director Gore Verbinski with the skeleton of his narrative and audiences with a core of expectations for the film. Certainly, like many more traditional films in this vein, such as *The Black Pirate* (1926), *The Sea Hawk* (1940), *The Buccaneer* (1958), and even the more recent *Master and Commander: The Far Side of the World* (2003), it could have relied on elaborate sets and historically authentic detailing to build a story squarely within the genre's conventions. The theme park ride, however, generated another set of expectations, particularly that it would recreate some portion of the ride *experience*, that it would, as Pierson suggests, also give special attention to the "audience's perception" of its fantasy world. This concern meant that the film would have to manage a fusion of the ride's historical, supernatural, and even comic elements, while also providing viewers with some sense of their own, nearly visceral participation in its fantastic world. That sort of fusion necessitated a series of compromises— once again, both stylistic and thematic—that would lend the narrative its own sense of wonder.

Early in the film, a young Elizabeth Swann catches a fleeting glimpse of the fabled pirate ship, *The Black Pearl*, just before it disappears in a swirling fog bank. At least she *thinks* she has seen it, as do we, since her view is coded as a subjective shot. However, we also understand that this momentary sighting could just be her imagination at work, cobbling together the tales of "cursed pirates [that] sail these waters," told to her by the mate Mr. Gibbs, her own fascination with the subject of pirates, something she finds both "exciting" and "fascinating," and an encounter with the wreckage of a merchant ship that *might* have been destroyed by pirates. In any case, a reaction shot of her face is followed by the apparent disappearance of the ship, and then an extreme close-up of her eyes as she shuts them tight, as if she herself could not quite believe what she has seen, followed by a match cut to her eyes opening, many years later, as she awakes in her room, now a grown woman. A most effective transition, that match cut across the years brings together childish imaginings and adult realities, while also establishing the agenda for the rest of the film, as it must accommodate both perspectives, that of the child who inhabits a world of "exciting," fantastic possibilities and that of the adult who lives within a strictly limited, reality-circumscribed world—in short, the vantages of the typical theme park riders.

And the film as a whole seems thoroughly informed by what we might term a "ride aesthetic," as it draws into its narrative a variety of effects that typify both the original *Pirates* ride and a host of others that have followed on its model. The characters are broadly drawn and invariably visually characterized, almost caricatured, as in the case of the pirate with the wooden eye. The narrative is marked by a succession of visual surprises, all of which, though, are mediated by a through line, in fact, several through lines: Captain Jack Sparrow's quest for his ship, Will Turner's romantic pursuit of Elizabeth, Captain Barbossa's efforts to lift the curse on himself and his fellow pirates, and even that provided by the *Pirates* theme song, which recurs both on the soundtrack and, diegetically, within the narrative (it is sung three times). Like the ride, the film has a kind of compromise tone, repeatedly shifting between the scary and the comic, thereby accommodating its great variety of visual surprises—a skeletal hand suddenly reaching into a pool of moonlight or a fork sticking in a pirate's wooden eye. It is, as well, a narrative that never stands still. In fact, the entire story seems to be *about* motion, and not just because of the various pursuits it details, but also because of its emphasis on escaping from the constraints—or, as Elizabeth styles it, the corset—of culture. And finally, like all good rides, it offers no real closure, only the promise of other adventures that might come, an invitation to take the ride one more time, the certainty of a cinematic sequel, such as 2006's *Pirates of the Caribbean: Dead Man's Chest* and 2007's *Pirates of the Caribbean: At World's End*.

This aesthetic, though, is effectively accommodated thematically here, thanks to both the possibilities of a digital cinema and the very context the film establishes, one that invites a kind of tension or compromise: the historical conflict between British colonial rule with its fixation on order and those pirates who ranged throughout the Caribbean and are precisely defined by their defiance of all order. This situation provides the motivations for its central characters, such as Governor Swann and Commodore Norrington, who desire order and precision above all else, and Captain Barbossa and his pirates, who are bound by no laws, not even the laws of nature, thanks to the curse they are under for stealing Aztec gold; as Barbossa simply puts it, "We are not among the living." And it also establishes the plight of the film's central characters, who cannot be contained within either of these extremes: Captain Jack, the pirate who is an outcast of the other pirates; Will, the apprentice blacksmith who is also the son of a pirate; and Elizabeth, the governor's daughter who refuses to "act like a lady"—or wear a corset—despite her protective father's efforts to prescribe her future, her behavior, and even the clothes she wears. Together, these three characters have to stake out a place for themselves that is both inside and outside of the law, a fluid sense of identity (pointedly expressed in Jack Sparrow's campy costuming) that permits the audience that identifies with them to feel, as if they were actually on the theme park ride that inspired the film, both adventurous and safe at the same time.

While *Pirates of the Caribbean*'s digital effects are a bit less simply schematic than its narrative, they seem aimed at generating the same sort of "wondrous" effects noted in *Toy Story*. While Elizabeth refuses to be intimidated by stories of the pirates' curse and informs Barbossa that "I hardly believe in ghost stories anymore," he suggestively responds that "You'd best start believing in ghost stories, Miss Turner. You're in one," and explains that "the moonlight shows us for what we really are," as he reaches towards her and suddenly reveals a skeletal arm. Reeling from that frightening revelation, she flees to the deck of the ship, where, in full moonlight, she then sees the rest of the pirates under the aegis of the curse—as skeletons, as fantastic figures who, like the toys in *Toy Story*, still go about their mundane tasks of scrubbing the deck, trimming the sails, and fixing the rigging. That vision is a triumph of CGI effects, suggesting—as the virtual regime of the digital always implicitly does—that there are multiple sorts of reality here, while also creating the nightmarish sense that she is *within* a ghost story, caught in a kind of ultimate thrill ride, as she is then tossed and passed about by these ghoulish figures.

The effect as Barbossa reaches towards her, though, bears some special consideration, in part because it is an effect that recurs several times in the film, but also because it so neatly illustrates that power of the digital, particularly how it can evoke those "deeply held beliefs about . . . visualization," as Elsaesser terms them, for narrative effect. For in one apparently seamless motion, a real hand and arm move across real space, becoming in the process something quite other, a skeletal image that seems a simple continuation of the real image, the arm of Barbossa and of the actor Geoffrey Rush who plays him. Not only in the transformation, but in the simultaneous presence of the real and the fantastic, with each a seemingly natural and convincing extension of the other, we see the capacity of the digital, both to convince and to question, to fashion a reality illusion and to beg the question of the real and, by extension, of the cinema. In that dual movement—or rather, in the sort of compromise effect that these movements together implicate—it affords its own kind of pleasure.

Like Méliès' wondrous play with his own new toy in the 1890s, like his many amazing *toy stories*, as we might term them, the digital work in *Pirates of the Caribbean,* as in a number of other recent films, does not so much serve to "dissolve" the real or render it all "simulation," as Baudrillard might suggest. Rather, it takes us on its own sort of ride, inviting us to see its world in the light that Virilio, in his own analysis of the impact of the digital, describes as "not simulation, but substitution," such that we increasingly find ourselves confronting other realities, virtual ones that seemingly stand alongside the "actual" (L. Wilson, "Cyberwar") and threaten to crowd it out. Through its own "surface play," a film like *Pirates* lets us momentarily enjoy the experience of something "better than real," the experience of "wonder" that we have at certain points found in the toys of childhood, perhaps even in the best amusement park rides, but also in that constantly evolving technological toy that is the cinema.

As Disney further pushes these combinatory efforts in films like *Sky High* (2005) and the two sequels to *Pirates of the Caribbean,* we see the studio once again committing itself to the possibilities of a new technology, perhaps, given the digital's potential for transforming film, even the ultimate cinematic technology. But if our digital technology, as Michele Pierson nicely puts it, "endows the cinematographic image with a distinctly electronic elasticity" (87), thereby opening up film's fantasy potential, it also challenges filmmakers to negotiate the best uses of that "elasticity." For Disney those uses would not simply involve the creation of more science fiction narratives like *Tron* or efforts that would visualize a synthetic, photo-realistic realm like *Final Fantasy,* but works that, in the best Disney—and fantasy—tradition, strike a bargain between this potential and a more conventional sense of the real or the representational. But for Disney, it seems, that has always been the essential opportunity of technology: not a point of "crisis" but one of compromise and possibility, and in that respect the company has negotiated a situation that could produce something that its audiences might well find "better than real."

Conclusion

> Our business has grown with and by technical
> achievements. Should this technical progress ever come
> to a full stop, prepare the funeral oration for our medium.
> That is how dependent we artists have become on the
> new tools and refinements which the technicians give us.
> Sound, Technicolor, the multiplane camera, Fantasound,
> these and a host of other less spectacular contributions
> . . . have made possible the pictures which are the
> milestones in our progress.
>
> —Walt Disney, "Growing Pains"

As early as 1938, in an address to the Society of Motion Picture
Engineers, Walt Disney initiated the discourse that informs this study.
In his talk "Growing Pains," he emphasized that, in his mind, numerous
technical accomplishments were every bit as important, as much "milestones" in his studio's development, as were the films by which both the
industry and the public had primarily come to measure its achievements.
That emphasis suggests that any effort to formulate a history of the studio
or simply to better understand the larger achievement of the Walt Disney
Company should take into account the sort of complementary trajec-
tories Walt described in order to see how the studio's embrace of technological development has, over the years, influenced the way it makes
its films, the sort of films it produces, the significance that attaches to
those works, and even the manner in which it "sells" its products to a
constantly expanding audience. This connection, as my introduction
suggested, tells us much about Walt's own enthusiastic attitude towards
the technological, but ultimately more about the company's continued
expansion of its technological thrust under subsequent regimes, while it

also points us towards a better understanding of why the Disney product has found such broad appeal.

Certainly, just incorporating technology or routinely pursuing its latest forms hardly guarantees the sort of success Disney has found over the years, as the very history of film attests. For while developments like two-strip Technicolor, Vitaphone's sound-on-disk system, early wide-screen processes like Polyvision and Grandeur,[1] and the 3D craze of the 1950s found brief acceptance or short-term popularity, they ultimately proved to be little more than minor footnotes to film history, generally exploratory technological steps that were soon forgotten, rather than the great leaps forward they were often trumpeted as. What Disney's efforts throughout its history—and particularly Walt's emphasis on *constant* development—point up is the importance of that difficult process of ne-gotiation underlying that technological partnership. It is a process that in some cases simply involves a bartering with time, as audiences gradu-ally come to accept or find meaningful certain technical changes or even particular types of narrative, such as science fiction. But also implicated, as this study has repeatedly illustrated, are two particular dimensions necessarily involved in such negotiation: with aspects of the technology that makes the studio's work possible and with the audience at which that work is aimed.

We might think of these different concerns as contributing an im-portant dynamic to Disney's history, as the company has continually tried to balance these two sorts of negotiation. Obviously, Disney has had to develop and learn how to work with the technology itself, using it to most effectively support and develop the studio's film, television, and park projects; and in some cases it has had to determine how to avoid or negate technology's less desirable consequences. Thus Disney developed the practice of "mickey mousing" music and sound effects to assist—and even to carry—its early sound narratives, and when it adopted Technicolor it had to determine which colors to avoid, because they registered poorly or unnaturally, and which ones to emphasize. Yet this sort of negotiation invariably implicated another, that is, Disney's effort at addressing an audience for whom technology is never simply a neutral device or empty experience. Technology has to be made to fit into our world, to seem a natural part of it rather than a challenge or intrusion. In some instances a rhetoric had to be developed for talking about the technology and what it could offer, as we see in Disney's treat-ments of space technology in its television shows of the 1950s, or in the way Pixar carefully drew out an aesthetic for digital animation in the 1990s. And in some instances, Disney has had to bargain between the demands of both terms, balancing off the promise of technology against the real or perceived attitudes of its audience—and here we might recall the studio's abandoning of its Fantasound system, its shift from educational to broadly comic visions of science and technology in the 1950s and 1960s, or the more recent "taming" of some of its most popular and technology-intensive theme park rides.[2] In either case, I would suggest, we are seeing the working of a historically determined policy, a kind of industrial *politique de rapprochement* that has characterized Disney's efforts.

We should also recognize another dynamic component to this situation, and one that, because of its complexity, has intentionally remained a bit vaguely articulated here. It is the very nature of what I have simply labeled "negotiation," a term that clearly has multiple—yet ultimately related—implications. Certainly, at no point have I tried to suggest that one might simply strike a bargain with a piece of technology. Rather, I have most often used negotiation allusively, to refer to a kind of trade-off or set of compromises, such as those we see at almost every turn in Disney's history. They might have been largely financial in nature, such as when Walt cashed in his life insurance to help finance the building of Disneyland, or they might have involved fundamental narrative change, such as the shifting emphasis from pantomime to aural information that the adoption of sound necessitated. But I have also tried to suggest a set of strategies or a process of maneuvering employed by Disney to bring about a desired end. Roy Disney's bargain with ABC to create a new television series in exchange for park financing is the obvious example, although Roy's successful behind-the-scenes financial dealings throughout the company's history could provide many others, as could those of his son Roy E. Disney and his financial advisor Stanley Gold, as they worked to keep the company intact in the face of financial raiders in the early 1980s,[3] or more recently as they mounted a campaign to bring about a regime change at Disney, resulting in the deposing of Michael Eisner and the installation of Bob Iger to lead the company. In the close discussion of various Disney texts in each of the chapters, though, we have seen another dimension to this process of maneuvering. Scott Bukatman has observed how our technological texts often take as one of their tasks the development of a "narrative process of technological accommodation" (28). That observation suggests how the various Disney narratives, including those "texts" represented by the theme park rides and attractions, frequently tell us stories about the technology they depict and/or employ. Bearing a weight of encouragement or persuasion, they prime audiences to buy into the technology that is involved, and often not in the subtle ways usually associated with ideological work, but in the sort of blatant manner that Byrne and McQuillan have identified. This kind of negotiation is an ongoing process and a sign of the company's inherent understanding that its success follows not, as some have suggested, simply from the various ways in which it reifies the cultural status quo or exploits what Howard Segal terms a "technological plateau" (33), but from its ability to adapt to changing audience concerns or interests—as the introduction suggested, like a magic mirror that provides viewers the sort of reflections they desire. Disney's technological prowess and foresight have simply allowed it constantly, and often easily, to manage that kind of accommodation.

In addition to this convenient but rather necessary vagueness, this study has adopted other limitations as well, as I have tried to emphasize the variety of technological developments that have had the greatest impact on Disney's evolution, without simply surveying all of the ways in which the company has, throughout its history, pursued a technological agenda. In part I have taken a lead from Walt's own early litany of such influences—"Sound, Technicolor, the multiplane camera, Fantasound"—but I have also focused on other developments that seem equally important as steps in Disney's gradual transformation from a small, Poverty Row animation studio to a major motion picture company and eventually to its current position as one of the world's foremost entertainment and communication conglomerates. The movement into television, the progress in live-action CGI, and the turn to 3D digital animation are all obviously crucial to this development. Additionally, this book has emphasized Disney's growing interest in certain *types* of narrative, such as the science fiction film or the sort of technologically focused text that the company's theme park attractions have increasingly featured, since the discourse about technology bound up in such narratives invariably reveals much about the company's attitudes towards the technological. It is a link neatly formulated by Garrett Stewart as he observes how inherently self-conscious the science fiction genre consistently is, specifically how "science fiction in the cinema often turns out to be . . . the fictional or fictive science of the cinema itself" (159). Disney, it seems, well understands that insight.

Yet in taking this larger view, in trying to remain focused on the studio's growth and metamorphosis, I have obviously had to omit or give only brief mention to several other noteworthy technological developments. While for most of its history Disney was a relatively small studio, it has significantly contributed to the technological development of the film industry and received Academy Awards for several such developments. Among them we might note the multiplane camera (1938), the creation of a key noise-reduction device (1947), and Ub Iwerks's optical printer for special effects work (1960). One particularly ambitious effort in this direction that never found widespread application was Disney's invention of Circle-Vision, a technology suggested by Walt as a new approach to live-action filmmaking—and indeed to the basic film experience. This technology was conceived in the mid-1950s as an "attempt to out-do the popular wide-screen formats" of the era, such as CinemaScope and Cinerama, by fashioning a 360–degree image that is projected in the round (Imagineers 128). A nine-camera device (originally eleven), with all of them aimed at a central mirror to produce a consistent focal point, Circle-Vision was never widely adopted in part because of the way it overwhelms the audience with its surrounding visual information, and at least in its earliest version, as Circarama, with some amount of cyestrain as well. However, it has found its way into a variety of attractions throughout the theme parks, offering a paean to America in Disneyland's Circle-Vision Theater with the film *America the Beautiful*, providing a unique travelogue experience for visitors to the Canadian and Chinese pavilions at Epcot through the *O Canada* and *Wonders of China* documentaries, and supporting the Magic Kingdom's now defunct "Timekeeper" and Disneyland Paris's "Le Visionarium" attractions. While Circle-Vision proved no more successful than the highly publicized Cinerama at altering the way we experience film, Disney has found a significant niche for it as a kind of cinematic ride, precisely by recognizing that part of its difficulty—that of audience reactions to the multiple and constantly changing perspectives it emphasizes—could be turned to capital because of the way they mimic the typical ride experience.

In this same context we should also briefly consider Disney's move into cable television, beginning with the launch of The Disney Channel in 1983 to serve as an outlet for the company's extensive archive of older material and to advertise Disney's other offerings. While initially offered as a premium channel, requiring a special subscription, the Disney Channel quickly drew enough viewer interest and demand to warrant switching it to regular service in most cable systems, as Disney came to recognize that its initial approach to cable—as a subscription cognate to broadcast television that would direct its video product to a special audience—might have been shortsighted, and that it might better use cable to build audiences, to sell advertising, and generally to push the Disney brand, much as Walt had originally done when the company entered into television in the 1950s. Consequently, that early success has been followed by efforts that reflect this realization, by the creation of new channels, such as Toon Disney, and, following Disney's purchase of the Capital Cities/ABC group in 1995, the company's acquisition of or partnership in a host of established cable outlets. Disney's cable holdings now include ESPN and its various offshoots, the ABC Family Channel (acquired from Fox News Corp.), and SOAPnet, while its equity interests include Lifetime Television and Lifetime Movie Network (in partnership with the Hearst Corp.); the A&E Network, which includes the History Channel, A&E, and the Biography Channel (in partnership with Hearst and NBC); E! Entertainment Channel (in partnership with Comcast and Liberty Media); and other cable sites. These diverse outlets have not only created opportunities for program development in areas new for Disney, but have also allowed the company to target a wider array of audience segments.[4] In fact, Disney has, very simply, become a major worldwide presence in cable and satellite broadcasting, reaching into more than seventy countries, entering television viewers' homes through various platforms, and, synergistically, building an ever wider discourse about Disney products.

Finally, we need to acknowledge Disney's increasingly important and fast developing online presence, wherein we can see the company constantly trying to balance off informational needs and marketing possibilities. Directing this presence is the Walt Disney Internet Group (formerly organized as GO.com), which oversees the company's large portfolio of news and entertainment Web sites, including Disney Online, ESPN.com, ABC.com, ABCNEWS.com, and Movies.com, while it also coordinates and controls all of Disney's online business operations. A recent survey has listed this group as one of the top twenty-five Internet companies, with its multiple venues helping Disney rank among the top five most-trafficked businesses on the Web.[5] As we should expect, the company supports Web sites for all of its movie releases—sites that are created to be not only informational but also entertainment experiences in themselves, providing viewers with online games, quizzes, film clips, and free downloads, while also directing them to local theaters showing the newest Disney films. And Disney continues to expand its Web marketing efforts, providing sites for, among others, Disney Travel, Disney Vacation Club, Disney Cruise Line, Disney Stores, the Disney Institute, all of the theme parks, and even Disney Auctions, where the company gives visitors a chance to own a piece of the mouse by bidding on film, theme park, and even hotel artifacts. Like the company's other technology initiatives, its Web presence has proven to be an ambitious move, marked by an effort at balancing the need to provide information *about* Disney and its many products with a desire for selling, in a new way and on demand, all that is Disney, in fact, by a recognition that providing information about Disney is an essential part of the selling of Disney. While neither these Web activities nor the cable and other technological efforts seem crucial to understanding the company's growth and development, all of these elements further sketch the larger Disney technological picture, underscore its fundamental technological commitment, and illustrate its simultaneous negotiations with both the latest entertainment and informational technology and its ever expanding worldwide audience.

There remains one other sort of technological negotiation that has, in recent times, become crucial to the success of the Disney enterprise and that also bears mention. For as it has expanded into other areas, the company has also recognized the benefit in partnering with other studios and technology companies—ones that can provide it with content, talent, or even technical support in exchange for Disney's marketing power and the prestige of its branding. Two of the most important such partnerships are those with Pixar and Miramax, small independent film producers that in some ways recall Disney in its early days, and that have opened up new possibilities for the studio in the areas of animation and live-action films. As the previous chapter noted, the relationship with Pixar has resulted in a string of highly profitable and critically praised releases under the Disney banner, including the groundbreaking *Toy Story* (1995), Pixar's first feature effort, the Academy Award-winning *The Incredibles* (2004), and the last film under the original Disney-Pixar agreement, *Cars* (2006). While this partnership has launched Pixar as a major force in the world of animation, it has also enabled Disney to move beyond its foundations in traditional animation through the joint development of digital projects, the acquisition of key Pixar-developed software for CGI work, and the cultivation of talent and experience for Disney's own digital animation program, the first result of which was the film *Chicken Little* (2005) and the second, the ambitious 3D release, *Meet the Robinsons* (2007). But the ultimate measure of the importance of this partnership was most dramatically demonstrated with Disney's recent purchase of Pixar for a reported $7.4 billion, in the process establishing a partnership with Apple Computer founder Steve Jobs—a partnership that has also flowered in Disney's recent deal to provide video content for Apple iPod downloads. Miramax, already one of the most successful independent studios, opened rather different doors for Disney with its line of more adult, often violent, live-action projects, that is, with film types not traditionally associated with the company's family brand. But the partnership has arguably added to the prestige of both studios, thanks to such major and award-winning releases as *Chicago* (2002), *Cold Mountain* (2003), and *Cinderella Man* (2005). By assisting in the production and distribution of such films—through its Buena Vista distribution arm—Disney has been able to reach out to a more mature audience segment. And in both instances these affiliations have allowed Disney to retain much of its core identity while also diversifying the product it offers to moviegoers, and even developing—at relatively small risk—new licensable figures and products, such as Buzz Lightyear and the various other Pixar characters, for additional gain and as further inspirations for theme park rides.

In a different vein, Disney has, over the years, invited relationships with a broad range of companies, such as Monsanto, TWA, Exxon, Federal Express, General Motors, and Hewlett-Packard, not only to obtain sponsorship for various theme park rides, but also to gain needed technical support for both the company's core activities and its latest initiatives, including its expansion into digital filmmaking and the Internet. Hewlett-Packard, in particular, has a long relationship with Disney, dating back to the studio's purchase in 1937 of the electronics company's first product, a customized version of its Model 200B audio oscillator, which was used in sound recording on *Fantasia*. In 2003, HP announced that it was joining in "a broad corporate alliance" with Disney (Tharp), at the base of which was Disney's adoption of a wide range of HP equipment, including approximately seventy thousand personal computers, fourteen thousand printers, and more than ten thousand workstations and servers—numbers that have only grown recently.[6] HP has also redesigned Disney's worldwide e-mail system, provided the Help Desk for the company's internet group, and developed a wireless headset to automatically provide non-English speaking guests at the Disney parks with translations of dialogue and story material as they enter various attractions (Tharp). Most recently, the company has sponsored and helped design one of Epcot's most elaborate and successful attractions, "Mission: SPACE."

But just as significant as these material contributions is HP's support for Disney's increasing emphasis on CGI in both animated and live-action films. One of the great limitations to digital filmmaking at present is the rendering process itself, that is, the addition of fine detail and realistic effects into each animated frame. In an effort at addressing what has become the most costly and time-consuming part of the production process and an industry bottleneck, HP has created a 1,000–server Rendering Farm, time on which it makes available to Disney (as it has also done to one of Disney's major animation competitors, Dreamworks). That ability to tap into massive amounts of utility computing power, practically on demand, has allowed the studio to speed up and make more cost efficient this increasingly important element of the filmmaking process (Firth). However, this corporate alliance is hardly a one-sided relationship. For while HP has provided Disney with access to technology that allows the studio, as Joan Tharp offers, "to create more and better magic," HP has in turn gained access to Disney products for future projects, learned "about making consumer products that are simple and fun to use," and tried to push a new corporate image, as what a spokesman rather ambitiously terms "a cool and exciting company" (Tharp).

Of course, in all of these situations the bargains that have been struck have also carried some dangers, trade-offs whose value is yet to be determined. While the partnership with Miramax, for example, has allowed Disney to target a rather nontraditional audience and even to garner some awards that have typically seemed off-limits to family films—*Chicago* received six Academy Awards, including that for Best Picture—the move into pointedly adult territory carries some risk of tarnishing the family brand. If the Pixar relationship helped strengthen Disney's reputation as the industry leader in animation, it has also prodded the studio to de-emphasize if not totally abandon its traditional 2D animation program, so that what was once the studio's core strength had become one of its weaker divisions. Consequently, in order to avoid having Pixar walk away from the Disney alliance—and from the generally unfavorable terms Disney had imposed in its initial agreement with the company—Disney has had to purchase its partner for $7.4 billion in one of the largest deals in media history. And while HP's technology today helps make Disney run, there is always the fear that such powerful companies might exercise undue control over Disney. In this context, we might note that, in recognition of its partner relation, an HP representative now sits on the Walt Disney World Technology Architecture Council (Tharp), helping to determine how that group employs the latest technological advances in computing.

Yet as we have seen, Disney has historically proven most adept at striking successful bargains—with other companies, with changing audiences, and with the demands of the technology itself. Certainly, one of the keys to its success over the years resides in that very ability, or rather, in what we might describe as a dynamic capacity for creating trade-offs and developing effective strategies of accommodation, in a mediatory policy that is part of the company's character and, I would suggest, a possible reason for those seemingly "unstable ideological codes" (Byrne and McQuillan 5) found throughout its offerings. By examining this sort of dual ability, this study should help us not only to better understand the Disney model of media success, but also to see beyond the horizon of the media giant that Disney has become. For Disney is just one of several media conglomerates—like Time–Warner Bros. and the newly configured GE (now majority owner of NBC Universal, Universal Theme Parks, and a variety of cable channels)—that have come to dominate the international media landscape through their ownership not only of film studios, but also of print publication companies, television networks, cable and satellite companies, distribution organizations, record companies, software houses, and so on, and in the process have both spurred various sorts of technological development and helped shape our attitudes towards that development. Examining that Disney negotiation with technology as a pattern for many others in the entertainment industry can thus provide the perspective we need to understand how entertainment and technology have arrived at the sort of partnership that typifies today's media environment and, indeed, much of contemporary life.

But that perspective requires that we foreground two most telling impulses that characterize the Disney-technology relationship. On the one hand, the company models, in both the film and entertainment industries and, more broadly, in modern culture, the sort of relentless pursuit of technology that has so fundamentally marked life in the twentieth and early twenty-first centuries.[7] For Disney has obviously helped push forward film's boundaries by advancing the techniques that together constitute this technological art, while it has also branched out into other areas of what we might simply term technological entertainment, taking us further down the path towards André Bazin's oft-cited "myth of total cinema" (22). And on the other hand, it has repeatedly struck a note of prudence, of not simply accepting but finding an *accommodation* with technology as part of what, Postman reminds us, is our culture's "inescapable" task. Thus it has also helped audiences negotiate a technological world by providing them with examples, in some cases with a rhetoric, and in its theme parks with a most appealing venue for working through their often uncomfortable relationships with an increasingly technological world.

One of the aims of this study is to help us see Disney in the context of both of these impulses. In fact, I want to suggest that Disney's trajectory roughly traces the technological necessity of contemporary times, of our own cultural desire for technology measured with a note of hesitancy, as we recognize the need to strike deals with it, partly as a condition for helping us understand what it means to be human in this age. Perhaps this closing claim seems a bit ambitious, rather outsized for a company still symbolized by an animated mouse and, as I have suggested, largely dedicated to offering us the reflections—personal and cultural—that we most want to see. But Disney has grown to become one of the world's largest and most influential entertainment companies, and that stature, along with the body of texts Disney has produced, merits large claims, at least more than just the suspicion of its motives that many commentators almost reflexively voice. When seen in this light, the mouse machine appears to speak both loudly and even usefully about and to the sort of technological mindedness that is a fundamental part of contemporary life. While obviously a powerful part of that larger "vision machine" Paul Virilio has described, Disney, I believe, can also help us to understand the nature of that machine and perhaps to better work out our own relationship to it.

NOTES

Introduction

1. The "utilidors" quite literally underlie the surface of the Magic Kingdom in Walt Disney World, as well as several walkways in Epcot and other Disney parks, for the surface is actually fourteen feet above the ground on which the park was constructed. These miles of corridors that snake beneath Main Street—and many of the other streets throughout the theme park—allow for resupply, waste removal, cast-member movement, air conditioning and heating, and storage, and they contain the various machines and computer systems that make all that is above work, as if by magic.

2. In *The Vision Machine*, Virilio describes in detail how the Futurists early on heralded the advent of this new technologically inflected culture, which was forming particularly under Mussolini. As he offers, "They had come a little too close to the bone in exposing the conjunction between communication technologies and the totalitarianism that was then taking shape before 'newly anointed eyes'" (*Vision* 12).

3. As examples of texts that discuss the agency effects of technology itself, I would recommend Virilio's *War and Cinema*, Neil Postman's *Technopoly*, and Edward Tenner's *Why Things Bite Back*, among many others.

4. Reading this attraction from a Marxist vantage, Alexander Wilson finds that "it is hard to tell what this is supposed to be about," and can only suggest that it constitutes one more Disney effort to obscure the real social conditions of Western capitalist existence (120). That reaction seems a bit disingenuous, for "Spaceship Earth" is pointedly situated so that, much like the Main Streets in other Disney parks, practically every visitor passes through it, not because it is a vague mishmash of ideas, but precisely because it does so effectively convey the central theme of communication, one that in various ways ties together the rest of Epcot, and especially the many countries represented by the national pavilions that comprise the park's World Showcase. A 2006 Disney company publication, *The Imagineering Field Guide to Epcot at Walt Disney World*, offers a behind-the-scenes guide to the park's workings and notes that one of "the core philosophies" of Epcot is communication; in this context, Spaceship Earth "makes sense as an iconic attraction . . . because communications are the basis for everything else that comes after—it's how we retain and pass along knowledge, it's how we work together to further that knowledge, and it's how we share the benefits of this knowledge going forward" (Imagineers 34).

5. See Dyer's essay "Entertainment and Utopia" and Segal's *Future Imperfect* 1–2. That utopian promise, Segal argues, all too easily slips away because of the

always "indeterminate relationship between technological progress and social progress" (2).

6. It is worth noting one of the instances in which Disney did, quite pointedly, foreground such "revenge effects," in part because it recognized that there was both educational and entertainment elements that might be derived from doing so. The *Disneyland* television episode "Our Friend the Atom," broadcast January 23, 1957, incorporates footage of *20,000 Leagues Under the Sea*'s apocalyptic conclusion and pointedly identifies the images as nuclear in nature. It thus foregrounds that very problem of control over technology and the powers it might unleash—a theme that surfaces increasingly in later Disney texts.

7. The special "Keys to the Kingdom" tour of Walt Disney World's Magic Kingdom carefully spells out the Main Street "progress" theme and points up the various "signs" of that progress that have been built into the Main Street structures.

8. This concern with a "global culturalism" and Disney's possible role in fostering it forms the key focus of Wasko, Phillips, and Meehan's collection, *Dazzled by Disney?: The Global Disney Audiences Project*. For an introduction to this issue, see especially Wasko's contribution, "Is It a Small World, After All?" 3–28.

9. The introduction to each episode of the original *Disneyland* television series explained that the program offered stories drawn from these four lands, and then indicated which of the lands was the source for that particular episode's show. For background on the series, see my volume, *Disney TV*.

10. For a detailed examination of some of the similarities between Disney and Warner Bros., especially in terms of their approach to the new technology of television in the 1950s, see Christopher Anderson's *Hollywood TV*.

Chapter 1: Sound Fantasy

1. Merritt and Kaufman note how much the first Mickey Mouse cartoons "resorted to familiar territory," describing how in *Gallopin' Gaucho*, for example, "Mickey's visit to the cantina, his meeting with Minnie, her abduction by Pete, and Mickey's attempts to pursue them on his drunken ostrich were all borrowed from the 1927 cartoon *Harem Scarem*, in which Oswald had faced the same situation in the Arabian desert (with a camel instead of an ostrich)" (121).

2. As Leonard Maltin explains this process, Walt Disney, along with his top animators, Ub Iwerks and Wilfred Jackson, "calculated that if film ran at ninety feet a minute (twenty-four frames a second), they could animate their silent cartoon to a musical beat by planning it out in advance. Their simple tunes could be played at two beats a second, so markings were made on the film every twelve frames, both as a guide to the animator, and, later, as an indicator for the orchestra, which would synchronize the music track" (4).

3. Among the many accounts that detail Powers's unsavory reputation in the film industry, we might note Watts (30), Thomas (*Building* 61–66), and Schickel (99).

4. Maltin, *The Disney Films* 367. The actual origin of the Silly Symphony series is the subject of some historical debate. Richard Schickel largely avoids the question by emphasizing Walt Disney's desire for further differentiating his product from other cartoons of the era, all of which focused on individual "stars," and

his desire to address "the technical challenge that complex music presented to the animator" (103). Both Thomas and Watts indicate that it was Stalling who "suggested a different kind of cartoon" (Thomas, *Walt* 99). And Maltin allows that, while Stalling himself claims to have initiated the idea, one of Disney's early animators, Wilfred Jackson, has described how Walt Disney originated the concept as a kind of negotiation of an internal debate at the studio, as part of "an effort to soft-pedal Stalling's desire to have music take precedence over action in the Mickey Mouse cartoons" (4).

5. The final official Silly Symphony cartoon would be released in the following year, 1939, but that film, *The Ugly Duckling*, seems almost an afterthought, since it was a remake of a 1931 Silly Symphony of the same title.

6. Among these issues were the looming war, union rules that obstructed installation of the equipment, and the limited size of the projection booth area in many theaters.

7. For the 1990 rerelease of *Fantasia*, Disney returned to its pioneering surround-sound technology, dubbing it "Fantasound '90." This update of the original technology began with a restored and remixed soundtrack, which was then put through Dolby encoders and placed in a six-channel magnetic soundtrack. For a description of this effort to resurrect and update the original sound system, see Klapholz's "*Fantasia:* Innovations in Sound."

Chapter 2: Minor Hazards

1. A similar theoretical argument against the adoption of color was offered in 1933 by Rudolf Arnheim. He suggested that black and white fostered a more artistic development of the cinema, since "when the film artist has to depend on black and white," he is compelled to create, from the imagination, "particularly vivid and impressive effects"—effects that would not arise if the film simply reproduced the colors of the natural world (*Film as Art* 65).

2. Michael Barrier, in his history of the animated cartoon, notes that there is some disagreement about how much *Flowers and Trees* was affected by the decision to rework it as a Technicolor production. While Bob Thomas indicates that the film was "half completed" when the decision to redo it in color was made (*Walt* 115), Barrier claims that the cartoon "had already been shot" in black and white, and he cites Disney cameraman William Cottrell's description of how the filmmakers "took all the [black-and-white] cels and carefully washed all the reverse side" to remove the white and gray paint, and then "repainted them in color on the back" (80).

3. Disney archivist Dave Smith indicates that separate contracts with Technicolor covered the studio's first color films, and that the exclusive contract for use of the process only began on September 1, 1933, and ran through August 31, 1935. See Barrier, 585n.

4. In his biography of Roy Disney, *Building a Company*, Bob Thomas indicates that it was at Roy's insistence that the Technicolor process would initially only be used for the Silly Symphony cartoons and not for the Mickey Mouse series. Since the Mickey cartoons were already a proven success, he felt that they did not need the sort of costly "boost" that Technicolor offered (81).

5. For background on color design in *Becky Sharp*, see Scott Higgins's essay,

"Demonstrating Three-Strip Technicolor: *Becky Sharp.*" One of the problems in that film, he suggests, resulted directly from the effort at using it to "show-case" color, as color was given "too high a priority in the hierarchy of film style" (157).

6. Bill Cotter, in his in-house history of Disney television, emphasizes the influence of RCA on the Disney move. He describes NBC's embrace of the new partnership as an effort to "help parent company RCA sell more color televisions" and notes that when ads began appearing, announcing that Disney programming would soon be available in color, television sales "began to increase even before the show began to air" (67).

Chapter 3: Three-Dimensional Animation and the Illusion of Life

1. The key touchstone for the discussion of early cinema is certainly Tom Gunning's classic essay in which he describes the film product from the time of Edison to approximately 1920 as a "cinema of attractions."

2. The study of the institutional practices of classical Hollywood cinema by David Bordwell, Janet Staiger, and Kristin Thompson, *The Classical Hollywood Cinema*, offers another vantage on these various histories.

3. Rotoscoping, as developed by Max Fleischer, involved the photographing of live action and then tracing over that filmed movement frame by frame. It produced a highly naturalistic image, although one that lacked the sense of imagination that attached to free-hand animation, and it resulted in little real economies of time or effort over traditional animation. See Maltin's discussion of Fleischer's rotoscope device in *Of Mice and Magic*, 80–81.

4. In *Hollywood Flatlands*, Esther Leslie chronicles the shifting critical response to Disney's work, emphasizing in particular the links between Disney's perceived realism and the political implications of the cartoon. While early on embraced by a leftist avant-garde and endorsed by such figures as Sergei Eisenstein and Walter Benjamin, the move towards an illusion-of-life aesthetic, coupled with a movement away from the spirited nature of the animal (the mouse) and towards a precise imitation of the human, resulted in rejection. As Leslie sums up, there was simply "too much of man in a medium that belongs to the 'subhuman'" (250).

5. Walt Disney's comments were first offered on an early episode of the *Disneyland* television series, "The Story of the Silly Symphonies," which aired October 19, 1955. They are also included as additional material on the DVD release of *The Silly Symphonies*.

6. Disney would later work another variation on this approach with its documentary *Nature's Half Acre* (1951). This Academy Award-winning film also used a variety of new technologies, including the telephoto lens and time-lapse photography, to provide viewers with a newly intimate view of the natural world just outside their doors.

7. This film not only drew on the original South American tour arranged by the Office of Inter-American Affairs, but also involved three later trips to Mexico by various animators and members of the Disney staff. For background on the trips,

see especially J. B. Kaufman's "Norm Ferguson and the Latin American Films of Walt Disney."

8. Dali's work with Disney has recently been resurrected, as Walt's nephew, Roy Disney, has restored and completed the short, *Destino,* on which Dali had worked while at the studio. After its release in 2003, the short was nominated for an Academy Award.

9. For full background on the Alice comedies as well as a descriptive filmography, see Russell Merritt and J. B. Kaufman's *Walt in Wonderland.*

10. As Merritt and Kaufman note, human action often seemed slow in comparison to the animated figures in the early Alice films. To compensate, the Disneys "instructed their cameramen to undercrank" the live action scenes, so that once combined with the animated characters, the live figures would seem to move faster (66).

11. For examples of this technique, see *Alice the Peacemaker* (1924), *Alice's Wild West Show* (1924), and *Alice Cans the Cannibals* (1925). Also see the discussion of this technique in Merritt and Kaufman, 65–66.

12. For background on this three-part process, I have relied on the contemporaneous account, "How Disney Combines Living Actors with His Cartoon Characters."

13. See page ix in his *Art and Flair of Mary Blair.* As Canemaker further notes, Blair felt that this rather abstract sequence "was the only time her own artwork and style appeared uncompromised in animation on the screen" (18). Given the stark contrast it creates with the live-action elements of the film, Blair's imagery seems a curious highlight here.

14. In her study of Hollywood female images, Julie Burchill describes Carmen Miranda's typical persona as "hysterically happy and mindless," nearly "a parody of condescending and cretinous US relations with Latin America" (94). What she omits from this description, though, is the carefully contrived and caricatured sexual appeal of Miranda's character, an appeal that consistently relegated her to comically ineffectual roles. This also ensured that she would never be seen as sexually dangerous to the male protagonists in her films, and instead would serve as a kind of empty signifier of sexual allure, a status most clearly imaged in her number "The Lady in the Tutti-Frutti Hat" in *The Gang's All Here* (1943).

15. For detailed commentary on the shooting of *The Three Caballeros,* see Kaufman's interview with Jack Kinney in "Norm Ferguson and the Latin American Films of Walt Disney," especially 267.

Chapter 4: A Monstrous Vision

1. Sontag, in her famous assessment of science fiction cinema of the 1950s and 1960s, suggests that it embodies "the deepest anxieties about contemporary existence," anxieties not only about "physical disaster, the prospect of universal mutilation and even annihilation," but also "about the condition of the individual psyche" faced with such new and global menaces (223).

2. Disney's *20,000 Leagues Under the Sea* was certainly one of the most ambitious films the studio had ever undertaken, as well as its most costly, requiring Roy Disney to request additional investments from the studio's bankers. However, it was an investment of money and resources that, like many other Disney

gambles, paid off. See Christopher Anderson's discussion of the film's success in *Hollywood TV*, 148–49, and Bob Thomas's description of the production's problems in *Walt Disney*, 235–38.

3. See Fleisher's "Underwater Filmmaking" essay, originally published in *Films in Review*. It is a focus that Disney also emphasized in its production of a documentary about the making of *20,000 Leagues Under the Sea*, which became an early episode of the new *Disneyland* television series, airing on December 8, 1954. This show, entitled "Operation Undersea," would, in fact, win the studio Emmy Awards for Best Individual Program of the Year and for Best Television Film Editing. See Cotter, 144.

4. We might note the more restrained version of Professor Aronnax's (the name is spelled differently in the novel) newspaper interview found in Verne's novel. Lacking the sensationalistic sketch, the article is one in which, as Aronnax recounts, he "discussed the question [of a monster] in all its aspects, political and scientific" (10). In fact, the novel quotes almost the entirety of the interview, so that readers gain a sense of the very measured and scientific message he offers to the newspaper readers and that the newspaper accurately reports.

5. Released on December 23, 1954, *20,000 Leagues Under the Sea* earned the bulk of its receipts during 1955. Its $8 million in box office during that year made it Disney's most successful film to date. See Cobbett Steinberg's listing of box office receipts for 1955 in *Reel Facts*.

6. Certainly the most famous of these efforts is the Disney short, *Our Friend the Atom* (1957), released theatrically in Europe and presented as part of the *Disneyland* television series in the United States. As its title suggests, this film sought to educate the public about the peaceful uses of the atom at a time when the specter of atomic warfare loomed large in the public consciousness.

7. Indeed, given the titles of other of Verne's "Voyages Extraordinaires," such as *Master of the World* and *Robur the Conqueror*, we might well argue that his work is in dialogue with this sort of postulated crisis of subjectivity, and that Walt Disney, in his efforts to fashion his own lands and worlds (Disneyland, Walt Disney World) was a natural descendant of Verne in this regard.

8. As an example, we might note the following passage from the novel, as it describes the *Nautilus* in "open waters," with no discernible point of reference. Undaunted by the lack of any visual orientation, Professor Aronnax explains that the ship "headed straight for the Pole, without deviating from the 52nd meridian. From 67° 30′ to 90°, we still had 22½° of latitude to go, about five hundred leagues, or more than a thousand miles" (Verne 349).

9. For background on Disney's financial situation in this period and on the making of *Swiss Family Robinson*, see Bob Thomas's *Walt Disney*, 295–96, and Steven Watts's *Magic Kingdom*, 300–302.

Chapter 5: Disney in Television Land

1. For accounts of these early Disney television efforts, see Anderson's *Hollywood TV*, 134–35, Cotter's *Wonderful World of Disney Television*, 3–4, and the introduction in my own *Disney TV*.

2. We should note that Walt Disney had, in 1950, already hired the research firm of C. J. LaRoche to study his studio's television prospects. For further background

on Disney's early efforts in television, see Anderson's *Hollywood TV*, 135–41, and my own *Disney TV*.

3. The anthology format must also have seemed to represent less of a risk than a more theme-specific show. As Cotter notes, "anthologies had done well so far" in the early history of television, ranking among the top series from 1949 through 1951 (59).

4. Among the many efforts at detailing and explaining the Crockett phenomenon of the mid-1950s, we might especially note Paul Andrew Hutton's "Davy Crockett: An Exposition on Hero Worship," William Eric Jamborsky's "Davy Crockett and the Tradition of the Westerner in American Cinema," Margaret J. King's "The Recycled Hero: Walt Disney's Davy Crockett," and Charles K. Wolfe's "Davy Crockett Songs: From Minstrels to Disney."

5. This list of licensed merchandise is, of course, only partial. For further commentary on the merchandising of the Crockett phenomenon and further listings of products, see Thomas's *Walt Disney*, 256–58, and Watts's *Magic Kingdom*, 314–21.

6. As another example of that synergistic linkage that was becoming a Disney signature, we might note that both Fess Parker and Buddy Ebsen were prominently featured in the opening of the Disneyland theme park, as well as the television special promoting it. To mark the park's grand opening on July 17, 1955, the studio produced a ninety-minute live program, "Dateline: Disneyland," which prominently featured the stars of the Crockett series. As that show depicts, Parker, Ebsen, and Walt Disney led the parade that opened Disneyland, and to inaugurate Frontierland, it featured Parker and Ebsen doing a musical number and leading guests on an early attraction, a mule ride.

7. The term "technoscience," as originally popularized by the sociologist Bruno Latour, is central to contemporary science studies. Aylish Wood, in his study of technoscience in contemporary film, explains that the term "encapsulates the processes through which any range of influences works on the practices of science and technology, and is not a shorthand collapse of the words science and technology" (3).

8. Virilio offers another formulation of this principle in his *Art of the Motor:* "Today it would be no exaggeration to say that, 'Whenever a people can be mediatized, they are!'" (6).

9. The articles ran in the *Collier's* issues of March 22, 1952, March 14, 1953, June 27, 1953, and April 30, 1954, with von Braun's contributions appearing in each of the issues. For further discussion of these pieces, see Randy Liebermann's "The *Collier's* and Disney Series."

10. "True-Life Adventures" was the series title for a group of thirteen nature documentaries that appeared between 1948 and 1960. Among them were the Academy Award–winning *Seal Island* (1948), *Bear Country* (1953), and *The Living Desert* (1953). For all of their efforts at providing audiences with a factual record of the natural world, these films too have been seen as unnecessarily mixing fact with distorting narrative touches for purposes of entertainment. See Maltin's discussion in *The Disney Films*, 18–20.

11. In his biography of von Braun, Dennis Piszkiewicz describes how the limitations on contemporary knowledge helped shape the narrative trajectory of the "Man and the Moon" episode (88–89).

12. In his history of Disney television, Bill Cotter describes how the deteriorated footage of the unpaved Lincoln Highway was obtained from the University of Michigan, carefully restored by Disney technicians, and then returned to the Michigan archives for the use of future researchers (131–32).

13. We might here recall President Kennedy's injunction to the nation that committed the country to the sort of space exploration project envisioned by von Braun and the *Man in Space* series. While President Eisenhower had in 1960 deferred approval of a moon landing project due to its projected cost, Kennedy, shortly after taking office, announced in a speech to a joint session of Congress that "This nation should commit itself to achieving the goal, before this decade is out, of landing a man on the moon and returning him safely to the earth. I believe we should go to the moon" (quoted in Logsdon, 152).

14. In addition to the Emmy Awards noted earlier, we should note that when the first episode of the *Man in Space* series was released theatrically, it received an Academy Award nomination for best documentary short.

Chapter 6: The "Inhabitable Text" of the Parks

1. For a discussion of the amusement zone of the 1939–40 New York World's Fair, see my chapter on the fair in *A Distant Technology*, 162–82.

2. Long before coming to work with Disney, Ebsen had been a headliner in vaudeville, doing a dance act with his sister, and, as a supporting player, had done featured dance numbers in a variety of MGM musicals during the 1930s, most notably *Broadway Melody of 1936* (1935), *Born to Dance* (1936), and *Broadway Melody of 1938* (1937).

3. The original mechanical prototype of this "dancing man" device still exists and has been, for several years, on display at the Disney-MGM theme park as part of a walk-through attraction, "One Man's Dream," a tribute to the life of Walt Disney.

4. See Steven Watts's account of the creation of the Audio-Animatronic Lincoln in his *Magic Kingdom*, 417–18. He describes this creation as "the most sophisticated expression of this technology yet developed."

5. In her *Shifting Gears*, Tichi describes how certain "machine-based values" (37) came to dominate American cultural life in the twentieth century. Her focus is primarily on Machine Age America, that period in the first half of the twentieth century when the machine was establishing its preeminent place in everyday life. Her observations are significant for our discussion, though, because they reflect on the period when Walt Disney was establishing his career, and on an era that is pointedly evoked throughout the Disney theme parks.

6. That sense of popularity is drawn from the invariably long lines that await anyone who wants to experience "Dinosaur." Bob Sehlinger, in his *Unofficial Guide to Walt Disney World, 2005*, rates this ride as a "super-headliner attraction" (564).

7. Of course, the link between the chairman of X-S and the flesh-eating alien seems quite intentional, given the initial presentation in which he apologizes for making so much profit from his company's technology and in which we see the animal Skippy—cute in the usual Disney tradition—practically "cooked" by the teleportation process.

8. We might note that the film *Raiders of the Lost Ark* inspired a television special, *Great Movie Stunts: Raiders of the Lost Ark* (1981), that involved several of the key figures from the film: Steven Spielberg, Harrison Ford, and Karen Allen. In another twist on the fake/real nexus that Umberto Eco describes, the Disney ride seems to have drawn as much on this show *about* the movie as on the movie itself for its own inspiration and model.

9. Disney's nearby competitor, Universal Studios–Orlando, has created its own stunt attraction, also ostensibly based on a film, "The Wild, Wild West Stunt Show." It is, very simply, a western-themed demonstration of traditional stunt skills—doing falls, throwing and taking a punch, using breakaway props, and so on. Apart from several references to Universal Studios, though, this show essentially omits the movies from its discourse.

10. The new "Lights, Motors, Action! Extreme Stunt Show" amplifies this effect by incorporating in its massive stadium a giant video screen on which are projected the various scenes we watch being staged and shot. No longer simply faking the movie-making, as does "Indiana Jones," this show uses the latest digital technology to shoot and instantaneously project the images of its own action, providing audiences with the sort of mastery—a liberation from the flow of time—always implicit in the "instant replay."

11. Dery, in his discussion of that preeminent amusement park, Coney Island, offers a valuable metaphor for its workings that speaks as well to the Disney project. Coney Island's combination of "escapist simulation and social reality" (39), he suggests, created a kind of "permeable membrane between fact and fiction, actual and virtual" (30) that has become a hallmark of modern technological culture. The major Disney attractions, it seems, traffic precisely in this sort of "membrane" effect and have developed it to a new level of sophistication, particularly in the Epcot attractions that try to combine education and entertainment.

Chapter 7: Course Correction

1. Drawing on *Variety* and other industry sources, Cobbett Steinberg's *Reel Facts* (394–95) provides year-by-year comparisons of earnings by the major American film studios, along with listings of the top twenty films each year for a fifty-year period.

2. Bill Cotter has described the role of audience testing in helping to reshape the Disney anthology show. He describes the heavy emphasis on animal and nature programming that was the result of "scientific scheduling," and he notes that, at least for the next few years, as Disney adhered to this program emphasis, television ratings continued to do fairly well. See his *Wonderful World of Disney Television*, 69.

3. John Culhane provides an overview of the film's elaborate production, with a special emphasis on Ellenshaw's work, in his article "The Remarkable Visions of Peter Ellenshaw." He notes, for example, that *The Black Hole*'s production costs were more than double those of the next most costly Disney feature, *Pete's Dragon* (1977), and he gives special attention to the pioneering effort at merging the computer with more traditional optical methods of effects production.

4. As another of his inspirations, Ellenshaw cites the Goldstone Deep Space Tracking Center, with its delicate metal framework holding "huge bowls, radio

telescopes" that look "almost like a spiderweb" ("Designing" 76). Obviously that image of the spiderweb further builds the visual characterization of Reinhardt as a predatory and threatening figure.

5. Bart Mills details the various changes in the Disney production environment during the late 1970s and early 1980s in his article "Disney Looks for a Happy Ending to Its Grim Fairy Tale."

6. For background on the production team involved in the creation of *Tron*, I have relied primarily on Sorensen's lengthy interview-essay "Tronic Imagery."

7. One sign of that still formative nature of the CGI industry was the lack of compatibility among the different companies involved in the production. As Richard Taylor notes, one of the hurdles he immediately faced as supervisor of visual effects was finding a way to work with the various systems involved: "I looked objectively at the film across the board, and it was immediately apparent that no one of the computer simulation companies was going to be able to handle the load. Each has its own hybrid system, and no one of them shares common software or techniques—each one has its own way of looking" (Sorensen 19).

8. While most CGI programs of this time fashioned objects out of a great many small and undifferentiated polygons, the MAGI Synthavision system drew on a number of familiar but different three-dimensional shapes—spheres, cones, cubes, etc.—that would be combined to produce more complex images. According to MAGI computer graphics head Larry Ellin, this approach "is a lot like building with blocks. Everything that we build in our system is built from these simple shapes. They can be added to each other or subtracted from each other, made larger or smaller and their proportions changed in any way, making it possible to make complex-looking things" (Sorensen 24).

9. *Tron*'s cost was approximately $18 million, while its revenues have been reported as between $27 and $33 million. It was simply one more in a line of feature-film disappointments for the Disney studio in this era. As Jon Lewis summarizes, during Ron Miller's leadership of the film division, even as production significantly increased, the company "posted losses of $33.4 million, studio overhead reached thirty-five percent (compared to the industry average of twenty percent)" and "earnings per share of Disney stock dropped ten percent" (98).

Chapter 8: "Better Than Real"

1. Of course, these are all the subjects of some of the best known and most frequently cited of the Lumière brothers' shorts of the 1890s.

2. Indeed, the move away from traditional animation would become a key rallying point in the struggle for control over Disney in 2004, as Roy E. Disney, Walt's nephew, led an effort to depose Michael Eisner as company CEO. In the previous year, the Disney Company, under Eisner, had laid off the majority of its traditional animators and hinted that it would completely abandon 2D animation in favor of the digital. Roy, who had previously headed the studio's animation program and oversaw the release of its *Fantasia 2000*, did suggest this shift was a betrayal of the company's successful tradition—a tradition that was central to its identity.

3. The CAPS program, or Computer Assisted Production System, is, as Rita Street explains, "a digital ink-and-paint system that employs a sophisticated

multiplane camera within a digital environment" (79). In 1992 the system earned an Academy Award for technical achievement, shared by Disney and Pixar.

4. Pierson's primary concern is with what she terms "the cultural reception of special effects" (4), that is, the discourse surrounding their use, publicity, and reception. That focus essentially leads her to a theory about the kind of spectatorial pleasure afforded by cinematic effects, proposing that they answer "a cultural demand for the aesthetic experience of wonder" (168).

5. As just one example of such economies of scale, we might note how the digital-effects-laden *Lord of the Rings* films repeatedly conjure up great armies of Orcs, Elves, and men through the computer's ability to model and multiply small groups of carefully made-up and fully costumed live actors.

6. See *Saving the Appearances*, 48. Barfield is exploring modernism's estrangement from the world of phenomena, which was resulting, he offered, in a decreasing sense of "participation" in the world (40). His approach looks forward to recent reactions to the digital regime, and particularly to suggestions that digital reproduction undermines our sense of the real, and potentially our sense of our own reality.

Conclusion

1. Polyvision was the multiple-camera/multiple-image process developed by Abel Gance and employed for his masterwork *Napoleon* (1927). Polyvision used three cameras and three synchronized projectors to create its super-widescreen effect. Working from a different principle, Grandeur was a 70mm process developed by the Fox Film Corporation. Requiring the specially designed Grandeur camera and projected with a Super-Simplex Projector, this process produced a 2.1:1 aspect ratio and was used most spectacularly in Fox's epic Western *The Big Trail* (1930).

2. In addition to the revamping of "Alien Encounter" as "Stitch's Great Escape," described in chapter 7, we might also note a similar sanitizing of the "Indiana Jones Epic Stunt Spectacular" in 2004. In an effort to make the attraction less disturbing to young audiences—and perhaps to render it potentially less politically troublesome—all swastikas were removed from the uniforms of those playing German soldiers and from the various Nazi vehicles, and the climactic confrontation between Indy and a German mechanic, a scene taken directly from the original Indiana Jones film, was reworked to remove the implication that the German was sliced to pieces by an airplane propeller. In another vein, several recent incidents, including a tourist's death, have prompted Disney to provide a "toned down" version of its "Mission: SPACE" ride at Epcot by turning off the centrifuge that provides its illusion of a multiple-G-force rocket experience.

3. For background on how Roy O. Disney effectively built the Disney empire through his shrewd financial dealings, see Bob Thomas's biography, *Building a Company*. John Taylor, in his *Storming the Magic Kingdom*, has chronicled the complex maneuverings of those who sought to dismantle the company and the countermoves of Roy E. Disney, Stanley Gold, and their financial backers—efforts that eventuated in the Bass Brothers buying a controlling interest in the company and inserting their own management team of Michael Eisner and Frank Wells, who managed to bring Disney back into prosperity in the late 1980s.

4. For background on Disney's entry into the cable field and a listing of its first decade of cable programming, see Cotter's *Wonderful World of Disney Television,* 291–326, and my own *Disney TV,* 82–90, which provides a brief survey of the various audience segments Disney has targeted with those television and cable offerings. Information on Disney's full range of holdings, including its various cable channels, can be found in the *Columbia Journalism Review*'s "Who Owns What: The Walt Disney Company," as well as in the company's own annual reports, the most recent of which is available at www.corporate.disney.go.com/investors/annual_reports/2006.

5. "Hoover's Online," a business-oriented Web site, describes the basic workings of the Walt Disney Internet Group. For the latest information on the Disney Group's ranking, consult *www.hoovers.com.*

6. For much of the background on the Disney-HP relationship, I have relied on Hewlett-Packard's internal newsletter, *hpNOW.* Particularly useful was the issue of October 14, 2003, "Racing Through Space," in which the company's then-CEO, Carly Fiorina, formally announced its "10-year strategic alliance" with Disney.

7. We should note in this context that new Disney President Bob Iger has identified the "application of technology" as one of the company's new "strategic priorities"—along with "creative innovation" and "global expansion." See his "Letter to Shareholders" in the Walt Disney Company 2005 Annual Report.

WORKS CITED

Agee, James. *Agee on Film: Essays and Reviews by James Agee.* Vol. 1. New York: Grosset & Dunlap, 1969.

Altman, Rick. "The Evolution of Sound Technology." *Film Theory: Sound and Practice.* Ed. Elisabeth Weis and John Belton. New York: Columbia University Press, 1985. 44–53.

Anderson, Christopher. *Hollywood TV: The Studio System in the Fifties.* Austin: University of Texas Press, 1994.

Armitage, John, ed. *Virilio Live: Selected Interviews.* London: Sage, 2001.

Arnheim, Rudolf. *Film as Art.* Berkeley: University of California Press, 1971.

Attebery, Brian. "Beyond Captain Nemo: Disney's Science Fiction." *From Mouse to Mermaid: The Politics of Film, Gender, and Culture.* Ed. Elizabeth Bell, Lynda Haas, and Laura Sells. Bloomington: Indiana University Press, 1995. 148–60.

"The Automatic Camera Effects System (ACES)." *American Cinematographer,* January 1980.

Barfield, Owen. *Saving the Appearances: A Study in Idolatry.* New York: Harcourt, Brace, 1957.

Barrier, Michael. *Hollywood Cartoons: American Animation in Its Golden Age.* Oxford: Oxford University Press, 1999.

Baudrillard, Jean. *The Ecstasy of Communication.* Trans. Bernard and Caroline Schutze. New York: Semiotext(e), 1988.

———. *Screened Out.* Trans. Chris Turner. London: Verso, 2002.

———. *Simulations.* Trans. Paul Foss, Paul Patton, Philip Beitchman. New York: Semiotext(e), 1983.

Bazin, André. *What Is Cinema?* Vol. 1. Ed. and Trans. Hugh Gray. Berkeley: University of California Press, 1967.

Belton, John. *Widescreen Cinema.* Cambridge: Harvard University Press, 1992.

Benjamin, Walter. "The Work of Art in the Age of Mechanical Reproduction." *Illuminations.* Trans. Harry Zohn, ed. Hannah Arendt. New York: Schocken, 1969. 217–51.

Biskind, Peter. *Seeing Is Believing: How Hollywood Taught Us to Stop Worrying and Love the Fifties.* New York: Pantheon, 1983.

Boddy, William. *Fifties Television: The Industry and Its Critics.* Urbana: University of Illinois Press, 1990.

Bordwell, David, Janet Staiger, and Kristin Thompson. *The Classical Hollywood Cinema: Film Style and Mode of Production to 1960.* New York: Columbia University Press, 1985.

Brown, John Mason. "Mr. Disney's Caballeros." *Saturday Review,* February 24, 1945, 22–24.

Bukatman, Scott. *Matters of Gravity: Special Effects and Supermen in the 20th Century*. Durham: Duke University Press, 2003.

Burchill, Julie. *Girls on Film*. New York: Pantheon Books, 1986.

Burton-Carvajal, Julianne. "'Surprise Package': Looking Southward with Disney." In Smoodin, *Disney Discourse*. 131–47.

Byrne, Eleanor, and Martin McQuillan. *Deconstructing Disney*. London: Pluto Press, 1999.

Canemaker, John. *The Art and Flair of Mary Blair: An Appreciation*. New York: Disney Editions, 2003.

Comolli, Jean-Louis. "Technique and Ideology: Camera, Perspective, Depth of Field." Trans. Diana Matias. *Narrative, Apparatus, Ideology: A Film Theory Reader*. Ed. Philip Rosen. New York: Columbia University Press, 1986. 421–43.

Cook, Robert L., Loren Carpenter, and Edwin Catmull. "The REYES Rendering Architecture." *Computer Graphics* 21.4 (1987): 95–102.

Corn, Joseph J., and Brian Horrigan. *Yesterday's Tomorrows: Past Visions of the American Future*. Baltimore, M.D.: Johns Hopkins University Press, 1984.

Cotter, Bill. *The Wonderful World of Disney Television*. New York: Hyperion Press, 1997.

Culhane, John. "The Remarkable Visions of Peter Ellenshaw." *American Film* 4.10 (1979): 18–24.

Daly, James, et al. "Hollywood 2.0." *Wired* 5.11 (1997): 200–215.

Darley, Andy. "Second-Order Realism and Post-Modern Aesthetics in Computer Animation." In Pilling, *Reader in Animation Studies*. 16–24.

Deming, Barbara. *Running Away from Myself: A Dream Portrait of America Drawn from the Films of the Forties*. New York: Grossman, 1969.

Dery, Mark. *The Pyrotechnic Insanitarium: American Culture on the Brink*. New York: Grove Press, 1999.

"Designing a Deep Space World for *The Black Hole*." *American Cinematographer*, January 1980.

Disney, Walt. "Growing Pains." *American Cinematographer*, March 1941.

Drotner, Kirsten. "Denmark: 'Donald Seems So Danish': Disney and the Formation of Cultural Identity." In Wasko, *Dazzled by Disney?* 102–20.

Dyer, Richard. "Entertainment and Utopia." *Genre: The Musical*. Ed. Rick Altman. London: Routledge, 1980. 175–89.

Ebert, Roger. Review of *Sky Captain and the World of Tomorrow*. http://rogerebert .suntimes.com/apps/pbcs.dll/article?AID=/20040917/REVIEWS/409170301/ 1023.

Eco, Umberto. *Travels in Hyperreality*. Trans. William Weaver. New York: Harcourt Brace, 1986.

Elsaesser, Thomas. "Digital Cinema: Delivery, Event, Time." *Cinema Futures: Cain, Abel or Cable?* Ed. Thomas Elsaesser and Kay Hoffmann. Amsterdam: Amsterdam University Press, 1998. 201–22.

Firth, Simon. "Movie Mogul: HP Labs Launches a New Experiment in 3–D Animation." *hpNOW*. http://hpnow.corp.hp.com/news/05q1/050107m1.htm.

Fischer, John. "The Embarrassing Truth about Davy Crockett." *Harper's*, July 1955.

Fjellman, Stephen M. *Vinyl Leaves: Walt Disney World and America*. Boulder: Westview Press, 1992.

Fleischer, Richard. "Underwater Filmmaking." *Hollywood Directors, 1941–1976.* Ed. Richard Koszarski. Oxford: Oxford University Press, 1977. 200–205.

Foucault, Michel. *Language, Counter-Memory, Practice: Selected Essays and Interviews.* Ed. Donald F. Bouchard. Ithaca, N.Y.: Cornell University Press, 1977.

French, Lawrence. "*Toy Story.*" *Cinefantastique* 27.2 (1995): 16–37.

Garity, William E., and J. N. A. Hawkins. "Fantasound." *Journal of the Society of Motion Picture Engineers* 37 (Aug. 1941): 127–46.

Garity, William E., and Watson Jones. "Experiences in Road-Showing Walt Disney's *Fantasia.*" *Journal of the Society of Motion Picture Engineers* 39 (July 1942): 6–15.

Geduld, Harry. *The Birth of the Talkies.* Bloomington: Indiana University Press, 1975.

Gifford, Denis. *Science Fiction Film.* New York: Dutton, 1971.

Gitlin, Todd. *Media Unlimited: How the Torrent of Images and Sounds Overwhelms Our Lives.* New York: Henry Holt, 2002.

Gomery Douglas. "Disney's Business History: A Reinterpretation." In Smoodin, *Disney Discourse.* 71–86.

Gunning, Tom. "The Cinema of Attraction: Early Film, Its Spectator, and the Avant-Garde." *Wide Angle* 8.3–4 (1986): 63–77.

Haas, Robert. "Disney Does Dutch." *From Mouse to Mermaid: The Politics of Film, Gender, and Culture.* Ed. Elizabeth Bell, Lynda Haas, and Laura Sells. Bloomington: Indiana University Press, 1995. 72–85.

Handzo, Stephen. "A Narrative Glossary of Film Sound Technology." *Film Sound: Theory and Practice.* Ed. Elisabeth Weis and John Belton. New York: Columbia University Press, 1985. 383–426.

Higgins, Scott. "Demonstrating Three-Strip Technicolor: *Becky Sharp.*" *Color: The Film Reader.* Ed. Angela Dalle Vacche and Brian Price. New York: Routledge, 2006. 154–60.

"How Disney Combines Living Actors with His Cartoon Characters." *Popular Science,* September 1944, 106–11.

Hutton, Paul Andrew. "Davy Crockett: An Exposition on Hero Worship." *Crockett at Two Hundred: New Perspectives on the Man and the Myth.* Ed. Michael A. Lofaro and Joe Cummings. Knoxville: University of Tennessee Press, 1989. 20–41.

Imagineers, The. *The Imagineering Field Guide to Epcot at Walt Disney World.* New York: Disney Enterprises, 2006.

———. *Walt Disney Imagineering: A Behind the Dreams Look at Making the Magic Real.* New York: Hyperion, 1996.

Iwerks, Leslie, and John Kenworthy. *The Hand Behind the Mouse: An Intimate Biography of Ub Iwerks.* New York: Disney Editions, 2001.

Izod, John. *Hollywood and the Box Office, 1895–1986.* New York: Columbia University Press, 1988.

Jackson, Kathy Merelock, ed. *Walt Disney: Conversations.* Jackson: University Press of Mississippi, 2006.

Jamborsky, William Eric. "Davy Crockett and the Tradition of the Westerner in American Cinema." *Crockett at Two Hundred: New Perspectives on the Man and the Myth.* Ed. Michael A. Lofaro and Joe Cummings. Knoxville: University of Tennessee Press, 1989. 97–113.

James, Edward. *Science Fiction in the Twentieth Century.* Oxford: Oxford University Press, 1994.

Jones, Robert Edmond. "The Problem of Color." *The Emergence of Film Art.* Ed. Lewis Jacobs. 2d ed. New York: Norton, 1979. 206–9.

Kalmus, Natalie. "Colour." *Behind the Screen: How Films Are Made.* Ed. Stephen Watts. London: Barker, 1938. 116–27.

———. "Color Consciousness." *Color: The Film Reader.* Ed. Angela Dalle Vacche and Brian Price. New York: Routledge, 2006. 24–29.

Kaufman, J. B. "Norm Ferguson and the Latin American Films of Walt Disney." In Pilling, *Reader in Animation Studies.* 261–68.

Kindem, Gorham. "Hollywood's Conversion to Color: The Technological, Economic, and Aesthetic Factors." *The American Movie Industry: The Business of Motion Pictures.* Ed. Gorham Kindem. Carbondale: Southern Illinois University Press, 1982. 146–58.

King, Margaret J. "The Recycled Hero: Walt Disney's Davy Crockett." *Davy Crockett: The Man, the Legend, the Legacy.* Ed. Michael A. Lofaro. Knoxville: University of Tennessee Press, 1985. 137–58.

Klapholz, Jesse. "*Fantasia:* Innovations in Sound." *Journal of the Audio Engineers Society* 39.1–2 (1991): 66–70.

Kozlenko, William. "The Animated Cartoon and Walt Disney." Rpt. in Lewis Jacobs, ed., *The Emergence of Film Art.* 2d ed. New York: Norton, 1979. 246–53.

Leslie, Esther. *Hollywood Flatlands: Animation, Critical Theory, and the Avant-Garde.* London: Verso, 2002.

Lewis, Jon. "Disney after Disney: Family Business and the Business of Family." In Smoodin, *Disney Discourse.* 87–105.

Liebermann, Randy. "The *Collier's* and Disney Series." *Blueprint for Space: Science Fiction to Science Fact.* Ed. Frederick I. Ordway III and Randy Liebermann. Washington, D.C.: Smithsonian Institution Press, 1992. 135–46.

Logsdon, John M. "The Challenge of Space: Linking Aspirations and Political Will." *Blueprint for Space: Science Fiction to Science Fact.* Ed. Frederick I. Ordway III and Randy Liebermann. Washington, D.C.: Smithsonian Institution Press, 1992. 147–54.

Maltin, Leonard. *The Disney Films.* 4th ed. New York: Disney Editions, 2000.

———. *Of Mice and Magic: A History of American Animated Cartoons.* New York: New American Library, 1980.

Manovich, Lev. "'Reality' Effects in Computer Animation." In Pilling, *Reader in Animation Studies.* 5–15.

Merritt, Russell, and J. B. Kaufman. *Walt in Wonderland: The Silent Films of Walt Disney.* Baltimore, M.D.: Johns Hopkins University Press, 1993.

Mills, Bart. "Disney Looks for a Happy Ending to Its Grim Fairy Tale." *American Film* 7.9 (1982): 52–56.

Mosely, Sydney A., and H. J. Barton Chapple. *Television: Today and Tomorrow.* 4th ed. London: Pitman and Sons, 1934.

Neale, Steve. *Cinema and Technology: Image, Sound, Colour.* Bloomington: Indiana University Press, 1985.

Neupert, Richard. "Exercising Color Restraint: Technicolor in Hollywood." *Post Script* 10.1 (1990): 21–29.

———. "Painting a Plausible World: Disney's Color Prototypes." In Smoodin, *Disney Discourse.* 106–17.

Nightingale, Virginia. "Australia: Disney and the Australian Cultural Imaginary."
In Wasko, *Dazzled by Disney?* 65–87.

Oliveira, Carlos. "Global Algorithm 1.7: The Silence of the Lambs: Paul Virilio
in Conversation." *Ctheory.* www.ctheory.net/articles.aspx?id=38.

Orvell, Miles. *After the Machine: Visual Arts and the Erasing of Cultural Boundaries.* Jackson: University Press of Mississippi, 1995.

Penley, Constance, and Andrew Ross. "Introduction." *Technoculture.* Ed. Penley
and Ross. Minneapolis: University of Minnesota Press, 1991. viii–xvii.

Phillips, Mark. "The Global Disney Audiences Project: Disney Across Cultures."
In Wasko, *Dazzled by Disney?* 31–61.

Pierson, Michele. *Special Effects: Still in Search of Wonder.* New York: Columbia
University Press, 2002.

Pilling, Jayne, ed. *A Reader in Animation Studies.* Sydney: John Libby, 1997.

Piszkiewicz, Dennis. *Wernher von Braun: The Man Who Sold the Moon.* West-
port, Conn.: Praeger, 1998.

Plumb, Edward H. "The Future of Fantasound." *Journal of the Society of Motion
Picture Engineers* 39 (July 1942): 16–21.

Postman, Neil. *Amusing Ourselves to Death: Public Discourse in the Age of
Show Business.* New York: Viking Penguin, 1985.

———. *Technopoly: The Surrender of Culture to Technology.* New York: Random
House, 1992.

"The Producer Talks about *The Black Hole.*" *American Cinematographer,* January 1980.

"Racing through Space." *hpNOW.* http://hpnow.corp.hhp.com/news/03q4/
031014m1.htm.

Real, Michael R. *Mass-Mediated Culture.* Englewood Cliffs, N.J.: Prentice-Hall,
1977.

Ross, Andrew. *Strange Weather: Culture, Science, and Technology in the Age of
Limits.* London: Verso, 1991.

Sarnoff, David. *Pioneering in Television: Prophecy and Fulfillment.* New York:
Radio Corporation of America, 1946.

Schickel, Richard. *The Disney Version.* New York: Simon and Schuster, 1968.

Schneider, Mike. "Disney World Emphasizes New Technology Over New Rides."
USA Today, May 10, 2005. www.usatoday.com/travel/destinations/2005-05-
10-disney-tech_x.htm.

"Screen Magic from *Snow White* to *The Black Hole.*" *American Cinematographer,* January 1980.

Segal, Howard P. *Future Imperfect: The Mixed Blessings of Technology in America.*
Amherst: University of Massachusetts Press, 1994.

Sehlinger, Bob. *The Unofficial Guide to Walt Disney World, 2005.* Hoboken,
N.J.: John Wiley, 2005.

———. *The Unofficial Guide to Walt Disney World, 2001.* Foster City, Calif.:
IDG Books, 2001.

Smoodin, Eric. *Animating Culture: Hollywood Cartoons from the Sound Era.*
New Brunswick, N.J.: Rutgers University Press, 1993.

———, ed. *Disney Discourse: Producing the Magic Kingdom.* London: Routledge,
1994.

Solomon, Charles. "Will the Real Walt Disney Please Stand Up?" *Film Comment*
18.4 (1982): 49–54.

Sontag, Susan. "The Imagination of Disaster." *Against Interpretation.* New York: Dell, 1966. 212–28.

Sorensen, Peter. "Tronic Imagery." *Cinefex* 8 (1982): 4–35.

Steinberg, Cobbett. *Reel Facts: The Movie Book of Records.* New York: Random House, 1978.

Stewart, Garrett. "The 'Videology' of Science Fiction." *Shadows of the Magic Lamp: Fantasy and Science Fiction in Film.* Ed. George E. Slusser and Eric S. Rabkin. Carbondale: Southern Illinois University Press, 1985. 159–207.

Street, Rita. "Toys Will Be Toys." *Cinefex* 64 (1995): 76–91.

Stuart, Fredric. "The Effects of Television on the Motion Picture Industry: 1948–1960." *The American Movie Industry: The Business of Motion Pictures.* Ed. Gorham Kindem. Carbondale: Southern Illinois University Press, 1982. 257–307.

Taylor, John. *Storming the Magic Kingdom: Wall Street, the Raiders, and the Battle for Disney.* New York: Knopf, 1987.

Telotte, J. P. *Disney TV.* Detroit: Wayne State University Press, 2004.

———. *A Distant Technology: Science Fiction Film and the Machine Age.* Hanover: Wesleyan University Press, 1999.

Tenner, Edward. *Why Things Bite Back: Technology and the Revenge of Unintended Consequences.* New York: Random House, 1996.

Tharp, Joan. "Behind the Magic: HP Technology Helps Disney Dreams Come True." *hpNOW.* http://hpnow.corp.hp.com/news/03q4/030912m2.htm.

Thomas, Bob. *Building a Company: Roy O. Disney and the Creation of an Entertainment Empire.* New York: Hyperion Press, 1998.

———. *Walt Disney: An American Original.* Rev. ed. New York: Hyperion Press, 1994.

Thomas, Frank, and Ollie Johnston. *The Illusion of Life: Disney Animation.* Rev. ed. New York: Disney Editions, 1995.

Thompson, Dorothy. "On the Record: Minority Report." *New York Herald Tribune,* November 25, 1940, 13.

"The Three Caballeros." *Time,* February 19, 1945, 91–92.

Tichi, Cecelia. *Shifting Gears: Technology, Literature, Culture in Modernist America.* Chapel Hill: University of North Carolina Press, 1987.

Verne, Jules. *20,000 Leagues Under the Sea.* Trans. Mendor T. Brunetti. New York: Signet, 1969.

Virilio, Paul. *The Aesthetics of Disappearance.* Trans. Philip Beitchman. New York: Semiotext(e), 1991.

———. *Art and Fear.* Trans. Julie Rose. London: Continuum, 2003.

———. *The Art of the Motor.* Trans. Julie Rose. Minneapolis: University of Minnesota Press, 1995.

———. *A Landscape of Events.* Trans. Julie Rose. Cambridge, Mass.: MIT Press, 2000.

———. "The Last Vehicle." *Looking Back on the End of the World.* Ed. Dietmar Kamper and Christoph Wulf. New York: Semiotext(e), 1989. 106–19.

———. *The Lost Dimension.* Trans. Daniel Moshenberg. New York: Semiotext(e), 1991.

———. *The Vision Machine.* Trans. Julie Rose. Bloomington: Indiana University Press, 1994.

———. *War and Cinema*. Trans. Patrick Camiller. London: Verso, 1989.

Virilio, Paul, and Sylvere Lotringer. *Crepuscular Dawn*. Trans. Mike Taormina. New York: Semiotext(e), 2002.

Walker, Alexander. *The Shattered Silents: How the Talkies Came to Stay*. New York: William Morrow, 1978.

Walt Disney Company 2005 Annual Report, The. www.corporate.disney.go.com/investors/annual_reports/2005.

Wasko, Janet. *Hollywood in the Information Age: Beyond the Silver Screen*. Austin: University of Texas Press, 1994.

———. *Understanding Disney: The Manufacture of Fantasy*. Cambridge: Polity Press, 2001.

———, Mark Phillips, and Eileen R. Meehan, eds. *Dazzled by Disney?: The Global Disney Audiences Project*. London: Leicester University Press, 2001.

Watts, Steven. *The Magic Kingdom: Walt Disney and the American Way of Life*. Columbia: University of Missouri Press, 1997.

White, Timothy R. "From Disney to Warner Bros.: The Critical Shift." *Film Criticism* 16.3 (1992): 3–16.

"Who Owns What: The Walt Disney Company." *Columbia Journalism Review*. www.cjr.org/tools/owners/disney.asp#broadcast.

Wilson, Alexander. "The Betrayal of the Future: Walt Disney's EPCOT Center." In Smoodin, *Disney Discourse*. 118–30.

Wilson, Louise. "Cyberwar, God, and Television: Interview with Paul Virilio." *CTheory*. http://www.ctheory.net/articles.aspx?id=62.

Wolfe, Charles K. "Davy Crockett Songs: From Minstrels to Disney." *Davy Crockett: The Man, the Legend, the Legacy*. Ed. Michael A. Lofaro. Knoxville: University of Tennessee Press, 1985. 159–90.

Wood, Aylish. *Technoscience in Contemporary American Film: Beyond Science Fiction*. Manchester, U.K.: Manchester University Press, 2002.

INDEX

J. P. TELOTTE is a professor of film and media studies in the Literature, Communication, and Culture program at Georgia Tech. Author of more than one hundred articles on film and literature and co-editor of the journal *Post Script,* Telotte has published seven books, including *The Science Fiction Film* and *Disney TV.*

The University of Illinois Press
is a founding member of the
Association of American University Presses.

Composed in 9.5/12.5 Trump Mediaeval LT Std
at the University of Illinois Press
Manufactured by Sheridan Books, Inc.

University of Illinois Press
1325 South Oak Street
Champaign, IL 61820-6903
www.press.uillinois.edu